BECAUSE *Mom* ASKED

the power of a cup half full

BECAUSE *Mom* ASKED

the power of a cup half full

RW HERMAN

Giro di Mondo

Published by Giro di Mondo Publishing,
a subsidiary of LHI Technologies, LLC
Toccoa, Georgia
https://www.girodimondo.com

Printed in the United States of America.

Cover and interior by Roseanna White Designs
Editing by Emily Carmain, Noteworthy Editing
Author photo by Kathy Herman

FIRST EDITION (Hardcover print)

ISBNs: 979-8-9904398-9-4 (Hardcover)
       979-8-9904398-8-7 (Paperback)
       979-8-9904398-7-0 (Digital)

Library of Congress Control Number: 2024913778

DEDICATION

To all those on the
HERMAN FAMILY TREE
and everyone who wants to preserve
its branches, its roots and its memories

PREFACE

I FELT WONDERFUL, AND MAYBE A LITTLE RELIEVED, when I finished my first book in 2021. Although it took fifty years, I had fulfilled a commitment: My mother had asked me to write a book someday. Now, content with what I had accomplished, I considered my writing days over. Even though *The Unopened Letter* would win the Florida Authors and Publishers Association President's gold medal, I certainly didn't consider myself an author.

Giving in to the pressure of family, friends, and, I guess, fans, I reluctantly wrote *Against the Current in the Silent Service* to appease their curiosity and answer questions that my first book had left them with. Once again, I was content to put away the pen. Then I won my second gold medal, and my life was different. For one thing, I finally accepted that I was an author, and second, I discovered I was actually missing writing every day. However, not enough to commit to another book. All that was about to change.

A day I remember just like yesterday, and one that will forever be engraved in my heart, arrived on Christmas Eve 2022. Our family—twenty-three of us this time—were celebrating our tenth annual holiday get-together, and that morning two of my grandchildren asked to speak to me in my office.

"Yes, PopPop," Dawson said, "Alexis and I talked it over and we want you to write a third book."

D, as I call him, my grandson, was now eighteen, a college freshman who has really grown up these past several years. He must be six-two now and 200 pounds. Seems like just yesterday I was attending his Little League baseball games and watching him, his bright, curly red hair sticking out from under his baseball cap, struggling to fit in. He glanced over at his cousin, gesturing for her to join in.

My granddaughter, also eighteen and a college freshman, flashed her beautiful smile at me and knew I would melt. Unlike D, she had never seemed awkward and since birth had been the model child. She was downright stunning at about five-seven, slender, with a smooth, lovely, light brown complexion (the child of a Caucasian father and African-American mother).

"Yes," she added much to her cousin's relief, "your books are great, but...." She looked at D, who was nodding in agreement.

"The books tell us a lot about our family heritage," Alexis said, "but now, we'd really like to learn more. Actually, we've got even more questions now than we had before you wrote them. Like, it seems my great-grandma and great-grandpa Herman faced a lot of challenges when you were growing up in Minnesota. I'd like to know more about all that."

"Even if I'm not a Herman by blood," Dawson chimed in, "you know how proud I am of you, your military career, and being able to call you Grandpa. From what I've heard, I think your mother also could have a book devoted just to her life ... it would be neat to read more about her."

He gave me that irresistible, quirky grin that always makes me smile. "And for my own benefit—and my kids, if I ever have some—I'd like to know more about what happened to you after you retired, how you met Mimi and became our grandfather."

Alexis jumped back in. "You were retired before my mom and dad met, so I'd like to know about those years too. See, you have a lot left to tell us." She glanced at Dawson, and then they both turned to me as if the ball was back in my court.

Their faces beamed enthusiastically. Although they hadn't seen each other often in the past few years, always during the Christmas holidays, they had been communicating on social media and created a close bond. Both being A students and competitive (their college

SAT scores only four points apart) had nothing to do with it, I'm sure.

"Why couldn't you two just ask for money for Christmas?" I sighed dramatically. I couldn't hold back my smile. "Truthfully, you make me one very proud grandfather. Maybe there is more to tell, a few more branches to place on our family tree, and I'm sure my stories can fill those branches with leaves."

The kids did a high-five, hugged, and then turned it into a group affair.

"For the time being, let's keep this between us," I said. "I don't want to continuously be asked how the book is coming. Now let's rejoin the family before they miss us."

They left, closing the door behind them. I hoped I hadn't shown the tears in my eyes for them to see. I sat back into my chair, closed my eyes, and envisioned Book 3.

What was it Alexis said about the challenges her great-grandparents had faced raising me? That sounded like a great place to start. Maybe I wouldn't personally recall many details about my first few years, but I do have a good memory. In her later years, my mother also told me many stories of my childhood, often revealing major surprises. With my sister Marlys to help fill in the blanks, I was confident I could write an accurate account of my early years.

I couldn't help chuckling a little as I realized how many books would come from a simple request ... because a mom asked her son.

THE YOUNGER YEARS

June 1948 – December 1965

"I found him slipping into a diabetic coma and drove him to the emergency room. ... I called my father; he was busy ... My mother gave me the same response. I called Uncle Sherm .... I had collapsed."

CHAPTER 1

June 23, 1948, South Minneapolis, Minnesota

"MRS. HERMAN?" A WOMAN ASKED WHEN MY MOTHER answered the phone. "I'm calling from the mayor's office, please hold for the mayor."

Earlier today, a messenger from the mayor's office had picked up a rough draft of a speech my mother had edited for the mayor. Just a couple of years older than my mother, Hubert H. Humphrey had started out as an assistant pharmacist working for his father, but in 1937 went to the University of Minnesota and then later earned his master's in political science from Louisiana State University. He had returned to the U of M to work on his doctorate but got involved with politics, eventually being elected mayor of Minneapolis, never earning his Ph.D.

Humphrey had first met my mother, Angeline Herman, in 1938 when he hired her to type his essays and other important college papers. He and his wife, Muriel, a political force in her own right, were so impressed with her work ethic, editing ability, and political savvy that when he reentered the U of M to work toward his doctorate, he again hired her. When Humphrey became mayor, my mother became his personal confidant, with her now good friend Muriel's approval. At my mother's insistence, and it was never betrayed, this relationship remained confidential.

"Yes, Angie here, sir." She paused to listen. "Yes, sir, I know you want me to call you Hubert but, with you leading a major city, I'm more comfortable with mayor. I'm glad you like my input for your speech. I think we can easily wordsmith it to use for your senate race also." She was listening again. For a long time.

"Well, sir, this is my thought process. Next month, you're going to be addressing the Democratic National Convention in Philadelphia in prime time, giving possibly the speech of your life. You'll not only have their attention but the entire country's, on live television. It's time to step up to bat, sir." She knew he liked her straightforwardness, never sugarcoating or playing to his ego.

My mother listened intently, taking notes. She took a deep breath, looked down at me and winked. "Yes, sir, I know it's taking a chance, but isn't that why you consult with me? Give a moment to think, what has to be done in order to move the country forward? Isn't that why you got into politics? No one believes in civil rights more than you. You're going to upset and probably lose the Southern Democrats, but if President Truman is to get elected again, he has to accept the big picture of the future and not try to stay content with the status quo of the past."

After another pause, she broke into a big smile. "Of course, Mayor, the final edition of your speech will be yours. I only wanted you to know my personal opinion. You represent the people, never forget that."

Another pause. "No, sir, I have no desire to join you and Muriel in Philadelphia. Yes, sir, I am considering your offer. Let's see how the speech goes and then get you elected U.S. senator this fall first, then we'll see. Good luck, Mayor."

The phone rang as soon as she hung up.

"Yes, Clayton, I know what time it is," she said quickly. "I'm just finishing up, and we'll pick you up in half an hour." She hung up the phone and breathed out heavily. "Your father, young man, never in a hurry when he has the car, but when I've got it, he expects me to be right on time. I guess I shouldn't be too hard on him, he's anxious to hear how your medical exam went this morning. And it's your birthday so let's go enjoy it, shall we?"

She reached down and picked up my bassinet. "If Clayton only knew what I was doing the rest of the day ... I doubt I'll ever tell him—but you, Richard William Herman, someday I am going to tell you all about how your mother secretly worked for Mayor Hubert H. Humphrey, soon to be a United States senator from Minnesota."

Driving along, Mom murmured some phrases over and over, then said, "Richie, the speech is either going to be one of the greatest ever delivered in the history of American politics, or my good friend is going to soon be a nobody and forgotten. I'm betting it's going to be a steppingstone for Mr. Humphrey to become president of the United States one day." She was smiling and seemed very happy, reaching over and patting me on the head.

My mother pulled the car into the loading dock area of George A. Clark and Sons, Plumbing and Hardware Supplies Inc., where my father had worked for nine years and was now the warehouse foreman. He was talking to a bunch of men, all relatively short, muscular with rough facial features, who spoke with heavy Polish and Italian accents. It was easy to tell he was the boss.

My dad, thirty-four years old and generally considered handsome, was almost six feet tall, thin, with long, wavy brown hair and a fair complexion. Mom, four months older than him, stood five-foot-four, had a slim build and black hair and, as my dad would say, was easy to look at. Together they made an attractive couple.

Dad waved to us and headed our way. Opening the driver side door, he said, "Move over, I'll drive." Reaching into the back seat, he put his lunch pail next to me and said, "Happy birthday, young man," patting me on the head.

"How was your day, Ange, and how did Rich's doctor's appointment go?"

"Everything checked out good at the doctors. I'll fill you in later. The rest of the day was same old, same old, nothing exciting to talk about." Mom winked at me. "Remember, we need to pick up Marlys at dance lessons. She's looking forward to celebrating her baby brother's second birthday." We drove in silence until I heard Mom, "Here we are. Go ahead and park, I'll get our ballerina."

Marlys, my almost seven-year-old sister, with her ballet slippers hanging around her neck, jumped onto the back seat next to me.

"Is Grandma making a birthday cake?" she said, patting me on the head. "Is anyone coming to our party? Can I decorate?" she chattered non-stop.

"Whoa, young lady," Mom said smiling. "Yes, Grandma is making a cake, yes, your cousins Arlo and Jackie will be there. Finally, yes, you can decorate." That seemed to satisfy my sister, and I slept the rest of the way home.

Dad pulled into the driveway of a huge two-story farmhouse, converted into a duplex, in Spring Lake Park, a small community just outside the city. Old family friends, the Muellers, owned the farm and all the buildings, and Grandma Nelson rented out half of the duplex. She was my mother's mother; my grandfather had died before I was born. We were staying here while Mom and Dad saved enough money to buy a home of our own. I loved it here with the pigs, chickens, and cows, as well as several dogs and a cat named Blackie.

The party was enjoyed by everyone, although all Jackie, eight months old, and I did was crawl around and rub chocolate birthday cake in each other's hair while my sister and six-year-old Arlo ran around the house breaking balloons and blowing paper horns. Being Wednesday and a work night, our company left early. Grandma and Marlys volunteered to put me to bed so my parents could talk. It had something to do with someone called Louie, but I hadn't met him yet.

I would hear about all this when I was several years older. My parents' older son, Louie, had been in Mayo Clinic Rochester for almost three years, receiving the best possible care from the top doctors in the world for juvenile diabetes and complications.

"What did Dr. Petry say?" Dad asked, handing Mom a Grain Belt beer and an ash tray.

"All tests were negative for diabetes." She took a sip of beer and lit a cigarette. "He gave Richie full glucose tolerance checks, and all looks good.

"With his brother's situation, Dr. Petry said we will need to do this testing with Richie every six months, at least until he's a teenager," Mom said. "I said that was a small inconvenience in his life considering what it could prevent if we diagnosed diabetes in the early stages."

"Finally, some good news, Ange."

"Yes, and now for the not so good news." She shook her head, frowning.

"I received a bill for almost forty thousand dollars today," she said. "Mayo is asking for a substantial payment or they will be forced to turn it over to a collection agency. Unless we find out one of us is related to the Rockefellers, there's no way we'll ever pay this off, let alone future costs to keep him there." She hesitated, and when Dad said nothing and looked away, she got very serious.

"Look, Clayton, we can't hide our heads in the sand, and I've decided to go on the offensive. I've made an appointment to see the clinic's head of billing and financial policy. I promise you I will bend but I won't break, and we will leave with our dignity, no matter what happens. If you're not up to it, fine, but I'm not letting anyone threaten Angeline Herman's son with less care over money."

She put out her cigarette, poured what was left of her beer down the drain, looked and saw a dejected husband staring at the table. "I'm going to say goodnight to the kids, put the lights out when you come up, and please don't burn the house down." As usual, my dad said nothing.

CHAPTER 2

June 25, 1948, Northeast Minneapolis

"WE SHOULD BE HOME SUNDAY BEFORE BEDTIME," Mom said, hugging my aunt. "Be good, Richie." She walked out the door, and once again I would be staying with Aunt Margy and Mom's older brother, Irving, for the weekend while she and Dad visited my brother in the Mayo Clinic. I was already playing with Jackie and Arlo, happy as ever.

"Is Marlys staying with Sherm and Joyce?" Irving said, entering the room. He had just gotten home from another week on the road selling farm equipment. He was shorter and heavier than my dad and didn't have a hair on his body. I heard someone say he lost it all when he battled shingles when he was young. Sherm was my mom's youngest brother and Joyce his wife.

"Welcome home and yes," Margy replied. "Angie thinks it's just too much for your mom to take care of them all the time and likes to give her a break. Did she tell you she was meeting with the financial committee at Mayo tomorrow? That's why they're driving down to Rochester tonight. She and Clayton sure are in a tough place right now with all those bills."

"Well, knowing my sister, she'll make out just fine. In fact, it wouldn't surprise me if she convinces that hospital their son is such a unique case, having survived almost four years now after his diagnosis of diabetes, twenty-three operations, and being told he'd probably never see his second birthday, that they should be paying Angie and Clayton to have him there for someone to study."

"Get real, Irving." Then Margy started laughing. "Although she was the one to convince Clayton to allow Louie to be put on that new drug, insulin, when it hadn't been tested on babies. Not many parents would be willing to make that call. I'd love to be a fly on the wall when Angie talks to them. Her passion alone would be worth the price of a ticket."

"Well, my money is on my sister. Everyone in the family agrees she is the smartest of us all, and lo and behold, watch out if someone or something is standing in her way. In fact, if they ever allow a woman to be president of the United States, it will be a descendent of hers or someone just like her. Actually, if she lives long enough, it could be her." He looked at Margy expecting her to agree.

"Until then," she said, shaking her head, "we'll do what we can helping with Marlys and Richie, trying to make their lives as normal as possible as their brother fights for his life." She looked at me and smiled. "I think Richie is going to be as close a brother to Jackie as Arlo. He already seems protective of her and he's only two." They both laughed.

Saturday morning, Angeline Herman stood at a podium in the Rochester, Minnesota, Mayo Clinic Hospital Board of Directors conference room. Seated before her at the table were six board members and the director of finance, Sam Abrams. A female stenographer sat at one side recording the meeting.

"Gentlemen," Mom started, "thank you for seeing us this morning to discuss our financial situation regarding our son. First of all, I would appreciate it if you refer to him as C. Louis Herman, better yet as he is known to us all as Louie, rather than Case H-3209."

"Louie it shall be, Mrs. Herman," Sam Abrams said. He smiled and you could tell he liked her immediately.

"Thank you, sir." Mom had no notes and looked directly at each board member before continuing. "I want you to know that my husband and I will always be grateful for the care our son has received here—it is a fact that he would not be alive without it. And we fully understand that medical care, especially the best in the world, is not cheap. That too is a fact. Unfortunately, our bill approaching forty thousand dollars, and no end to its growing in sight, is also a fact." All the members smiled at this, and several took a sip of water anticipating what was coming next.

"There is nothing Clayton and I won't do to help our son live, as long as he can look forward to some degree of quality of life with a chance to join his family, learn to love and be loved and experience life to its fullest within his capabilities. I am also pragmatic, gentlemen, and it is also a fact that my husband and I will never be able to pay off this bill. I would not insult your intelligence by telling you otherwise. So, what do we do?" She let that sink in and watched the members look at each other, noticing none of them seemed anxious to answer her. She liked that.

"Not only will I not insult you, I will not waste your time. I stand here today to tell you we can afford and are proposing we pay you five dollars a month for the rest of our lives, regardless of how long Louie lives. It is not an offer that comes without much thought and it is an honest one and from our hearts. Thank you for listening and for any and all consideration you give us." She sat down. My dad took her hand and actually had tears in his eyes.

"Mr. and Mrs. Herman," Abrams said, "the board will need a little time to digest your son's case. If there are no objections, let's adjourn for now, you can visit your son and his doctors, and let's reconvene at two o'clock this afternoon." No one spoke up and the meeting was over, for now.

Everyone was back in their seats at two. "Mr. and Mrs. Herman," Abrams began, "speaking for the entire board, that was an amazing presentation this morning, unlike anything I've seen in my twenty-seven years as finance director. Like you said, what do we do? There is no easy answer when it comes to medical bills, and I like to think nothing should be cut and dried or carved in stone when it comes to human beings and their health. I believe that the Mayo brothers, when they founded this hospital, put the patient first above all the rest, they were compassionate and also considered the families involved and the impact on the entire family structure. That being said ..." he hesitated, took a deep breath and continued.

"Louie is an exceptional case. You and your husband are to be commended for how you approached his illness and willingness to sacrifice so much of yourselves to try and save your child, where many parents would have accepted his fate and let him die. He is not only one of the first toddlers to be treated with insulin for his diabetes, he is one of the few survivors. From him we are learning tremendous knowledge on treatment and care for juvenile diabetes, and because of your love and dedication to him, thousands if not millions of children have a better chance at a normal life in the future. It is the unanimous decision of this board that in the best interest of all involved, Mayo Clinic will accept your proposal, at five dollars a month as a 'sign of good faith' with intent to pay."

"*Yes!*" the stenographer shouted out. Realizing she had gotten carried away, she quickly added, "I'm sorry, Mr. Abrams, but that was beautiful." Everyone started clapping and shaking hands.

"Mr. Abrams," Mom said, shaking his hand. She hadn't realized until now how impressive a figure he was, maybe sixty years old at about six-three with silver-black wavy hair. "Thank you. I think William and Charles Mayo are looking down on you right now and are proud of your decision."

"Please, call me Sam, Angie," he said with a broad smile. "I was wondering, would you and your husband please join my wife and me tonight for a small dinner party? Casual attire. I'd like you to meet some other people involved with the hospital. I could send a car for you."

"We would love to, Sam. Right, Clayton?" Dad stood there dumbfounded, nodding yes.

"Great, my secretary will work out the details with you. See you tonight." He shook their hands and was led out the door by an associate, probably to the next big meeting.

"Ange, what have you gotten us into?" Dad asked. "We don't have anything in common with these people."

"Sure, we do," she shot back. "This hospital and our son. Just be yourself, you may actually have a good time. And keep in mind, Clayton, I believe that this decision today by the Mayo Clinic Board of Directors will set a precedent for the future of this institution. Today, many consider it the best health care provider in the world. They have the best doctors, the best equipment, the best research, and most importantly, an amazing success rating. Within twenty years, I predict Mayo Hospital will have clinics throughout the United States with their name and backing, making it easier for people from all walks of life, from all areas of the country and probably the world, hoping to get seen by them for their care."

As always, my dad nodded in agreement. He couldn't remember when he disagreed with her last. He knew from the time they met, when she hit him with a bowling ball while he was setting pins, that not only was she beautiful, she was one of a kind. Little did he know at that time just how unique she actually was. Now, nine years and three children later, he was content to let her be at the forefront, fighting the battles that she seemed to thrive on. He loved her unconditionally and, in his own way, was comfortable with how his family was living their lives.

Mom knew Dad was relieved that Mayo Clinic was no longer a threat to his family's stability. Unlike him, she felt it was an obvious decision and that she'd just had to show Mayo Clinic what the right answer was. She smiled to herself, and was already thinking of her next challenge.

After our parents got home from Rochester, we all returned to the family's daily routine for a few weeks.

"Clayton, come listen to some of the Democratic National Committee speeches," my mother hollered to him in the basement. Hubert Humphrey was giving the keynote speech that July evening, next to the last day of the convention, and Mom was anxious to see what the final edition of his speech would say. Of course, no one knew that she was his behind-the-scenes speech writer. She had the radio tuned to CBS, and Edward R. Murrow would be the commentator. Grandma was teaching Marlys how to make donuts from scratch in the kitchen, and I was sitting next to Mom playing with a toy.

My father credited the unions for helping get this country back on its feet after the depression and World War II. When it came to voting, he would wait until the Teamsters met and then vote the way they recommended. There was no changing his mind. Dad came up to the living room, handed Mom one of two beers he was carrying, and sat in his easy chair. "I'm only listening because I know you like Humphrey. I'll vote with the Teamsters Union."

My mom smiled and winked at me. "Yes, he's good people and we should hear all parties, Clayton."

My father seemed more interested in his beer and cigarette than the speech being given, but he remained silent. Mom, on the other hand, had moved forward in her chair and was staring at the radio, nodding in agreement with everything being said. "What a great speech," she shouted when it was over. "Way to go, Hubert." My dad just stared at her like he didn't recognize her.

"Wow," Edward R. Murrow said. "For those of you listening, this audience may have just heard one of the most moving speeches of our lifetime. As I look around, they are sitting stunned by what they just heard. Wait, several are clapping now. And more ... now cheers are going up, and they're starting to give a standing ovation. Oh-oh, the Louisiana delegation is storming out, and so are some of their Alabama colleagues. No surprise, they are die-hard segregationists, and this speech was all about civil rights and the equal rights of blacks and other minorities. I need a minute to gather my thoughts. We'll be back after a quick break for our sponsor."

In a minute or two, the announcer was back. "The Philadelphia Convention Hall is rocking following that explosive speech by Minneapolis Mayor Hubert H. Humphrey," Murrow said. "He's also running this year for U.S. senator from Minnesota, and during the break I heard many delegates and my colleagues here say Minnesota will be electing their first Democratic senator since the Civil War. Our time is short, but let me leave you with this. His statement, quote, '*The time has arrived in America for the Democratic Party to get out of the shadow of states' rights and to walk forthrightly into the bright sunshine of human rights,*' unquote, will either lead this party to victory or bring it crashing down, along with the career of Hubert H. Humphrey. Good night and good luck."

Mom heard Dad in the kitchen trying to get a fresh donut. Even Grandma was laughing at him as he teased my sister. Mom picked me up, held me, and whispered, "Did those words sound familiar, Richie? I suppose not, but between you and me, I have high hopes for this country and your future. If we can just stay out of wars."

CHAPTER 3

August 8, 1951, Northeast Minneapolis

"THIS IS IT, RICHIE, YOUR NEW HOME," MOM SAID, pulling up in front of a huge house on Pierce Street in lower Northeast Minneapolis. I got out of the car and saw Marlys on the front porch. She had dance classes across town earlier today and had taken the streetcar here. "Any problem getting here, sweetheart?" Mom asked.

"No," she said, "except I didn't know it would be a four-block walk from where the streetcar dropped me off. When's Daddy and all our stuff getting here?"

"Daddy and Uncle Irving are loading up the truck we borrowed from Daddy's work. They should be here shortly. Come on, let's check out your bedrooms."

The house was light tan stucco with dark brown wood trim. It was a two-story, three-bedroom, one-bath home with an enclosed back porch upstairs and the kitchen, pantry, dining room, living room, entry room, sunroom, and front porch downstairs. It had a full basement and large backyard with a garage.

I couldn't believe how big it was. Then Mom said the bedroom upstairs on the left side of the bathroom was my sister's and the other bedroom with the long walk-in closet was mine. The enclosed porch off my room would be my brother's, when and if he came home from the hospital. I could hardly wait to have cousin Punky, my nickname for Jackie, come over to visit and explore with me.

The week before school we went shopping for clothes, and Marlys was excited because she was told she was old enough to pick out her own three outfits, except shoes. As I was only five years old, Mom picked out my clothes, and we went to the shoe store. My mother was adamant that children must always wear good shoes, no matter the price. My dad didn't see it that way because we outgrew them so fast but could never win against her logic: "God gave us one set of feet, and they have to last a lifetime—take good care of them."

We settled in, and on September 4, 1951, I attended my first day of school at Pillsbury Elementary School, Mrs. Sodergren's kindergarten morning class; Marlys, who just turned ten two days ago, was in the fifth grade. School was only seven blocks from our house and with Mom and Dad both working, my sister and I walked to school together. Grandma had moved in with us and saw us kids off to school each day. I, only going half-days, always had lunch with her, and I grew to be very close to her.

On September 18, I walked home as usual, but when I got there, Grandma wasn't making my lunch and she wasn't alone. My mother was home and I was right, that was Aunt Margy's car out front. "Richie," Mom said, "your sister isn't feeling well, and your dad has taken her to the hospital to be checked out. I came home to get a few things, and your aunt and I are going there now. Nothing serious, honey, and we should be home later. Take care of Grandma."

"Later" ended up being over a week for Marlys. She had been complaining of a toothache for several days. What I didn't know was the morning before she went to the hospital, she had gone to the dentist, who took one look at her and said she needed to be seen by an oral surgeon.

At the University of Minnesota Hospital, they diagnosed her with a rare giant cell mandible tumor (GCT) and, even rarer, that it was on both sides of her jaw. Immediate surgery was performed, and along with both tumors, permanent removal of her wisdom and rear molar teeth was necessary.

During post-operation recovery, the surgeon asked if Marlys had siblings. This led to my brother and I being scheduled to be seen for the same medical problem. I was looked at the next day, and the results were negative.

Louie, still a resident at Mayo Clinic, was examined the same day, and when the results showed the exact same tumors, in the exact same location, and requiring the exact same surgery, history was about to be made. GMT was rare, and even less frequently discovered in siblings—but no recorded case could be found matching my sister's and brother's identical results.

Surgeons from both the University of Minnesota and Mayo Clinic had seen cases of GMT before. But it had never occurred with siblings, born on the same day two years apart, who had the exact same x-rays, tumor size, and removal required. A research project was agreed upon, and the "Giant Cell Tumor 1951 study of Marlys Louise and C. Louis Herman" by the University of Minnesota and Mayo Clinic, Rochester, was documented and copyrighted for the American Medical Association distribution.

For my sister, this was a big deal, but for my brother and my parents it was just one more of many studies conducted and forever to be available to researchers of medical anomalies and miracles.

In December, we learned my brother was going to be allowed to come home for two days at Christmas. With such a short visit, Mom wanted to make it a special time for as many family members and friends to see Louie as possible, and invited everyone to a Christmas brunch open house from seven a.m. until noon. She and Dad drove the ninety miles to Rochester on the morning of December 24 and brought their other son home.

I met my brother for the first time, other than waving to him in the third-floor window of Mayo Hospital. He was a little taller than me, even thinner, with black hair and black-rimmed glasses.

"Hi, I'm Richie," I said. He looked at me but remained silent, walked to the couch and sat. If he was glad to be here, he didn't show it. Marlys also said hello and received the same response.

"Your brother is just tired, kids," Mom said, sitting down next to him. "That's a long ride in the car for him. You'll get to know him better tomorrow ... now, off to bed, everyone. It's late and we have a big day ahead of us tomorrow. Do you think Santa will remember where we're living?" With that we were off. I'd almost forgotten about Christmas. Well, almost.

Early Christmas morning, we opened gifts and got ready for our guests to arrive. Several were prompt, the doorbell rang at exactly seven, and throughout the morning everyone enjoyed bacon, sausages, eggs, pancakes, waffles, and their choice of beverage cheer, including Tom and Jerry's and Bloody Mary's. Everyone made a fuss over Louie while Marlys and I played waitress and waiter helping Mom and Grandma by delivering plates of food, removing and washing dishes.

Mom's oldest brother, Floyd, his wife, Eileen, and two daughters, Sharon and Holly, arrived. Floyd, over six feet tall and barrel-chested, had on a suit. Eileen, also six feet tall, wore a fancy dress, high-heeled shoes, and a hat with a veil, while carrying a cigarette holder. Our cousins Sharon and Holly, maybe a year or two older than Marlys, wore dresses, patent leather shoes, and hats. We didn't see much of this uncle, aunt, and cousins, although they lived only a half-block from Aunt Margy and Uncle Irv. My dad said they thought they were too good for us, a statement I wouldn't understand until years later. Mom was happy to see them, and that was good enough for me.

The Newsoms, my dad's best friend and his wife and kids arrived, and Dad's enthusiasm picked up. So did the drinking.

About twenty people were milling about and enjoying the festivities when the front door opened and Uncle Sherm walked in. He was barefoot, in shorts and a short-sleeve shirt, a University of Minnesota ball cap, and sunglasses. It was twelve degrees outside with a foot of snow on the ground. He left the door open. "Merry Christmas, everyone," he shouted.

My dad and Irving walked across the room, each grabbed an arm and started to push him outside. "How dare you come here Christmas morning drunk," Irving said. I thought it was funny, but then I saw Grandma looking at her youngest son and tears filled her eyes. Mom rushed forward and took Sherm's hand.

"Irving, Clayton, let go of him," she demanded. "He's not drunk. This is just something that clinical psychologists might experience while going through psychoanalysis for their doctorate. He'll be fine, and remember, he'll be Dr. Sherman E. Nelson in the spring—the youngest student, just twenty-four, to receive a Ph.D. in clinical psychology from the University of Minnesota." She led my laughing uncle into the kitchen. I don't think any of the people grasped what Mom had said, but she had spoken with authority, and that was it.

Sherman Nelson, fourteen years younger than my mom, had been taken under her wing when their father died. She recognized her brother was exceptionally bright and found school boring. When he turned sixteen, she made a fake high school diploma and enrolled him at the University of Minnesota. He doubled classes there, even while still attending high school, and graduated with his bachelor of science degree at age nineteen. He breezed through his master's degree in psychology and now was near receiving his doctorate.

Dad never left the drink table, played bartender, and was his own best customer. Even with the short interruption, the brunch was a tremendous success, even Santa (Uncle Irving) made an appearance, and it was decided this would be an annual event and a Herman tradition.

The next day, Louie returned to Mayo Hospital, and everyone was sure he would be coming home for good very soon. He didn't seem to care one way or the other. He was definitely a little different.

CHAPTER 4

September 1953

WE CELEBRATED LABOR DAY WEEKEND, WHICH officially closed out summer in Minnesota, and school started on the Tuesday after Labor Day. We had celebrated Marlys's twelfth and Louie's tenth birthday the week before, although he was still in the hospital.

As I was starting second grade, one thing was becoming very apparent. It seemed all the kids had grown, except me. The first night of school my sister, now in the seventh grade at Edison High School, went to a girlfriend's house to study after dinner, and it was my turn to help with the dishes.

I asked my mother, "Is there something wrong with me? I'm so small compared to my friends. I know Louie is little too ... do I have an illness like him?"

"Not to worry, Richie," she said, looking at my dad. "You're a little small for your age, but so was your father when he was young and look at him now. Almost six feet tall. You'll shoot up one day."

"Okay." I was satisfied. "Can I turn on the TV now?" My dad had bought a used RCA black-and-white TV from his boss last month, and we no longer had to go to Aunt Margy's to watch theirs. "There's a new show the kids are talking about called 'Superman' and it starts in a little while."

"I'll turn it on, son," Dad said, and he and I went into the living room. Grandma saw us turn the set on and left the room. She didn't trust the TV and "people looking out at her," saying it was a fad and wouldn't last. She liked her radio.

As soon as the TV came on, our Siamese cat jumped on top of it and lay down. "Don't hit the antenna, Ginger," Dad yelled. "There, adjusted the set with the test pattern, and it looks pretty clear. Ah, here's the show now." He was as fascinated as I was and sat down with me.

At seven o'clock my mother joined us in the living room and lit a cigarette. Dad said, "Well, we know what time it is." It was a family joke that no matter where she was, Mom always lit her first cigarette of the day at seven p.m. When asked why, she said it was time to relax.

The doorbell rang, and I ran to answer it. It was our Prudential insurance man, Mr. Rudy Banks, who came every other Tuesday after dinner to collect the insurance premium. Mom and Dad gave a friendly greeting; he had been with us for several years, and he took a seat next to the TV. Mom got her purse, counted out the money in cash, and handed it to him. Thanking her, he began writing out the receipt.

All of a sudden, Mr. Banks jumped, and his briefcase and papers went everywhere. He screamed something and ran out of the room, only to trip before he got to the front door and hit his head on the piano. We didn't know what was going on, and Grandma entered the room holding a rolling pin.

"Rudy, what's the matter?" Mom said, running to help him up. "Richie, go get a wet cloth, his head is bleeding."

"The *cat*! The *cat*!" he said shakily. "MY GOD! That *cat* came to life. I thought it was a statue, and all of a sudden it stood and stared at me. Oh, Sweet Mother of Jesus!"

My parents and even Grandma started laughing. "Oh, Rudy, Ginger is our pet Siamese. She likes to sit on the TV because it is warm. Are you okay?" Mom said, trying not to laugh.

I handed Mr. Banks the wet towel, and he wiped the blood from his head. "I'll be okay," he said. "I think I'm the one who needs the insurance." With that he started to laugh too. I knew this would be a story I'd never forget and gave a purring Ginger a big hug.

"I think that was enough excitement for one night," Mom said.

Mr. Banks assured her he was all right. He did call his wife to tell her he was canceling his other appointments and coming home early.

Marlys came home and she, Grandma and I went to bed for the night. Dad brought Mom a Presbyterian drink (whiskey on ice with ginger ale and a splash of water for mixer) and sat at the kitchen table with her, drinking a beer.

"Thanks, Clayton, I think I need this tonight." She took a sip of the drink and lit a cigarette. "That call we got today is going to bring a major change to our lives starting Saturday."

"We've been preparing a long time, Ange, and still, wow, it's for real this time. When do you want to tell the kids and Grandma?"

"Friday will be soon enough. Any earlier and that's all they'll think about until then. Let them get settled this week in school, and we'll have a family talk Friday night after dinner. It's up to you and me to do this right. They'll follow our lead and so will my mom."

Yes. C. Louis Herman was finally coming home to live.

Friday evening, September 11, Mom and Dad talked to us about Louie coming home and what to expect. Although I was only seven, his illness and prognosis had been discussed so many times I actually began to feel I understood what he was going through. The technical talk made no sense to me, but I did know that he had been very sick and would have died, had my parents not agreed to allow him to live at Mayo Clinic to receive constant care while being treated with a drug called insulin.

Juvenile (Type 1) diabetes took the lives of children under five years of age within months of their being diagnosed. Insulin was first tested successfully in 1922, but to date, it still just prolonged some lives a few months and in rare cases, years. Because of the uncertainty of success, the possible pain and suffering the patient and family would go through, and quite honestly, the cost, many families chose to let their child live what little life they had and accept the inevitable, death. This was not Angeline Herman's outlook on life, and with her husband at her side, she had agreed to have their little son receive the treatment.

Now, eight years later, my brother was coming home. Although I had met him last Christmas, I was sure this time would be different, and I was excited. Grandma Dea and I made up the bed in the sunroom adjacent to my bedroom. Dad had installed storm windows, and the room, overlooking the back yard, could now be used year-round. The view included the apple tree, garage, and alley.

Saturday morning, I heard the horn and saw our car pulling into the driveway. I ran downstairs and out the door to meet them. "Hi," I said. "Welcome back, Louie." He looked at me but gave no response of any kind, just like before.

"Richie," Mom said, breaking the silence, "can you handle your brother's bag? Let's get him settled. Clayton, get his insulin into the refrigerator, and make sure there is fresh orange juice made."

I managed to drag the suitcase up to the sunroom and showed Louie the view. He didn't say a word, only stared out the window. In fact, he didn't seem curious about anything. I guessed he was just tired. Then he saw Mom unpacking his things, and he ran over and took what she had out of her hand. "I'll put those away. I have a certain way I like them."

He didn't have much, and we watched as he neatly placed each piece of underwear neatly in one drawer with his socks lined up in a straight line. He then refolded his shirts and placed them neatly in another drawer. "Do you have hangers for my pants?" Mom showed him the closet, and he hung all three pairs of his jeans, separated so they didn't touch.

"Very nice, son," Mom said. "Richie, take a look, you can learn from your brother." I was speechless. "Now, let's go downstairs to get you a snack and your next insulin shot." They left me standing there, and I thought about going to straighten my drawers and closet. Instead, I followed them downstairs.

In the kitchen, Mom had me and Marlys sit at the table for our first lesson on treating our brother's diabetes. Grandma stood at the sink, staring at the floor. "You're young, but it's important for you both to know how to give your brother his insulin shot in case one day you have to do it."

She took his insulin out of the refrigerator, and from a small leather pouch she removed what I learned was a hypodermic needle. She pointed at a red line on the tube. "Louie needs this much insulin four times a day. Because of so many shots, he goes to a different spot on his body each time. He will inject himself in his thighs, arms, stomach, and butt." We giggled, but our parents' look told us this was serious. "Go ahead, son."

My brother pulled up his shirt, and I saw a scar that ran from his belly button all the way up his chest. I knew he had a lot of operations, including one that removed two-thirds of his stomach, but I never expected this. He drew insulin from the bottle to the red mark on the tube and stuck the needle into the left side of his stomach. He pushed the plunger down until all the medicine was gone and then pulled out the syringe. He removed the needle, dropped it into a jar containing alcohol, and put a new needle on the syringe before putting it back in the case.

Next, he put the insulin bottle back in the refrigerator in a place Dad had made on the door for it to fit snugly. He turned, smiled, and bowed. It was the first time he had shown real emotion, and we all clapped and laughed. I had just witnessed my first insulin injection, not realizing I would be administering hundreds, if not thousands, in the future. I noticed Grandma was still staring at the floor.

"That's enough lessons for today," Mom said. "It's best to have something to eat in half-an-hour after his shot, so why don't you kids go play and I'll let you know when it's ready." She didn't have to tell us twice, and we were off to catch up on years of being apart. Dad got himself a beer and sat back down at the table while Mom and Grandma prepared a snack.

"The kids didn't flinch when Louie had his shot," Dad said. "I think you're right that Richie is old enough to learn how to do it in an emergency. Let Marlys do it for a couple of days and see if he volunteers."

"Sounds good," Mom said, smiling at him for admitting she

was right. "It's not too early to teach responsibility and work ethic. Remember, you had a job delivering ice at age six." She saw him smile and knew a little positive reinforcement always went a long way with her husband.

Monday night, Grandma fixed a roast beef dinner with mashed potatoes and gravy and creamed corn. It was fun watching her cook. A little taller than my mom, maybe five-foot-six, and heavier, she would whip those mashed potatoes like she was killing a wild animal. Her silver hair, always in a bun, would start to get in her eyes, but she never stopped.

Mom was in a great mood. "The meeting went very well at school today about what grade Louie will go in," she announced. "Miss Dalton, the education specialist, talked to Louie and me about his time in the hospital and how he was taught his subjects by volunteer student teachers, usually at night, and about the hospital's working relationship with the local school system to give the patients their tests. I was very impressed and so was the principal. Then she took Louie into a classroom by himself and did her own assessment."

"What was the outcome?" Dad asked.

"I'm getting there, Clayton." No one said a word. "She has recommended, and we all agreed, Louie will be placed with his ten-year-old peers in the fifth grade. I'll take him tomorrow when he meets his teacher and classmates, and then he can start walking to school with Richie. The school year has just started, so he basically has no catching up to do. I think it's wonderful and just another reason we can be so grateful to Mayo Clinic."

The second week of school, my teacher noticed I wasn't paying much attention to her and had me move up to the front of the class, in front of her desk. I responded by showing more interest in what she was teaching on the blackboard than looking out the window. Apparently, she talked to the school's nurse, and one day I was sent home with a note for my parents.

"Clayton," my mom said as soon as Dad came in the door.

"Richie's teacher sent him home with this note." She waved it in the air. "She thinks Richie has been distracted in school because he can't see well enough. She recommends we get him tested."

The following week, I showed up at school with my new black-rimmed glasses, and the teasing began. I had an easy fix and decided I'd put them in my pocket during school hours and wear them only at home. This lasted two days and, when I sat on them and they broke, I found myself waiting in my room for my father.

Like all the times I faced punishment, my father came when he was ready, always after dinner. He entered with the two pieces of my glasses, sat next to me on my bed, and said, "Well, Bub, what do you think we should do?"

"I think I should pay for fixing my glasses out of my savings, Daddy, and never try to hide from wearing them again."

"Good answer, son." He stood, took my glasses, and said, "Grandma has your supper in the oven, you better eat. I'll bring your new glasses home tomorrow night."

He walked out and, as usual, I felt so guilty I wasn't hungry anymore. I also decided I was going to invest in a glass case for when I wasn't wearing my glasses. I just hated it when I disappointed my father. Why couldn't he just spank me and get it over with?

CHAPTER 5

October 1953

MARLYS WAS ATTENDING A DIFFERENT SCHOOL NOW, Edison High, so it was nice to have someone, my brother, to walk to school with again. Louie remained an average student, didn't socialize well, and I was still having to step in to prevent fights as kids liked to bully him. I was his little bodyguard, a role I took on as part of being his brother. I was pretty well liked, and most kids backed off when I stepped in. Unfortunately, this wasn't always the case, and he, I, or both of us would come home with some bruises. My dad would tell me to protect him better, and Mom just said to watch him closer.

Louie missed a lot of school because of doctor appointments and diabetic episodes of low-sugar levels leading to sweating, headaches, anxiety, with violent outbursts and sometimes going into shock. He always carried a packet of sugar, as did I, at school and there was a bottle of pure orange juice kept refrigerated for emergencies. If he felt like he was having an episode or started acting strange, giving him the sugar and juice would usually stabilize him until insulin could be administered.

We had testing strips at home that would determine his urine glucose level and help regulate his insulin, but sometimes he'd forget—or say he did—to test himself. I started to think he did it to get attention.

One day, my friends asked that I not bring him around anymore because he was weird and scared them. I told them he was my brother and was having a hard time being in school after living so long in the hospital. They decided they might catch something from him, and after that it was just me and my brother together on the playground and walking home. I saw no other choice.

———————— ❧ ————————

Several weeks later, Louie showed me a pocketknife he had found in Mom and Dad's bedroom. "You're not supposed to go in there," I said. "And what do you need a pocketknife for anyway?"

"To learn how to throw it," he said, tossing it into the ground. It stuck, and he bet I couldn't do that, handing me the knife. I tried several times but I couldn't get it to stick. He took the knife and said, "Watch this." He threw it, and it stuck in the garage door.

He laughed, pulled it out, and walked toward our neighbor's house. Taking aim, he threw it at a kitchen window and it stuck in the wood strip between the windowpanes. He laughed harder and stepped on an upside-down bucket to reach up and pull the knife out. "Here, you do it."

I didn't want to, but for some reason I took the knife, aimed and let it go. It crashed through the window and I froze. Mrs. Johnson came running out holding the knife. "Richie, what in the world are you doing? You could have seriously hurt someone, or yourself."

Louie was nowhere to be seen. She checked to make sure I was okay. "I'm going to hold onto this knife until you and one of your parents comes to get it and tell me how my window will be fixed. Today, young man."

"I think your father better handle this," Mom said when I came in. "Go to your room, and he'll come see you when he gets home." I told her what happened, except how I got the knife. I saw my brother laughing in the other room, saying nothing.

"Okay, Bub," my dad said, entering my bedroom. I realized he only called me Bub when upset with me. "Tell me what happened." I told him what I had told my mother. He looked at me, put his head down, and after what seemed forever, finally looked at me. "I am disappointed in you. How did you get my knife?"

Louie, who was sitting on his bed watching us, gave me a look like I better not tell on him.

"I saw a kid at school doing some tricks with a knife, and I thought it would be fun to try. I knew you had a knife in the dresser so I borrowed it. I didn't expect this to happen and thought I could return it before you knew. I'm sorry, Daddy."

"So you hoped to get away with it, did you? Sounds like you're only sorry you got caught. Come on, let's go see the Johnsons and sort this out. The first thing you are going to do is apologize for your behavior. What do you think you should do next?" Before I could say, he jumped in, "Don't tell me, tell the Johnsons."

"I'm very sorry, Mr. and Mrs. Johnson," I said when they answered the door. My dad stood at the bottom of the steps. "It was a stupid thing to do, and I won't ever do it again, believe me. I want to pay to have your window replaced, and if you want anything for me to do, I will."

"Thank you for the apology, Richie," Mrs. Johnson said. Her husband nodded in agreement. "We have some window glass in the garage, and if you and your dad agree to repair the window, we'll call it even and a lesson learned."

I looked at Dad, who said, "That's very fair, and we can fix it right now. Get my tool belt, Richie, you're about to learn how to repair a window." He shook hands with the Johnsons and got his knife back.

While repairing the window he said, "Just because the Johnsons let you off the hook, it doesn't mean I have. Go to your room after school tomorrow, and wait for me to come home. We'll discuss this further."

I was really mad at my brother that day. I couldn't believe he let me take the whole rap, especially taking the knife from the bedroom, which I would never have done and I knew really hurt my parents. The next day I sat in my room after school until my father came in. My stomach hurt, and I felt terrible. Why couldn't he just spank me like other fathers? The door finally opened. It was eight o'clock.

"I think you've punished yourself enough, son. Just know that every time you disappoint me it hurts me as much as it does you. No parent likes to feel like a failure, and that's how I feel. Now, get ready for bed. Tomorrow is another day."

My father left the room, and the subject was never discussed again. It didn't have to be. I had just experienced my father's worst punishment; he let me know I disappointed him. I would never forget that lesson.

"Do I have to?" I pleaded with my mom. For the past year I had been going to dance and acrobatic classes with my sister and my cousin. I enjoyed performing and we had a recital scheduled Friday night at Windom Park Bandstand, our local hangout. I didn't mind performing before a crowd of people I didn't know, but doing so before my classmates and neighbors terrified me.

"Richie, you're one of the lead characters," Mom said, "of course you have to go."

"I hate to say it," Marlys added, "but I need you there for my ballet routine so I can look good." She was one of the three lead dancers for one musical event and, although a minor role, I played a key character to make their routine a success. "Plus, Jackie will be performing too, and you two are always good together." She knew she had me as soon as she mentioned Punky.

The time came, and when I made my entrance on the bandstand, all my friends started yelling and screaming. I entered doing a cartwheel, followed by a somersault, and then I would fall flat on my face. Yes, I was a court jester. I had red pointed slippers, black leotard with red polka-dot shorts, and a three-pronged black-and-red hat—with bells on the slippers and hat. The crowd roared with laughter, I was never so embarrassed in my life, and Marlys shone with her dance routine.

Afterward, I told my parents I couldn't do this anymore. They accepted my decision, my dad was never keen on it anyway, and along with my knife-throwing act, I retired from show business at age seven.

On the first day of summer vacation, June 16, 1954, and a week before my eighth birthday, Aunt Margy, Arlo, and Punky were coming over to pick us up to go to the beach. Louie and I were in our rooms and he said, "Let's take a quick way down. I've tied my sheets together, and you can climb out my window, hang on to them, and I'll lower you to the ground."

"I don't think that's such a good idea," I said. After a little coaxing, and Louie telling me how cool it would be for me to surprise everyone, I agreed. He opened his middle window, put the first sheet over, and I crawled out and sat on the windowsill.

I took the sheet and started to turn around to brace my feet on the wall, and he yanked the sheet away. I fell two stories to the concrete blocks below. Hearing me screaming, Punky ran around the corner and knelt at my side.

"What happened?" she said.

My leg and foot were killing me, and I had a hard time answering, I was crying so hard. "I was going to climb down and Louie pulled the sheet away." We looked up at the windows, all closed.

Aunt Margy ran up to me and checked me for injuries. "I think it's just your lower left leg." Grandma looked out the back door, saying something in Norwegian, and my aunt called to her, "Dea, bring me some ice in a towel. Then call Angie and tell her I think he is okay, but I'm taking Richie to General Hospital to be checked out, just to be safe. Watch the kids until we get back." She picked me up and off we went. I never knew her car could go so fast.

"Hey, Superman," my mom said as she came alongside my bed in the emergency room. She hugged my aunt, then me. She took a good look at my sprained left ankle. "Louie told me what happened. That you wanted to see if you could fly like Superman. He said he thought you were kidding until you jumped, then was scared you were going to die." She and my aunt started laughing. "You're very lucky, young man."

"Superman?" I couldn't believe it. "That's not what happened, Mom."

"It's all right, all young boys do stupid things when they're kids.

Just learn from it. Your father isn't angry at all, and says he'll see you tonight. Good thing your aunt was there to help so quickly. Thank you, Margy. We appreciate it."

I decided not to push it. I was beginning to realize there was no way they would believe me over my brother. Besides, if I said anything, he'd just forget to take an insulin shot and they'd soon forget about my so-called accident.

Grandma had put a pillow and blanket on the couch along with something to prop my foot up. I was lying there watching TV when I heard Grandma tell Jackie where I was. It was good to see my buddy Punky, as she plopped down next to me.

"I didn't know what to say," she said. "I didn't see Louie and the sheets, and he told his side of the story before anyone asked me anything. I'm sorry, Richie, but I believe you, and we'll always know what really happened."

She gave me a quick hug and we had our first big family secret. "By the way, when does Superman come on?" She was laughing when she ran out of the room.

CHAPTER 6

Fall 1957

I'D LIKE TO THINK I HAD A GOOD CHILDHOOD. AS A family, we dealt with the occasional problems with my brother, and it became accepted as a way of life. Marlys had her friends, I had mine, and Louie remained pretty much a loner. We weren't wealthy by any means, but we were never hungry, and I don't remember not being able to have or do something because we couldn't afford it. Of course, we had our chores, and for special events, we were expected to find ways to earn extra money to help pay our own way.

Most of our vacations found us camping, but one time we ventured to visit friends in Detroit, Michigan, and it turned out to be memorable. Mom, as usual, made the driving plan with only one stop needed along the way. Marlys now had her driver's license and helped share the driving. It was about nine o'clock the first night traveling when Mom gave us our first big surprise and educational experience. She had my sister pull into the parking lot of a police station in the middle of Chicago.

"What are you doing, Ange?" my dad said, looking around confused.

"I did my research, Clayton," she replied, getting out of the car. "Cheapest and safest place to stay is in a jail. Come on."

"I'm not spending the night in a jail cell," Marlys said. She folded her arms in front of her and exhaled loudly.

"Fine," Mom said. "Make sure you keep the windows up, and don't open them or the door for strangers." She started walking to the entrance of the jail. Dad and I followed. My sister joined us before we got through the doors.

My mom and dad talked to the policeman at the desk, and the next thing I knew, we were escorted down a hallway, each of us got a blanket and pillow, and we were shown a cell with four cots. Dad went with the policeman for a minute and was shown where we could use the bathroom and clean up. All the comforts of home. I thought it was great. I think Marlys was in shock, and she stayed close to Mom.

In the morning, a different policeman came to our cell, bringing a pot of coffee and two cups. He also had orange juice and some donuts. We all cleaned up and were on our way by eight o'clock. Our pillows lay neatly on our folded blankets on the cell's cots along with the towels and washcloths we were given to use. Everyone was friendly and even went over our route to Detroit, pointing out construction areas and where to watch for speed traps.

Our visit in Michigan was anticlimactic compared to our night in jail, and Mom, after a four-day stay, agreed to stay in a motel on the way home. Always looking for adventure and educational experiences, she had us drive straight north from Detroit to witness history in the making. On November 1, 1957, we were the third car in line (behind the governor's two-car limousine group) to cross and officially open the Mackinaw Bridge, the largest suspension bridge in the western hemisphere, connecting lower and upper Michigan. Angeline Herman struck again.

I liked having my own money and, on my twelfth birthday, I became a paper boy delivering the Minneapolis-Star Tribune morning and Sunday papers. Mom wanted me to take the evening route because of the delivery time (and no Sunday deliveries), but the morning route already had thirty more customers, which meant more money. It wasn't long before I wished I had listened to Mom.

I would get up at five each morning, ride my bike to the paper delivery point six blocks from my house, and count out my seventy-eight papers. Once I accepted the papers, I was responsible for paying for them. Although not required, I would fold all my papers and deliver them between my customers' storm and front doors to protect them from the weather. I thought this was a good business practice, and after my first few weeks, my tips had more than doubled.

Word spread, and many former customers, who had stopped taking the paper because the delivery boy was unreliable or their paper would be ruined by rain or snow, called and renewed their subscriptions. My route grew to 103 papers, the largest in the Twin Cities.

I enjoyed my route, but it started taking its toll on me once school started and then the bad weather came. With the additional twenty-five papers to deliver, I wasn't physically able to carry all of them on my bike at once and was forced to make two trips from where I received them. I also had to start getting up at four-thirty a.m. I never asked for any help, but more than once Dad would warm up the car and drive me around my route. I made it through the Christmas holidays, making super tips, but my folks finally said enough was enough.

I had started getting up in the middle of the night, sound asleep, taking bills from my money box and folding them like newspapers before putting them outside my bedroom door, as if delivered. Mom discussed my actions with Uncle Sherm, who in turn talked to me and determined I was reacting to stress. My career as a paper boy came to an end.

Mom and Dad were able to buy a cabin on Lake Independence, twenty-five miles outside the city, and Uncle Sherm built us a fishing boat as payment for my dad wallpapering the living room, dining room, and bedrooms in his house. Most weekends during the summer—in Minnesota, that is Memorial Day weekend until Labor Day weekend—we would load up the car Friday afternoon and head to the lake. We learned how to swim (Uncle Sherm threw me in the lake one day, and I had no choice but to swim back to the dock or drown), waterski, and my favorite—fish.

Bowling was a big part of our lives, and many Saturday night family outings found us at the bowling alley. All of us kids were learning, I was in junior league, and we each showed promise to be better than average bowlers, especially Arlo, Marlys, and me. Our parents' individual averages in leagues were Mom (140s), Dad (170s), Irving (180s), and then there was Margy. Regarded as a professional, she was one of the best bowlers in the city, if not state. Every Tuesday night she would pick me up, and I would keep score on my homemade bowling score sheets as she competed in the city's Premiere League. Consistently averaging 190 or better, she also traveled with her women's team competing in pro events. I was her biggest fan.

As good as my aunt was at bowling, my dad was at horseshoes. Friday nights I would pester him to take me to his Loring Park League matches. Horseshoe pitching wasn't as popular as bowling, but almost all good players at one were also good at the other. Uncle Irving and Uncle Floyd were above average horseshoe players but never played competitively in leagues. They did provide a challenge to my dad in matches at family gatherings, but so did Mom and Margy. Dad, however, was an exceptional player and always ranked near the top in the city. Dad did have one claim to fame, and that was he won the qualifying tournament in 1956 and faced Horseshoe Pitching Champion and legend Ron Cherrier. Although Dad lost the match, he could always say he faced the world's best and gave him a run for his money.

The week following the exhibition match, Dad came home from his regular league outing and was sitting at the kitchen table, probably having a final beer for the night, when our neighbor started yelling, "Fire! Fire!"

I was in bed, got up, and ran to the window to see what was going on. Our car was on fire in the driveway, the back seat in flames. Suddenly, Dad appeared and tried to open the car's back door. After burning his left hand, he took his shirt off, wrapped it around his right hand and was able to get the door open. He reached in, grabbed his horseshoe case, and threw it to the ground behind him. Reaching back in, he picked up his bowling bag and did the same.

My mother was now beside him pulling him away. I'm not positive, but I had the window open now and I think I may have heard my mother swear for the first time. My thought was reinforced when Dad, who absolutely hated swearing and would not allow it in his house or around his family, looked at her, shocked at what came out of her mouth.

After the firemen extinguished the blaze and treated my dad's burn, the fire chief took Mom aside and explained what he found. A cigarette was on the back seat cushion, and he thought my father, who obviously had been drinking, probably threw a cigarette out the window just before pulling into the driveway, and it flew into the back seat. Mom shook her head, smiled and went with the chief to talk to the policeman on the scene. I don't know what took place with that conversation, but the next morning I heard her say to my dad, "Yes, Clayton, just an accident."

Aunt Margy had her own car and loaned it to us until we found a replacement for the purple beast, which was a total loss and towed away for junk. The new family car arrived the following week when we heard a car horn honking in the backyard. Standing in the driveway, with a big smile was my dad. "A beauty, isn't it?" he said. "A 1951 Hudson Hornet."

Before us indeed was a shiny new car, but it was the ugliest lime green color I'd ever seen. Unlike before, this time I was sure I heard my mother swear!

CHAPTER 7

Summer 1959

MARLYS, WHO GRADUATED FROM EDISON HIGH School in June, wanted to become a high school teacher and was excited about going to Mankato State College, located ninety miles south of Minneapolis, in the fall. She was moving mid-August to start a job at the college and move into her dorm early.

Although five years older, my sister and I were close, and she had always been a big help to me, especially with dealing with our brother. I was going to miss her, but I was proud of her, as she had worked hard, saved her money, and was receiving some scholarship money. I was also a little jealous because she was getting away from home.

Actually, to say I was going to miss her was a huge understatement. These past six years, with Louie at home, had been nothing short of chaotic. He had been in and out of the hospital dozens of times, as regulating his blood sugar was always a challenge. As he got older and his body changed, constant adjustments to his insulin dosage were required. I lost count of the number of times I personally had to bring him out of diabetic reactions, usually having to get him under control as he would fight all assistance. It is a wonder I never broke any bones running after him and wrestling him to the ground. But he was my brother.

One time I woke up at night to a strange smell, so strong I got up to see what it was. I found Louie on his bed, and his bedside lamp, minus its shade, had fallen on him. The light bulb was burning a hole through the skin on his chest, yet he lay there motionless, in diabetic shock, feeling nothing. I slapped away the light, called my parents, took two sugar cubes from the bowl next to his bed, and forced them into his mouth. I knew he was near going into a full-blown diabetic coma.

Mom, always prepared, arrived with orange juice, and I held him with his mouth open while she poured the juice in. Luckily, he started coming around. Of course, now he was in intense pain as well as getting violent as his adrenaline kicked in. Dad honked to let us know he was ready, and we carried Louie, wrapped tightly in a sheet, to the car. One more middle-of-the-night trip to the University of Minnesota Hospital ER.

Although we were in different schools, every day it was my job to check on Louie to make sure he got home all right and had taken a snack. Grandma had made it clear from day one that she would help with her grandson but didn't want the responsibility of his care. She never learned how to give him a shot or bring him out of a diabetic episode. My parents came to rely on me more and more, and by the time I was ready to enter seventh grade, I was his primary caregiver during the day. It became such a normal part of my daily routine that neither I, nor anyone else, ever noticed it could be having an adverse effect on me.

Early Saturday morning, August 15, 1959, we all helped load up the car, and Dad and Marlys headed to Mankato to get her settled for her freshman year. Louie, a couple of weeks shy of his sixteenth birthday, went to his room to build another model airplane, and Grandma was in the basement doing laundry. Saturday mornings usually had us all doing assigned chores to clean house, do yard work, and whatever needed tending to. Mom and Dad worked all week and no one expected Grandma to do everything, so no one complained, we just did it.

Today, Mom declared a special day off, and she and I went on a secret errand.

When Dad returned from Mankato, I was excited to share the

news and met him in the driveway. "Mom said to tell you she was successful and tomorrow is a go."

He smiled, walked into the kitchen saying hi to everyone, grabbed a beer, and told us about his trip with Marlys. Not a word about our secret errand and what he and Mom had been planning for over a year.

"Once Marlys met her roommate," he said taking a drink from his beer, "it was like I didn't exist. She's going to be fine. Here's the number to the school switchboard," he handed it to my mother. "The housemother said we can reach her room using this. And if we say it is an emergency, they'll send someone to find her. I was impressed."

The next morning, Mom told Grandma it was a nice day to take a ride and get some fresh air. Reluctantly, with my pestering her as well, she agreed, and Dad helped her into the front passenger seat of our car. Louie and I got into the back seat with Mom and off we went. After driving around a bit, Dad pulled up to the curb across the street from my school, Northeast Junior High.

"Let's stretch our legs," he said. As we all got out, he pointed to a little house, freshly painted dark green, on the lot, way in the back. "That's a cute place, isn't it, Dea?"

"I suppose," Grandma said. She pointed at the school, "So this is where you and Jackie go to school, Richie? Very nice."

My parents handed her an envelope. Confused, she opened it and pulled out a card, and read it aloud: "A Special Thank You. For all that you have done for us. Welcome to your new home. Love, Ange, Clayton and Kids." She held up a key, looked at the little green house, and as my mother hugged her, started to cry.

"You've given so much of yourself to us, Mom, and at seventy years old you deserve to have your own place where you can be independent and have the quality of life that you want. It's yours, no strings attached. Come on, let's take a look at your new home."

Grandma moved into the small one-bedroom, living room, kitchen/bath combination house with a fifty-by-seventy-five-foot front lawn the following week. Being across the street from my school, where I still had eighth and ninth grades to attend, I could visit her often.

As another positive, she was now living only five blocks from her two oldest sons, Floyd and Irving, and four of her other grandchildren. Yet, time would show, her only regular visitors were still just my parents and me. That was fine with me, because I loved her dearly and enjoyed having all her attention. I immediately volunteered and took over all her lawn care and sidewalk shoveling in the winter.

To show her independence, Grandma took the bus alone, transferring twice, to the Minnesota State Fair the following weekend. Go, Grandma!

I had a lot of interests, especially sports, while my brother was content with his model cars and planes. Surprisingly, one day he told Dad that he'd like to try hunting. A family tradition was that only the men would go hunting and fishing on the seasons' opening weekends. There were a few rules everyone had to agree to: First, no drinking when firearms were present. All guns had to be unloaded, safeties on, and stored before the bar opened. Second, all sons, as a rite of passage, had to wait until they were twelve to join the men, and, for hunting, they had to pass the National Rifle Association Safety Course.

You had to be eighteen to take the course by yourself so Dad attended the course with us. We passed the course, and Irving and Arlo scheduled a pheasant hunting trip to a farm owned by a client Irving had sold farm equipment to. The farmer's only price was asking us to use his hunting dogs to keep their skills sharp. They turned out to be well trained, more excited than us, and great hunters.

Unlike duck and deer hunting, in the spring and winter where it was usually cold and you had to keep quiet, pheasant hunting was in the fall and generally warm, and you were expected to make noise. We all lined up on the end of a corn field, facing into the wind, about six rows apart. Uncle Irving and Dad were on the ends, holding the dogs, and I was in the middle with Louie on my left and Arlo on my right. We started walking and the dogs were let loose.

About twenty feet in front of us a pheasant flew up and started flying into the wind. It suddenly turned and headed toward us when BAM! Someone fired.

"I got it," Arlo yelled. One of the dogs brought it to Irving. We all cheered, congratulating my cousin.

We started walking again, and another pheasant flew up about ten feet ahead of me. Startled, I began to bring up my gun, but tripped. The gun went off, and I lay there not saying a word. *No, no, no,* I thought. *Please, Louie, don't be shot.*

All of a sudden, I heard the pheasant coming back right over where Louie was. BAM! The bird exploded in the air and feathers went everywhere. "I got it," we heard him yell. I was never so happy to hear his voice. The dog retrieved what was left of the bird and brought it to Irving.

Irving burst out laughing. "Looks like we got about a third of a bird and over 200 pellets, Louie. I think you're supposed to wait until they are a little further away."

Now, everyone was laughing. I was the only one whose tears weren't from laughter. I put the safety on my gun and never tried to fire it again. We got six good eating pheasants that day, and I was the only one skunked. It was a great trip home, and I never told anyone how close I came to killing my brother.

I remained active in bowling and led the Saturday junior league for boys with an average of 183. The owners of East Side Bowl, Ed and Helen Mellon, were impressed with my ability, and Helen became my personal instructor. Ed hired me in my freshman and sophomore years to work part time as a desk clerk, bar server, and go-fer for whoever was on duty as manager.

When Ed was there, I would assist him with trouble calls like stuck bowling balls, resetting fallen pins, or minor mechanical problems with the automatic pin-setters. Helen confided in me one day that Ed enjoyed my company, filling in for the son they never had. She also said, if I stuck with her, I could have a future as a pro bowler. I'm not sure whose dream it would have been, hers or mine.

Since I can remember, Dad and I would tune in the radio and listen to his favorite, "Friday Night Fights," and then baseball and football games while doing chores on the weekend. We loved the Minnesota Gophers, but not having our own pro teams, we cheered for the Green Bay Packers and any pro baseball teams we could get on the radio. All that was about to change.

Spring and summer of 1961 brought pro sports to Minnesota at the top level for the first time since the Minneapolis Lakers basketball team and George Miken left for Los Angeles the previous year. I was good at saving money and enjoyed giving gifts. One of my best surprises was taking Dad to see our new team, the Minnesota Twins, at their opening baseball game April 21 at Metropolitan Stadium. We lost to the Washington Senators 5-3, but to the over 24,000 fans present, it was a win, win, win.

I planned to treat Dad to the first game of our first professional football team, the Minnesota Vikings, in the fall.

CHAPTER 8

Summer 1961

LOUIE WOULD HAVE SPORADIC INSULIN INCIDENTS, which we usually could handle at home, and more and more, I became the one to be first on the scene to help him stabilize before going into diabetic shock or coma. I was sure he manipulated his insulin regimen to get attention, but I could never prove it, and he always had an excuse for missing his shot or snack. I tried talking to my parents about it, but they didn't want to hear anything negative about their elder son, so I quit trying.

Remarkably, he attended enough classes to satisfy state attendance requirements and he did manage a C average, so in June, he graduated with the Edison High School class of '61. I graduated the next week from ninth grade at Northeast Junior High and turned fourteen, but that was overshadowed by his accomplishments. My saving grace was when Marlys came home for two weeks, bringing her friend Darcy with her. Darcy was beautiful and very nice to me, becoming my first crush. My sister thought it was silly but knew it was harmless and let me have my moment in my own little world.

My brother's interest in building models and engines, almost everything electrical and mechanical, continued. He was so good that he was accepted as a student at the Chicago DeVry Institute of Technology and began home courses, including building a color television from scratch. He also found a job where he learned how to make false teeth. He was being productive, and his life seemed to be taking shape.

On September 5, 1961, I started tenth grade at Edison and was officially in high school. Over the years at school, I had made a lot of friends, but now everyone seemed to be breaking into groups. We had students from lower Nord'East (mainly Italian, Polish, and Russian descent); Upper Nord'East (mainly Irish and Scandinavian descent); and those of us (myself and kids in the middle of the Northeast area and of all descents) suddenly all in one school. I wasn't comfortable picking sides so remained neutral, using my humor and gift of gab to get along with everyone. At least at first.

Most of my time I spent with my best friend, Todd, who, at six feet tall, blonde, and energetic, was one of the school's best athletes, very popular, and boyfriend of Pam. Todd, Pam, and I had been friends since we started going to sixth grade together at Pillsbury. Throughout junior high, we were in many of the same classes, and Todd and Pam started dating regularly now in high school. Pam never minded me tagging along, and we really bonded when I would be the one to patch up their arguments, which were frequent.

I tried out for the hockey team, gave it my best shot, but finally had to accept that size matters. As long as we were at practice, I could hold my own by outskating and stick-handling my peers, but in game conditions, the other players would just hip check me and I'd go flying. No way my athletic ability could compete with guys a foot taller and a hundred pounds heavier. Who knows what would happen if I faced real opposition? Everyone wished me well and gave me an A for effort, but I retired my hockey skates and this dream to the shelf along with my knife-throwing, dancing, and delivering papers.

My sister did well in college, even though she faced challenges from none other than her own cousin Arlo. While she was at school to get an education and a teaching degree, Arlo enrolled at Mankato State one year after her, majoring in having a good time and specializing in party event organization. He was so good at throwing keg parties that they became more popular than the entertainment of local businesses.

Marlys worked evenings as an operator at the school phone switchboard. Several times she had taken calls from Margy or Irving and, having recognized their voices, would disguise hers to say, "Please hold a minute while I ring Mr. Nelson's room." She'd come back on the line saying, "I'm sorry, but Arlo Nelson has signed out to the library for study group until ten p.m. I'll leave a message you called." She always felt guilty hanging up, but Arlo thought it was hilarious.

At one point, the management of the Norse Lounge, the local college hot spot and home to the Minnesota Vikings during training camps, complained to the college about unfair competition. By his sophomore year, Arlo was asked to leave school and find his education elsewhere or face criminal charges. He took the hint, dropped out of school, and went into construction.

Our social studies class was studying different cultures, and we were given an assignment to develop our family tree and explain how we fit into our society's structure. I was excited because Grandma Dea was my only grandparent living, and I had a lot of questions about the family. I told my folks about it, and Mom said they would set aside some time to talk to me and try and answer my questions. My dad didn't seem too enthusiastic and offered no help.

Interviewing my mom, I was able to go back several generations of her Nelson family heritage. I learned many were of Norwegian descent and, like many Scandinavian families, immigrated to the United States and settled in the Midwest, mainly Minnesota and Wisconsin.

Grandma was first-generation American; both her parents had migrated from Norway in the late 1800s. This explains her first language being Norwegian.

I was amazed how much I learned about my grandfather, Albert Nelson, being an inventor. Although he didn't get the credit for it, never getting a patent, he actually invented the turn signal for automobiles. Like most inventions, this came from necessity—he wanted a way for drivers to alert others of their intentions without having to open the window in bad weather, especially during freezing winter.

I also learned that Uncle Floyd took after his father with inventions. Floyd owned his own plumbing and electrical supply company in Minneapolis. He built a unique water circulation pump that, when placed in the bathtub, would provide hot, moving water over your body, helping to relax tense muscles by increasing blood flow. In the spring of 1952, a man had come to see my uncle, and after a brief meeting, history was about to be made. That man was Candido Jacuzzi.

In 1949, Candido's fifteen-month-old son, Kenneth, was diagnosed with rheumatoid arthritis and was being treated with hydrotherapy. Mr. Jacuzzi had invented a pump to circulate water, and after hearing about my uncle's pump, he asked if he could see a demonstration. Not only was he impressed with it, he got excited at the prospect of what could be done by working together toward advancing treatment for muscle-related illness and injury. The two men found mutual respect in one another, saw great value in merging their talents, and shook hands on a short-term business venture. To celebrate, Candido and his wife, Inez, came to dinner at the Nelson house, and the Jacuzzis met my aunt Eileen.

Mr. Jacuzzi, at forty-nine, was medium height and stocky while his forty-two-year-old wife was several inches taller, slim and stunning. Arriving in full make-up, she wore an evening gown, long white gloves, and hat with veil, and held a long cigarette holder. If she was shocked when she met Aunt Eileen, it didn't show; she was too classy for that. But my aunt, who was even taller, also was fully made up, wearing a fancy dress. When she saw Inez, she picked up her own cigarette holder and had Floyd light her cigarette. The two women swapped kisses on their cheeks, accepted drinks from my uncle, and sat down talking like they were old friends.

For the next several weeks, while the men worked on their secret project—secret from the public anyway—the women got together almost every day to have lunch, shop, or just enjoy each other's company. I had often wondered about my family's relationship with this aunt and uncle and their daughters because they rarely attended family get-togethers. I did hear Margy and my mom talking once about Eileen being from money and thinking she was better than everyone else. They also commented that she dressed up to do the laundry, vacuumed in high heels, and always had a scotch and soda nearby. So what? She was fun, and I liked her.

The day finally came and, before Christmas 1952, it was announced that the Jacuzzi company was patenting the Jacuzzi Pump. Although it was projected to take three to four years to fully market it, the stage was set for the future of indoor spas. Later, I asked Uncle Floyd one time why his name didn't appear anywhere on the Jacuzzi products. He just smiled at me and said, "It was part of the deal I made with their family. And, Rich, it was also a large part of their cost to buy me out." He laughed, and I had just learned a valuable lesson on negotiation.

After I finished my mother's side of the family tree, I asked Dad when it would be a good time for him to sit and help me with his side. He reluctantly came into the living room, looked at what my mom and I had accomplished on her family side, and took a deep breath.

"Rich, I don't have a family side to share with you. I don't know who my parents were, only rumors and what I was told by the people who raised me. You see, son, I'm nobody's child and wouldn't want to contaminate your tree. I'm sorry, but don't ask me any more about it."

I sat stunned, and very quiet. I knew it was a sensitive subject for him, but until now I didn't realize it really hurt him not to have family to call his own. Mom came into the room, tears in her eyes.

"Your father was tossed about when he was young," she told me. "It's amazing he stayed on the straight and narrow, becoming the great guy he is. Although I try to convince him otherwise, he thinks Louie is the way he is because of himself and something in his background. I even think this is one reason he may drink so much; it's an escape for him. Give him time, Rich. It's not your fault."

I went into the living room and hugged my father from behind his chair. "You have a great family, Dad, and I love you." I know he didn't like to show emotion, but he let me have my hug. I went upstairs and never brought the subject up again.

The summer I turned sixteen, between my sophomore and junior years, Dad got me a job at Clark's working full-time in the warehouse where he was foreman. I worked in the office taking orders, answering phones, and learning the plumbing parts business. We were able to commute together, which ordinarily would seem great, but almost every night before heading home, he would have to run across the street for cigarettes. What this actually meant was he would pop into the local bar and have a beer and a couple of shots before heading home. The irony of this was the whole summer, I think he thought I believed it was just for cigarettes.

Marlys and I compared notes once, and she told me that oftentimes, when Dad would pick her up from ballet class or school, he would have to stop for cigarettes. She would remain in the car while he ran into the store, and he'd always comment on how busy they were when he returned twenty to thirty minutes later.

I think my father's drinking had been a problem for a long time. I don't remember ever seeing him drunk, but I would overhear comments at family functions about them not knowing how long my mother would put up with it. I do recall her asking him if he found it necessary to drink every night and if so, he should seek help. I don't think he stood up to defend himself; he'd always just walk out of the room.

Saturday was still chores day, and once a month that included the checkbook task. Mom would take the monthly canceled checks and checkbook register and balance the books. Dad always found somewhere else to be. Until one Saturday I heard, "Clayton, you can't hide, get in here."

"I was just cleaning the basement," he said, sitting down at the kitchen table.

"I have five checks I can't account for. Each one of them in the register you initialed as taking. How many times have I told you to write down the amounts, dates, and who you made them out to?" Dad said nothing. "Okay, check 2103, around the fourth of last month," she said.

"I think I made that out to cash, twenty-five dollars at Monty's."

Giving him a stern look, my mother entered it into the book and continued. "Check 2107 ... 2113 ... 2122 ... 2126?" She looked directly at him. "Also, Monty's? Also, for twenty-five dollars cash? Along with the four others you did fill in? A total of $225 in one month?" She put down her pen and waited for an answer. It didn't come. "Well? Are we going to sit here all day, or are you going to tell me and get this over with?"

"One of them may have been for thirty-five." My father stood, looked totally defeated, and left the room.

"You can't keep doing this, Clayton. I love you, but I won't let you destroy this family, not when we can do something about it. Your decision." My father was out of hearing distance. The tension between them was building.

<hr>

Pam and I were watching Todd and our football team practicing one afternoon in the fall of our junior year when Mr. Brisky, a science teacher, approached me. "Herman, I know you tried out for the hockey team and it didn't work out, but the coach said you were a staunch competitor. He thought I may be able to use you on our wrestling team. I need someone in the 95- and 103-pound divisions. Practice starts in two weeks, so why don't you come out."

It was more like a statement than a question, and with Pam's encouragement, I agreed. That night I told my parents, and they said, "That's nice," but didn't even stop watching "Password" on TV.

When the season started, I was needed to wrestle in the 103-pound division, although I only weighed 98 pounds. The coach said he had someone he thought could win in the 95-pound division, so he wanted me to be a team player and try to get an upset or two during the season. I went 0-13; my only highlight was I managed to avoid getting pinned in two matches. The only person to come see me wrestle was Pam.

Marlys graduated with her teaching degree in June of 1963. She was hired as a math and physical education teacher at the high school in Goodhue, a small town just sixty miles south of Minneapolis, bought a brand-new light blue Chevrolet Nova, and drove off to start her new life. She also hinted at having met a really great guy.

On Sunday morning, August 4, my mom put down the newspaper and said, "Come on, Rich, let's go for a ride." Irving had picked up Dad earlier to help him fix a plumbing problem for one of Irving's clients at a nearby farm. No one knew more about plumbing than my dad.

Mom drove to upper Northeast Minneapolis, and we walked through a house that was for sale and open for viewing. Several couples were walking around asking the realtors questions. We were in the basement when Mom whispered to me, "You'll always take care of me, won't you?" I looked at her, and she winked. "Your father may kill me, but I'm not missing this opportunity."

The next thing I knew we were in the kitchen and my mother was handing the realtor a check. "This is my good faith money to hold the house until tomorrow. Agreed?" As we drove away, I saw one realtor standing with the check in his hand, scratching his head, and another removing the For Sale sign.

At home, I heard the exchange of goodbyes, and Dad came in through the kitchen as Irving drove off. He had grease on his face and filthy hands, but my mother handed him a cold beer before he could even say hello. "Okay, Angie," he said, "what did you do this time?"

My mother explained our day, and my father never said a word until she finished. "You a part of this, Bub?" he said, looking at me. However, this time he wasn't upset or disappointed in me, he was making an attempt at humor.

"Well, I guess I should have charged that farmer more for fixing his plumbing problems, so when do we move?" We all laughed, and my father received a very rare sign of affection in the open from Mom, who now also had grease on her face.

Our house on Pierce sold quickly, and we moved into our new home at 3219 Buchanan Street Northeast (Upper) in time for me to start my senior year. Our house was a single-level, with half-finished basement, three bedrooms, one bath, living room, and kitchen with a dinette. We had a nice-sized front and back yard with a single-car garage next to an alley. Uncle Floyd's family lived on the corner and Uncle Irving's a block over, all on Buchanan. Grandma Dea was just a short distance from us all.

On September 3, 1963, the day after my sister turned twenty-two and my brother twenty, Marlys started her teaching career, Louie was employed at a trucking firm, and I began my senior year at Edison High School, hopeful that a fun-filled experience was just ahead.

CHAPTER 9

Fall 1963

IT FELT GREAT TO WALK THE HALLS AS A SENIOR, wearing the dark blue jacket with cream-colored leather sleeves and the big gold E showing I lettered in wrestling. I hadn't grown taller, but I did gain some weight, mainly muscle, over the summer, up to 108 pounds. I was determined to be a wrestling winner and had been lifting weights for three months.

When the season was about to begin, I would fluctuate between 108 and 110 pounds, so I put myself on a diet of one meal a week, after a match, and drinking only water with some fruit and raw vegetables the rest of the week. I also started going to the sauna at a spa two blocks from the school, every other day and always the night before matches. Before match weigh-ins, I would force myself to throw up before getting on the scale, although I usually only coughed up phlegm. I would step on the scale, blow out all my air, and every time make exact weight.

The only senior in the city wrestling at 95 pounds, I was soon rated among the best! My coaches and parents never knew of my routine.

The last regular season match, I had my first fan other than Pam show up. When the whistle blew to start the first period, Marlys walked into the gymnasium. I was so shocked to see her I almost let my opponent take me down. I recovered quickly, pinned him in the second period, and ran to hug my sister. She had someone take over her afternoon classes and drove up just to see me wrestle. She put the icing on the cake for my winning season, seeming to always know when I needed that little recognition.

I made it to regionals and won a couple of early rounds, but when it came to the championship, with my parents in attendance, I didn't have enough left in the tank and fell 2-1 in overtime to the eventual state champion. The one and only match my parents ever attended, and I lost.

I made a point of visiting Grandma often. In the summer I would mow the grass, the winter, shovel her sidewalk, and many times I just visited to say hello and maybe see if she needed help with the Sunday crossword puzzle.

As her first language was Norwegian, she learned English late in her life. Mom got her to do crossword puzzles to help with the words and their meanings. To everyone's amazement, she got so good at it, she could now do the New York Times Sunday crossword using a pen! That didn't stop me from always asking if I could help. She would smile and hand over the already finished puzzle.

Grandma had some funny quirks, too. She loved to play cards, 500 and whist, but during games, she insisted on her chair sitting parallel with the bathroom tub and in line with the crack in the table. She was adamant about the tub rule but would allow the crack to be covered, if it lay perpendicular to the tub, so the game could be played.

One Friday night it was late, and I called my parents telling them I would be staying the night with Grandma. I was about to curl up on the couch when she asked me to come help her. I knocked on her bedroom door and when I entered, I saw she had unplugged her TV and was trying to turn it around to face the wall.

"What are you doing, Grandma?"

"I need to get the TV to face the wall so I can get ready for bed." She obviously saw the look of confusion on my face. "That announcer on WCCO, Dick Nesbitt, always starts his sports show saying, 'Hey, folks, you're looking good out there,' and I'm not about to let him or anyone else see me undress." I was actually able to hold back from laughing and did as she asked. After all, could she be right?

Grandma didn't drink, that is, except at Thanksgiving and Christmas dinner. A gallon bottle of Mogen David wine was always a fixture on our holiday table, and everyone got to toast the occasion. Dad allowed us kids to have a small glass after Mom convinced him it was as harmless as taking communion. Grandma always said no, but then, my dad poured her a glass, and when the toast was made, she would pick up her glass and drink all the wine in one gulp. Then she would put the glass in the center of the table as if no one would realize it was hers.

On February 24, 1964, Grandma asked that I help her plan some dinners. She told me that she thought it would be nice to have each of her kids and their families for dinner, one family at a time, the next four Sundays. (Her daughter Irene, living in Seattle, would have to miss out.) Grandma had me help her make actual invitations, and we walked to the post box together and mailed them. The schedule was Sherm's family, March 1; Irving's, March 8; Floyd's, March 15; and ours, March 22, Palm Sunday. Our dinner was great and I'm sure all the others were too. Little did we know that Grandma had a reason to have these dinners; she knew better than anyone what she was doing, saying goodbye.

On Tuesday, March 24, Grandma got sick and needed hospitalization. It was serious enough to call Irene and tell her if she wanted to see her mother alive, she had better come soon. Marlys said she would come home for the weekend to see Grandma and celebrate Easter. Irene was in the air when Grandma passed away Friday morning. Mom and I met her at the airport and as soon as the sisters' eyes met, Irene knew it was too late. When Marlys arrived that night, she walked in to see her aunt sitting at the kitchen table holding Mom's hand. She too knew she was too late. Dea Nelson, seventy-five, my grandma and last living grandparent, my friend, was now resting in Eternal Peace.

My senior year was fun, with some unusual experiences. Having enough credits to graduate, I convinced Todd and a couple of other buddies to take Home Economics with me. We were the first males to take the course in Minneapolis and, as a result, even got an article in the city's largest newspaper, my one-time employer, the Star and Tribune. The first day of class, Punky saw me enter and hid her head. As it turned out, we learned a lot, and although we did torment our teacher, we all got A's. Most of the kids in school thought we were crazy; I considered us trend-setters.

While everyone in the family played cards and bowled together, one of my mother's true loves was playing Scrabble. Always liking a good challenge, I used to play with her, but even after hundreds of games, and being fairly competitive, I had never beaten her. Mom would never intentionally lose a game and taught me that winning that way was worthless, as you learned nothing.

Then one Saturday morning she said, "No chores for you and me today, Rich, let's go for a ride." I had learned that Mom's "going for a ride" would always be exciting.

As we entered the Radisson Hotel, downtown Minneapolis, I saw a billboard outside one of the conference rooms saying "Welcome, Scrabble Players 1964." I knew I'd been set up. I looked at Mom. "You have to be kidding." She wasn't.

There was a sign-up sheet with registered entrants' names, which included ours, and we received name tags and a table number assignment. There were 256 players at 128 tables; Mom was at the fourteenth table and I at the seventy-fourth. She smiled, wished me luck, and was gone. I found my seat and had my ID checked by a young lady who turned out to be our scorekeeper.

"Welcome, Scrabble players," a gentlemen greeted us from the stage. "Although we have yet to form a sanctioning body to make our tournaments official, this two-day event, six matches today and two tomorrow, will be recognized by the Minnesota State Scrabble Council, not only for state but national rankings." The crowd cheered and clapped, and all I could think about was—two days.

He continued, "All national approved Scrabble rules apply.

Smoking of cigarettes and pipes allowed, no cigars. No alcoholic beverages. Games will be sixty minutes with each player having three minutes allowed to play between words. A player has fifteen seconds to accept or challenge their opponent's word before their turn starts. The clock will stop with a challenge, and each player is allowed two challenges each game." He stopped to take a sip of water.

"Four approved dictionaries are available for challenges and judges assigned to each one. A judge's rule is final. You will circle your choice of dictionary on the paper in front of you, show it to your opponent, and hand it to your scorekeeper." *Four dictionaries?* I thought. *I don't even know four different dictionaries.*

The tournament would be single elimination except for the final round Sunday determining our champion being a best of three series, he told us. "Please draw to see who goes first, then select your first rack of letters. Play begins in one minute at the sound of the bell."

Across from me sat an elderly lady, maybe Grandma's age, who introduced herself as Pat, gave me a limp handshake, and drew a tile from the bag first. I followed suit. When we showed our letters, mine was an O, while she had an A, so she would start. Replacing the tiles in the bag, we each drew seven new ones. On my rack I had B, E, G, I, K, N, and R. Not bad, I could work with that so felt pretty good. I looked up and Pat showed no emotion. The bell rang.

The scorekeeper turned over the three-minute timer, and within ten seconds Pat laid all seven of her tiles on the board. "QUICKLY, 120 points," she said.

What? You've got to be kidding. "Accept," I said, and the timer was turned.

I had never been under a timer before, Mom and I usually played fast enough we didn't use one, and I couldn't help but look at it. I heard a bag being ripped open and saw Pat put a handful of potato chips in her mouth. Immediately, the loud crunching and deliberate mouth-smacking irritated me, and I was totally distracted. I'm sure I was about out of time and quickly placed four letters around the I tile. "BRINK, twenty-seven points." I started to draw my new tiles.

"Accept," Pat said, laying down another word before I had my tiles on my rack. "Eighty-four points," I heard. The game went downhill from there.

It was probably good I didn't have a white hanky because I would have considered surrendering after the first five moves. As it was, when time was called, the final score on the board was 322-183. To put salt in the wound, as Pat was leaving the table, she said, "You should have challenged my play of PTARMIGIN, it's spelt with an A after the G, not an I."

Mom won her first game easily and moved on. She won the next five matches—including revenge for me, defeating my fierce opponent Pat—qualifying for the semi-finals and a return the following day. Sunday morning, the final four drew their opponents out of a hat, and play began.

Mom drew the reigning champion, number-one ranked player in the state and among the top five in the country. After the initial four plays at each table, the crowd started whispering. Almost everyone wanted to watch this upstart player challenging the heavy favorite. Play was stopped and the two tables rearranged to accommodate the large crowd who, as the newspaper articles would report, witnessed the greatest championship Scrabble game ever played. Yes, Mom would lose the match 331-312, but she won the hearts of the people and of the man who won it all, Edgar Thornberg, who would die two years later a virtual unknown.

Punky and I were more like a brother and sister than cousins, so when she found the love of her life, it seemed natural for her to want to get my approval. Uncle Irving liked her new boyfriend; after all, he grew up on a farm, was a Christian, and obviously had a good work ethic. Arlo liked him because he finally met someone worthy of his little sister. That left me.

The day finally came for me to meet Gary Irene. He pulled up out front of the Nelson house in his big, bright red Bonneville coupe and strode confidently to the door. I answered the doorbell and found myself with my nose in his throat, although he was standing on the stoop eight inches below. I looked up, he looked down and said, "I'm here to see Jackie and meet Rich."

"I'm Rich," I said.

This tall man stared down at me and burst out laughing. "What are you, about twelve?" He had a good point, as I was so small and did look like a little kid. Then he broke into a big smile and reached out to shake my hand. "Nice to meet you, Rich."

"Same here," I shot back, trying not to show the pain in my bones, realizing he was showing me who was in charge. Still, I immediately liked him and knew he would be good for my cousin. "Come on, Punky is in the living room waiting for you."

"Wait a minute," the big guy stopped me. "Why do you call her Punky? I never heard anyone else call her that."

I smiled. "When we were about three or four years old, Uncle Irving was helping us carve a pumpkin for Halloween. Jackie couldn't say pumpkin, it came out *punkin*, and I thought it was funny and started calling her Punky. It stuck. You're right, I'm the only one who calls her that, and it's kind of our little joke."

"That makes sense. I like it, but will let you two have your own nickname. Jackie said you guys were close."

Marlys had also found the love of her life, James Foster, from Gladstone in Michigan's Upper Peninsula. I really liked Jim, and when they announced they were getting married I was truly happy for them. The wedding took place on June 20, 1964, and was beautiful. For once, Louie didn't pull one of his stunts to grab the attention away from his sister, and the day went without a hitch. Jim was very protective of his wife and I think, realizing our family situation, couldn't wait to get his new bride to the UP. I would learn to realize just how good a decision that was.

For their wedding, I wanted to give a meaningful present. I decided what it would be, and with Aunt Margy agreeing to let me use their attic over the next two months, at night, I painted the "Lord's Supper" by number. I had it framed and gave it to them the night before their wedding. Although some jerk commented on a few small spaces I missed, Marlys had tears in her eyes when I gave it to her. She knew how much I loved her.

Surrounding her wedding date, I graduated with the Edison Class of '64 on June 18 and turned eighteen on June 23. Out of high school, with no real ties or commitments, other than enrolling at the University of Minnesota, my future was mine. It would be a start.

CHAPTER 10

Summer 1964

I FOUND MY DREAM CAR, A YELLOW 1957 CHEVROLET Bel Air two-door hardtop. With Mom's help, we negotiated an affordable price. When I got my license, I had passed the State Drivers Education Class, which gave us a ten-percent discount. I stayed on my parents' automobile insurance policy and paid them directly.

I was working nights at Briggs Trucking Company, verifying and filing invoices. Although I had my own car, Gary Irene worked down the road at another company and would drop me off and pick me up each night for work. After every shift, we would stop at White Castle and get twenty hamburgers, ten for a dollar. I would eat five or six burgers and Gary the rest. We became great friends, with Punky, now a senior at Edison, being our common thread. At family gatherings it would be Arlo, Gary, and me hanging together, a very close group.

Unlike Marlys, I remained at home where my parents said I could live rent- and board-free as long as I was in college. As planned, I enrolled at the University of Minnesota and when fall semester started, I had a place to live, a job that paid for my tuition, books, insurance, and my car. Louie was still at home, but he had been less reliant on me for quite a while.

That all changed in the spring of 1965.

I was maintaining a B average when Louie started having some minor insulin episodes. Little did I know how much they were affecting me, but I was finding it hard to concentrate and always seemed tired. More and more, I had to take care of him, a task my parents had just grown tired of over the years and were glad to have shifted the responsibility to me.

On the day of my final exam for calculus, I was running late and, if I had trouble parking, would miss the exam. Louie offered to drive me, and as we approached campus, he turned left, straight into the path of an oncoming eighteen-wheel semi truck. We were struck behind my passenger door, and the force of the impact caused us to spin around several times. No one was seriously hurt, and Louie told the policemen he had thought he had time to make the turn safely.

My brother received a ticket for failure to yield, but I knew it had been on purpose that he just overshot his distance a few feet. I kept my opinion to myself. After all, no one believed the kid who they thought once tried to fly like Superman, so why would they now? When I arrived late to the exam, the proctor was sympathetic but said either take the exam or fail the course. I fought a terrible headache and managed a C on the exam. Meanwhile, everyone felt sorry for Louie.

I continued to get more sluggish, saw my doctor, and was diagnosed with mononucleosis. Complete bed rest was required, and Marlys immediately came to get me, taking me to her and Jim's place in South Range, Michigan, to recover.

After I was well enough to return home, my sister insisted I stay there until my fall semester at the university started mid-September to ensure there was no relapse. There is no doubt in my mind that she and Jim saved my life by taking me in and keeping me away from the pressures at home, especially the responsibility of my older brother.

One day in mid-October after classes, instead of going straight home, I decided to join several classmates for a study group at a campus coffee shop. A while after getting there, I called the house to check on Louie and when I got no answer, drove straight home. I found him already slipping into a diabetic coma and drove him straight to the emergency room. After I'd convinced the ER doctor that he needed a shot of pure glucose or we could lose him, Louie finally came around and soon was out of danger. He would live to see another day.

I called my father; he was busy but would get there when he could. My mother gave me the same response. I called Uncle Sherm and, although I don't remember the conversation, convinced his secretary to interrupt a counseling session he was having, even with the DO NOT DISTURB red light on.

I had collapsed. Sherm dropped everything and came to the ER. When the staff on duty saw Doctor Sherman E. Nelson was coming to get me, they couldn't respond to his demands fast enough.

My uncle drove me to my parents' house to pack some clothes. Apparently, my father had finally gotten away from work; I heard him shouting in the front yard.

"You're not taking him anywhere," my father said, raising his voice.

"Get in the car, Richie," Uncle Sherm said. I started toward his car.

"Get back in the house," my father ordered, stepping between me and the car.

Uncle Sherm walked between us and, putting his hand on my shoulder, escorted me to the car, keeping his body between me and my father. He closed the door behind me as I got in the passenger seat. I was shaking.

"Clayton," Sherm said, "I know this is difficult, but we need to think about what's best for Richie, and right now, that is coming to stay with me for a while. I'll call you and Angeline tomorrow, but until then, accept my professional opinion."

We drove away. My father stood there alone, and I could see tears in his eyes. I think he was as confused as I was, but I loved my uncle and trusted his decision. I was still shaking.

The next morning, my uncle checked in on me and, realizing I was still overwhelmed by what took place yesterday, called his office. He said to cancel his appointments but he would take calls at the house. He poured us a cup of coffee and talked to me, not only as my uncle, but as my personal therapist.

"Rich," he started, "your mother and father are two of the most caring and unselfish people you will ever find. They took me, at age twelve, and my mother, your grandmother Dea, into their home when your grandfather died—and most likely saved us from a life with no future. These were difficult times for everyone, and then, when Louie was born and a year later diagnosed with juvenile diabetes, they were looking at raising a special needs child as well. They never complained and never asked for help from the family." He refilled our cups.

"Your father never would have survived without the strength of your mother, and she wouldn't have survived without the love and support of your father. Still, time was wearing them down, and as you got older, they saw someone who could help relieve much of the burden. The more responsibility you took on, the more they gave you. Yesterday, everything came to a head, and your mind and body said 'enough' and shut down. Your parents didn't realize what toll these years have taken on you."

"I don't even remember calling you yesterday," I said weakly. "Mom and Dad have to be pretty upset, I let them down."

"No, you didn't," Uncle Sherm said immediately. "And they'll realize that soon enough, either by your mom figuring it out or when I go see them and tell them exactly what has happened. Your father will be angry with me, probably for a long time if not forever, but your mom, who is as much a mother as an older sister to me, will accept it and, more importantly, own up to it. One thing, though, and you may not want to hear this." He paused a moment.

"Your mother is a wonderful person, smart, with an IQ of genius for sure, strong, compassionate, and I could go on and on, but she is human and does have one flaw. She is blind when it comes to Louie. For whatever reason, guilt or feeling she must protect him at all costs, she cannot see him doing wrong or even think he is less than perfect. She loves you and Marlys, but she'll always protect her needy son."

"Master Herman," I heard through the intercom several days later. It was my uncle's housekeeper, Darla. "Time to get up." I covered my head and moaned. Sherm had tasked Darla with getting me up to get to classes on time.

The night Sherm brought me here from the ER, I was given the master bedroom, located on the second floor of his beautiful home on Lake of the Isles. Sherm, divorced from Joyce, took a room off the kitchen, saying I needed the space and privacy more than he did. I was in no shape to argue, just thankful I had such a caring uncle.

"Be right there, Darla," I said and rolled out of bed. I knew she was following orders, and I didn't want to get her into trouble. I also happened to like her with her deep Slavic accent and funny expressions. She wasn't that great a housekeeper, but she was good with Sherm's kids—Shannon, Kyle, Matt, and Chrisanne—and was also a great cook. Her one downfall was she liked to drink the wine more than cook with it. Sherm said until it was a problem, she could stay on.

Living with my uncle was an education in itself. Never mentioning patients' names, he would share some of his cases with me, and I soon learned my problems were small compared to many others. Every case, although some would have similarities, had to be treated as a one of a kind and their treatment plans tailored for them. If nothing else, I learned that people could be possibly grouped into a labeled diagnosis (for example, paranoia, schizophrenia, and so on), but their treatment had to be tailored for their particular needs.

Sherm was the team psychologist for both the Minnesota Twins baseball and Vikings football teams. Many of the baseball players were Cuban, spoke little or no English, were uneducated and emotional wrecks trying to fit into a new culture that saw them as superstars. The football players were often overwhelmed by their newfound fame and fortune and, without a good family support system, found it hard to adapt.

Sherm conducted a study on football players and fear. He found that the professional quarterbacks were the most fearless—in fact, almost immune to danger. The quarterbacks also scored the highest on the IQ charts. Maybe boosting my ego, one day at lunch Sherm said, "Too bad you're not bigger, you could probably be a quarterback."

During one session, a Minnesota running back—who will remain nameless but was an All-Pro—was asked by Sherm how good his peripheral vision was. The player didn't know what that was, and Sherm explained that it referred to how much he could see to each side while running looking straight ahead. Sherm said he figured it had to be very wide and most likely when he ran, he reacted to the color of the opposing team's uniform to know when to cut and keep from being tackled.

Doing a non-scientific check, Sherm had the player follow his finger going side to side while looking straight ahead and say stop when he lost sight of it. Indeed, the player had an exceptional range of vision. The next game, that back, who only fumbled once the prior year, fumbled four times. He told my uncle he couldn't stop thinking about seeing the runners in his side view and lost all concentration. Luckily, the Vikings still won the game.

It was great to be free from the responsibility of being my brother's primary caregiver. I had talked to Mom and Dad, and they understood why Sherm did what he did. My dad might never forgive him, but Mom was realistic and knew it was actually for the best. For me, I still found it hard to concentrate in class and also found myself distracted by the world events and the great division in the country over a turmoil happening in Southeast Asia.

I soon started worrying about my grades and my future in general. To avoid failing out of the semester, I decided to take incompletes with the intent to return next semester and take the courses again. It sounded like a good plan to me.

One night I got a call from Punky, and my mind was taken off my problems as I focused on her and Gary. "We have a big favor to ask," she said. "Hang on for Gary."

"Hey, little guy," Gary said, "Do you have any plans for November 20th?"

"Not if you need me to help you with something," I replied immediately. I'd do anything for them.

"I'd like you to be my best man at our wedding."

A great wedding it was. Margy and Irv went all out for their only daughter, and she was a beautiful bride. Gary was nervous, and as best man I made sure he stayed that way. After all, he was marrying my cousin. When it came time for them to leave on their honeymoon, Gary drove up in front of the Nelsons' house in the shiny red Bonneville and ran into the house to get their suitcases.

I took this opportunity to say goodbye to my best friend, jumped in the driver's seat, and drove off with the bride. We returned about ten minutes later, to find a red-faced Gary was sitting, with the luggage, on the front steps. I pulled up, got out, and ran. Luckily, I could outrun him, and of course, he didn't chase me far, his priority was his new wife. I wonder why everyone was laughing, except Gary.

I was comfortable with my decision to take a semester off school. I continued to work but now I had ample time to think. Living with Sherm was great, and I found myself almost every evening talking to him and his fiancé, Denise, late into the night. Denise, a psychology doctoral candidate, was possibly as bright as my uncle, and even my mother. She didn't scare me, but I was always uneasy with her as it seemed she could look right through me when we talked.

Then of course, in me, she found someone who wasn't afraid to disagree with her, and I think she respected that. Her views on war and our country definitely didn't align with mine, and I often asked her, "Why do you live here—why not move overseas?" She would never give me a direct answer, only say that I'd see she was right some day. Unfortunately, that day might have already been predestined for me.

By December, talk was growing about the U.S. getting more involved in the Vietnam conflict. On the morning of December 7, 1965, I felt compelled to check my mail at my parents' house. No one was home, and I saw the mail on the floor as I opened the door. One envelope stood out from all the rest. My hand shook as I picked it up.

Yes, it was addressed to me. The return address of the U.S. Selective Service said it all. My life was about to change forever. I had received what would one day be known as: *The Unopened Letter.*

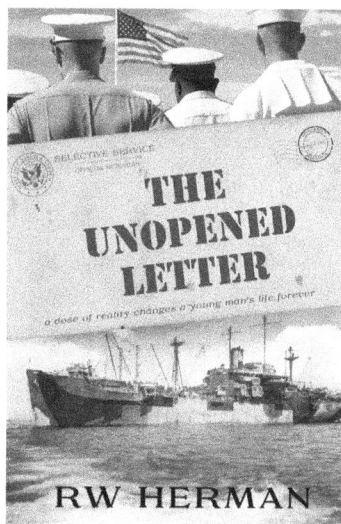

THE
UNOPENED
LETTER
a dose of reality changes a young man's life forever

RW HERMAN

Author's Note

As you just read, I had received my draft notice. I took that letter to the local Navy recruiter and joined the military. In 1970, when I returned home from my first enlistment, my mother handed me a box containing all the letters I had written home during this four-year period. She had one request: "One day, write a book about your experience so that others can enjoy your adventure as much as your family has."

The Unopened Letter, which fulfilled that request, is dedicated to Angeline Aldea Herman. It is a coming-of-age story during the Vietnam Era, when 27 million young men had to face reality and fateful choices, and I made a life-altering decision while remaining committed to serving my country. I embarked on a journey to many countries and cultures, witnessed historical events, and often found myself in unfortunate, but humorous, international incidents. The book follows me as I grew from teenager to the man I was upon my return—having answered one of life's vital questions: Would I be a leader, a follower, or just in the way?

Now, look forward to reading about my life after *The Unopened Letter.*

TRANSITION YEARS

January 1970 – September 1972

"I would be making a decision … Richard William Herman had come to the fork in the road at age twenty-four, just as his mother predicted …vowing never to look back."

CHAPTER 11

LAST FRIDAY MORNING, I HAD BEEN STANDING BRIG guard duty at the Naval Station, Philadelphia, the last stop on my way back from the Mediterranean Sea. My discharge was due to be processed here—but a personnel officer had brusquely informed me I was being detained on active duty, up to ninety days, for the needs of the Navy. There seemed no way to change this situation. Suddenly, last Saturday I was amazed to be told to pack up, people began treating me like a VIP, and I found myself on a plane home the next morning.

Sunday afternoon, my mother picked me up at the Minneapolis airport. I knew she must have had something to do with this change in orders, as she had hinted she knew someone who might help. But when I questioned her about it on the way home, she remained vague about details, saying we would talk about it later. I was just glad to be home and soon returning to college.

This morning, Mom took Dad to work and said she was taking me to lunch. I was surprised, but pleased, when we pulled into Martin's, a high-end steakhouse and lounge in Northeast Minneapolis. "It's time you and I have our own private conversation," she said.

The restaurant owner and my good friend from high school, Harry Trost, greeted us and led us to a back booth. He whispered something to my mom, gave her a hug, and welcomed me home with a firm handshake and slap on the back.

A waitress brought Mom a Presbyterian, a whiskey with soda water and ginger ale mixers, her drink of choice, and placed a locally made Grain Belt beer in front of me. Mom lit a cigarette, and I knew this moment was special because she never drank or smoked in the middle of the day. I didn't know why.

"For the past four years," she started, "every time you came home on leave, you honored your father by wearing your uniform to pick him up at work and then have drinks with all his guys. Your father would never say it, but he looked forward to that more than any other time during the year. Last night, I told him I wanted my own time with my son. Welcome home again, son." We clinked our drinks.

"I think you're a lot like me, Rich, and it's time you know a little more about the real Angeline Aldea Herman. I've never had this conversation with anyone, and I ask you to respect that for any communications you have in the future. You asked if it was Hubert Humphrey, the ex-vice president, I called about that Navy base trying to keep you three more months?" She looked at me and knew I was paying attention.

"No, it wasn't Hubert. Not directly anyway. I contacted his protégé, Don Frazier." She saw my blank look and laughed. "Oh, son, if you want something done, you go to the person who can make it happen. Don said he'd mention it to Hubert, and that was that." I raised my beer in a toast, and we both took a drink in appreciation.

"Let's back up," she continued. "When I graduated from high school, the country was in the Depression, and families were struggling. I wanted to go to college, but it wasn't in the cards. All five of my siblings and I worked, and our money went to the family. It's just the way it was. No one complained—like, who would listen?— and we survived and even managed some good times along the way. I did go to secretarial school at night—probably the best choice I ever made." She motioned for another drink, and I passed on a second beer. I wanted to remember this.

"I started typing university students' doctorate theses. I charged ten cents a page, with one carbon copy; the student provided the paper, carbon sheets, and typewriter ribbons they wanted used. I got so proficient that my reputation spread to the Law and Business School, and I was soon being asked to type court briefings and corporate merger briefs. My list of clients grew and included many new, up-and-coming lawyers and others destined for promising futures. Much of what I typed was privileged sensitive briefings. Do you see where this is heading?"

"I assume one of those young, aspiring clients was Humphrey? You had to do more than type a paper for him." Realizing how that sounded, I was totally embarrassed.

Mom burst out laughing. "We'll skip that remark. But you're right, I did more than type. I would also edit and make suggestions. As more people heard about me, I became a consultant to many others. And do you know what I am very proud of, son? Never, not once, did I breach their trust. Believe me, I had many an opportunity, but here's something I hope you will always remember. Nothing is more important than your word and reputation, Rich." I gave her a moment to collect her thoughts. I had never seen her so serious. Or drink so fast.

"What I'm about to tell you is probably the deepest secret I have. I'm sharing this with you because I think someday you are going to face a similar challenge that will define not only your life but you, as a person. I want you to know how I came to my decision and what I have lived with all these years. I never looked back, and I want you to be able to do the same when the time comes.

"Hubert Humphrey, when he became mayor of Minneapolis, asked me to be his executive secretary. As much as I wanted to say yes, I turned him down because I had a great job and didn't want to jeopardize the stability of our family. However, I believed in him and agreed to become his confidential advisor and sounding board, under one condition—his wife, Muriel, had to know and approve of the relationship, and no one else would ever be told. They both agreed immediately, and our close friendship has never wavered.

"I consulted on and edited his paper on the nation's first municipal fair employment law. Its success as a breakthrough in civil rights soon spread across the nation. On your second birthday, holding you on my lap, I made editing comments and opinions to the famous speech he gave in support of civil rights to the 1948 Democratic National

Convention—a speech that many credit with making Truman president and Humphrey a U.S. senator." She hesitated as if reliving that moment. "Then I had to make a life-altering decision. Hubert asked me to go to Washington as a special assistant for policy on his staff."

"Wow!" I blurted out. This story was getting more surprising every minute.

"I love your father with all my heart," she said. "He is a good man, even a great man in his own way. He could never have adjusted to the life in D.C. Your brother had medical needs I believe only Mayo Hospital in Rochester could fill. I like to think it was the hardest decision I ever had to make, but it was also the easiest decision I ever had to make. I couldn't put my career—a virtual secret up to now, and possibly even a dream—ahead of what I had in Minneapolis. I turned Hubert, and Muriel, down. They understood and told me they respected my decision, and if there was ever anything we needed, give them a call. So, I did. And here you are."

I embraced my mother and hugged her like I had never done before. All my life I had listened to others say how brilliant she was and that, had she been a man, she probably could have become the president of the United States. Everyone would laugh, but at this moment a thought struck me—if she had made a different decision that day and decided to go with Humphrey, just how far could she have gone up the political ladder? Neither of us noticed the new drinks before us.

She had more to discuss. "I think you've known for a long time your father has a dependency on alcohol. I can make all the excuses for him I want; Lord knows his life has not been an easy one. He's been knocked down, yet gets back up and never complains. He's always had compassion for other people. Even when we could hardly afford to take care of ourselves, he took in Sherm, who was twelve, and Grandma, because they were not coping well on their own after my father died," she said.

"Your dad has never been able to deal with not knowing who his birth parents are, and he blames himself for Louie's physical and mental health problems. He keeps things inside and to cope, I believe, finds an escape with drinking. I'm going to confront your father eventually and tell him I will not live with him like this when we retire."

Years ago, Angeline Herman had come to a fork in the road of her life at age thirty-five. She chose the path of her future and never looked back. It was her private story, yet she chose to share it with me. I listened, I heard every word, and I will never forget this conversation with this remarkable woman, and she was my mother, making me blessed for sure.

We ordered and enjoyed a wonderful meal, talking about the future and plans I might have. She let me know her boss wanted to talk to me about a job as social worker assistant, and I could work my hours around my school schedule. I took Mom home before picking up Dad at work. By the time he and I had a drink with the boys and got home, Mom was sound asleep in their bed. Maybe now I knew why she didn't drink in the afternoon.

CHAPTER 12

Wednesday, January 7

I CALLED MARY EHLERT, A GIRL I MET BRIEFLY LAST year when home on leave. She worked for my mother and had written to me while I was deployed overseas, and I had told her I would look her up when I got home. It was a joke really as I remembered her as a short, heavyset teen with braces and acne, not someone I was really interested in. But a promise was a promise.

That Friday night, I knocked on the door, and a young lady—I assumed Mary's sister—opened it. I told her I was there to see Mary. She said that would be her. I was speechless. Before me stood a cute girl, still short but now trim, with long blonde hair, nearly perfect teeth, and a smooth complexion. She introduced me to her father, Charles ("Bud"), older brother Bill, and younger brother Jim. Her mother, an RN, was at work at Fairview Hospital.

A little over six feet tall, Mary's father had wavy white hair and a white beard with a black streak on the chin. He wore a silk smoking jacket with matching scarf around his neck and looked like he was dressed to make a movie. Brother Bill was shorter, stockier, with short black hair and looked comfortable watching television and drinking his beer. Brother Jim, brown-haired and bigger than his dad, hardly looked up to acknowledge my presence.

Bud thanked me for my service, then reminded me that Mary wasn't twenty-one yet and I better keep that in mind. He also made the point of telling me she was the only girl in the family and I better keep that in mind, too. I smiled, told him I understood, and shook his hand. Although not totally uncomfortable, I gladly departed.

I intended to go to a local pizza parlor but changed plans and took her to Martin's. Harry Trost came over to our table, introduced himself, and I was able to thank him for taking such good care of my mom and me Tuesday. I could tell Harry liked Mary and as always, won her over, all the while praising me. I made sure I mentioned to Mary that he was our homecoming king, class of '64, and also my big protector, a story I would tell her someday.

Harry was what I think everyone calls a "man's man." Tall with wavy black hair, a great smile, and super personality, he also had a brilliant business mind. At eighteen, he had convinced his father to back him financially and purchased a liquor store and the restaurant. Not being twenty-one, he named both businesses after his brother Martin, also putting the liquor licenses in his name. He confided in me that on his twenty-first birthday, he paid back his father in full, got the liquor and food licenses in his own name, and was now sole owner of all the properties. He may not have been voted most likely to succeed, but there was no doubt in my mind he would be the first to earn a million.

We couldn't have had a better start to our first date. During dinner, I mentioned my folks had purchased three acres on the Pine River in Brainerd, about 120 miles north. They planned to build their retirement home there; in the meantime, they had transported the garage from our neighbor's back yard on Buchanan onto their riverfront property, turning it into a year-round cabin. It was a clear night, cold with the temperature below zero and about three feet of snow on the ground, but the roads were plowed. Why not? We headed north.

We arrived in Brainerd shortly after midnight. After a few missed turns, I found the sign saying "Pair-a-Dice." I turned down the half-mile dirt road to my parents' cabin, struggling a bit on the unplowed road, but the snow tires gripped well enough for me to make it safely.

The stars were out, with almost a full moon, and the river was flowing, although much was iced over. My folks had definitely named this place perfectly. I found the key to the cabin, and we made ourselves at home. It wasn't fancy, but Dad had gotten water (he was an expert and made extra money drilling wells), electricity, and heat hooked up. In no time we were comfortable, and I even popped popcorn. All was going well when the inevitable happened. Mary said she needed to go to the bathroom.

"What do you mean it's outside?" she asked in disbelief. "An outhouse? In below zero weather? No, no way."

"You can just go outside the door if you want," I said defensively. "I won't watch."

She looked at me, sat down, and started laughing. "This is going to make for a great story. Do you at least have toilet paper?" The only toilet paper was in the outhouse so I handed her a couple of napkins. "Oh, perfect." She was heading for the door when we heard a noise outside. We both froze.

I looked out and saw a large, dark figure run into the woods, toward the river. "We have company," I said. "Probably a deer, but black bears have been known to come out of hibernation now and then, so I can't be sure." I turned and Mary was in the small kitchen area. "What are you doing?"

"I don't see a gun so I'm looking for a knife and something to make a torch with. I'm not going down without a fight."

I started to laugh, then realized she was serious. "Whoa, back up, girl. Whatever it was, it ran away. It's more scared of us than we are of it." She didn't look convinced, and I wished I had a camera to capture this moment, hair falling over her face, holding a steak knife, and acting so brave. "You can go to the bathroom now, we're safe."

"I sort of went," she said, checking her pants. Laughing, she came over to smack me on the arm. "Great first date, sailor. Almost getting me killed."

We closed up, and I drove to the first open business I could find for her to freshen up. We stopped again for breakfast, so I got her home just after sunrise. No one was awake, but as I walked her to the door, a 1966 Plymouth Valiant, which was actually Mary's, pulled into the driveway. A short, heavyset, gray-haired lady in a nurse's uniform got out. I got to meet Mary's mother, Margaret, briefly and found her delightful. I immediately thought of how her personality was totally opposite to that of her husband.

Yes, it was going to be interesting if our dating continued. From my experience with our first date, I sure hoped we would.

CHAPTER 13

January 12

I STARTED AGAIN WHERE I HAD LEFT OFF IN 1965 AT the University of Minnesota. My plan was simple; at least I thought it was. I'd continue my education, live at home with my parents, and use the G.I. Bill to pay for my books and tuition. To cover other expenses, I got the job as an assistant for social welfare programs; I would be at the same agency where my mother was executive assistant to the director.

The moment I stepped into my first classroom, Physics 201, I could tell how different I felt from my first day in the fall of 1964. There was no doubt I had grown up a great deal during the four years in the Navy. Much more mature and confident in my abilities, I stood out from the majority of my classmates who were still finding their way and thought the conflict/war in Vietnam was the defining moment in their lives.

I settled into a routine and was doing well at school, liked my job providing aid to the less fortunate, and was comfortable being in a serious relationship. I became the new place-setting at the Ehlert Sunday dinner, a family tradition, and her family seemed comfortable that I was dating Mary. Especially her mother.

As spring arrived, so did more and more protests on university campuses across the nation, including the U of Minnesota. At first, I just ignored them. Before long, students started blocking the entrances to classrooms, and this is where I took my stand.

I always wore my flight jacket, one item of clothing I kept when discharged, which had the American flag on the back and the words

"Served My Country, and Proud of It." I would put my military pink ID card, showing that I had served honorably on active duty, on my forehead and push my way through the crowd. No one physically challenged me, other than a few shoves, but I was usually spat on and called "Baby Killer." I remained passive, but one day a group of protesters lay down blocking the road to campus, and a local biker group consisting of veterans, many having served in Vietnam, slowly ran over them. I cheered for the bikers.

At the beginning of April, I placed an engagement ring on Mary's finger and asked her to be my wife. After saying yes, she handed me the keys to her Plymouth, saying it was our car now, and we went to tell the parents. Of course, out of respect, I had already asked and gotten her father's blessing. A June wedding was planned, three weeks after her twenty-first birthday. Both our families were excited, but there was one glitch. To get Margaret and Bud's, and the church's, blessing, I had to attend five sessions with their priest and make certain concessions. Never to back away from a good conversation, I agreed.

I met with Father Patrick McCoy, he explained the church's position on mixed religion marriage, and we discussed what we needed to accomplish for our wedding to be blessed. I liked and respected Father Pat, who asked that I call him that, and he was gracious and respectful to me. At our second session, I explained that I was raised in the Unitarian Church where we studied most religions, a month at a time. At age eighteen, you were asked if there was one religion you preferred and, if so, they would help you with the transition. I could tell this priest wasn't prepared for that.

At the start of our third session, Father Pat said, "Rich, it is obvious you are well versed and comfortable with your religious beliefs and will not be joining the Catholic faith any time soon. And I, we the church, respect that." I think he knew I was waiting for the big *but*. He smiled and continued, "So all we ask is that you allow your children to be baptized as Catholics and be allowed to attend our services." He sat back, looking confident.

"Yes and no," I replied. His smile went away. "I will allow our children, if we are so blessed, to be baptized in a Catholic church, but they will be baptized as Christians, not as Catholics. And I will allow them to attend Catholic worship and catechism, but they will also be taught other religions." You could hear a pin drop.

He stood, opened the office door, and asked Mary to join us. With a serious look, he said, "We seem to have reached an impasse." I saw Mary begin to tear up. "But it is one that Rich has offered an acceptable solution to, and the Catholic Church will bless your marriage." He had a big smile and got a huge hug from the bride-to-be. "I hope you will consider me to officiate that glorious day."

The way I was treated at Sunday dinner, April 26, you would think I hit the winning home run for the Minnesota Twins in the World Series. My mom and dad were even invited to the traditional meal, this time a real feast. After dinner, Mary and I cleared the dishes and served coffee. Bud served Courvoisier brandy and cigars to me, my dad, and Bill, and sherry to Margaret and my mom.

He was about to make a toast when he stopped. "Margaret, don't look," he said. He poured and handed Mary and Jim drinks too. "It's a once in a lifetime occasion." Margaret blushed, winked, and smiled. "To the special couple." They all toasted and began talking at once. The Ehlerts and Hermans would get along fine.

Washing the dishes later, I asked, "Do you really think your mom doesn't know you've had a drink before?" Mary almost dropped the dish she was wiping and laughed.

"My dad may think I haven't," she said, "but Mom and I sometimes have wine in the evening when he isn't home. So does Jim, although he likes beer. Mom just asked us to keep it to ourselves, don't drink outside the house, and what Dad didn't know wouldn't hurt him."

The following week, campus protests grew larger and louder. It became a common sight to see fights break out, and injuries, mostly minor, grew in number. Then, on Monday, May 4, we received word of students being killed in Ohio, and classes were canceled for the day. Most of us went home, but the really die-hard anti-government protesters started to damage buildings, demanding withdrawal from Vietnam. I had talked to some of these radicals and, except for a few organizers, most of the students didn't have a clue what they were even against.

The evening news reported on the seriousness of the Ohio shooting. The Ohio National Guard had opened fire on students at Kent State University. Four students were killed and nine injured. With tensions on college campuses throughout the country already high, this incident resulted in an explosion of more violent activity.

Within two days, many institutions were in the process of shutting down, and the University of Minnesota followed suit. I was given an incomplete (I) for my courses, a whole semester gone with nothing to show for it. To make matters worse, there was no way to know when schools would reopen again.

We went through with our wedding plans and, on June 13, we drove off on our honeymoon, destined for Miami. The one surprise at the wedding was Gary didn't kidnap my bride as a payback for when I took Punky for a joyride on their wedding day. He said he didn't have to, because I would be so worried about it, I would be looking over my shoulder getting no peace the whole day. What he didn't know was Todd, my best man, had been tasked to watch over Mary to make sure she wasn't taken.

As a wedding gift, Mom and Dad Herman loaned us their 1969 Chevy Impala (no one trusted our Plymouth) with a credit card for all gas, meals, and motels. We drove to Wisconsin Dells our first night and stayed in the hotel's honeymoon suite.

I knew that Mark and Patti Newsom, my friends in Norfolk, Virginia, were away on vacation and Mary would have to wait until another time to meet them, but I planned to drive I-64 to I-95, past the Tidewater/Norfolk area and all the way down the coast to Miami. We crossed over the seventeen-mile-long Chesapeake Bay Bridge Tunnel when the car started overheating and making loud noises. I pulled off the interstate and found a motel with a gas station/garage next door. At least we were safe for the night, and I'd deal with the car in the morning.

"I'm sorry, young man," the mechanic said, "your water pump broke and with it took all the hoses. I can fix it, but I won't have the part until tomorrow."

He handed me the estimate. I called Dad, who said to put it on the credit card, get the receipt, and there was no doubt in his mind that Angie would get the money back from the dealer. In fact, he said, "She'll look forward to it as she hasn't had a cause to fight for in a while."

"What do we do now, sailor?" Mary said. "This is your stomping ground."

"I do have an idea," I said and started looking through the phone book until I found the number I wanted. "Cross your fingers I get an answer." Totally in the dark, she gave me a half-smile as I dialed the number. Thirty minutes later, a 1968 four-door Buick Electra pulled up in front of our room. "Our ride is here," I announced.

I opened the door and greeted my old friend and boss, Chief Leon Hill, his ever-present toothpick in his mouth. The handshake turned quickly into a hug and then I turned to introduce him. "Chief Hill, my bride of four days, Mary." I never got to finish.

"I know who this is," Mary said, "the one and only Chief Hill in the flesh. I can honestly say I know all about you, and it's great to meet you." They went right past the handshake and hugged.

"Please, call me Leon," he told Mary. "Now, you two pack up your belongings. Sami and I insist you spend the night, and we'll get your car tomorrow." Before we could argue, he told me to go check out and he'd help get the suitcases in his car. "Sami can't wait to see you, Herman, and meet the woman who actually got you to settle down." Mary liked him immediately, as almost everyone did, and had no problem leaving the motel.

Sami greeted us at the front door of their home in Chesapeake, one of the cities in the Tidewater area. Chief Hill, about five-ten, was maybe two inches taller than his wife. Both were athletically fit, outgoing, had great smiles, and I'm sure Mary also noticed they were black. Married fifteen years, they had four children, two boys and two girls. He was career Navy, and Sami was a schoolteacher. The kids were at their grandmother's house down the street; we'd see them in the morning.

Sami had fixed a platter of fruit and vegetables, and we all took seats in the dining room. Two bottles of wine, a red and a white, stood on the table, with a full bar along one wall. They were the perfect host and hostess, and as the girls sipped glasses of wine and the Chief and I, a few beers, a lot of sea stories were told. I could see Mary was completely won over by this couple, just as I had been years ago. I was almost glad that our car had broken down.

After dinner—steaks from the grill, salad, bread, and more drinks—we retired to the living room to relax. The Chief and I reminisced about our days on the USS Cambria and what we were doing now. The girls, who had been non-stop talking and laughing while doing the dishes, joined us when they were finished in the kitchen, and more stories flowed forth. I told my friend that he should apply to become an officer, and he told me I should come back into the Navy. We both decided neither was going to happen and left it at that.

When it was time for bed, Sami showed us to the master bedroom in the house, saying this was a wedding gift to us, and the closest they had to a honeymoon suite. After a mild protest, we accepted the offer and said goodnight.

"They may be the nicest couple I've ever met," Mary said, crawling into bed, a king-sized four-poster. There were even rose petals and two chocolates on the pillows. "Talk about class. Wow. I think it's just a crime what they've had to put up with because they're black."

"So, you did notice?" She hit me on the arm, and we both laughed. "Yeah, the Chief put up with a lot, and so did our shipmate

Stark. It almost got me killed once, but I'd do it again to have them as my friends."

"He's more than a friend, Rich. He told me, while you were in the bathroom, that as much as it pains him, you being white and all, he still loves you. Why don't you call him by his first name anyway, now you're a civilian? And what's with that toothpick?" She was asleep before I could respond. I did call him by his first name, Chief! And the toothpick? A story for another day.

In the morning, we were greeted with breakfast in bed. Our hosts delivered trays of eggs, waffles, bacon, sausage, toast, orange juice, and a pot of coffee. I started laughing and dug in. Mary was speechless, got out of bed, and hugged them both. That's when four children and a grandma entered the room, and everyone started talking at once.

When our car was ready, the Chief and Sami drove us back to the motel. Before pulling away, my old friend said, "Seriously, Herman, you've had a fascinating life up to now, and having survived those adventurous years on the Cambria, you should write a book." We were all laughing as they drove away. Like that would ever happen.

We cut our honeymoon short and headed back home. Three days later, we took up residence in my in-laws' basement, and both continued working at our jobs. We decided to stay put for one month, in hopes a decision would be made about the colleges and universities reopening. After all, what could go wrong in a month?

CHAPTER 14

July 7, 1970, Pillsbury House, South Minneapolis

"RICH, TELEPHONE CALL, LINE ONE," SOMEONE called down to the small lunch area of the building where Mom and I worked. We often had lunch together, but today she was off to a budget meeting with her boss and the Minneapolis City Council.

"Hello," I said picking up the phone.

"Mr. Herman," a man's voice said, "this is Detective Wills, Minneapolis Police, and I'm calling to let you know…" My head started pounding, as all I heard was "… your sister has been shot."

I ran to my car and headed home immediately. Marlys, Jim, and two-year-old nephew Steve had been visiting over the July 4 holiday weekend and were staying at the house. I made the usual thirty-minute drive in fifteen, and as I pulled up, I saw my sister standing on the front lawn talking to a policeman and an older man in civilian clothes.

Running up to her, I said, "I was told you were shot." She actually gave me one of her rare hugs while shaking her head no.

"Mr. Herman," the man in civilian clothes said, "I'm Detective Wills, the one who called you. It was your *sister-in-law* who has been shot. You hung up before I could clarify. Sorry. Do you have any idea where your brother is?"

"Louie? No. How is his wife?"

"She was shot once in the chest and is in surgery at General Hospital as we speak. Even being shot with a .22-rifle point blank, she was awake and alert enough to tell us her husband had shot her over a dispute about seeing their girls. He also fired at his mother-in-

95

law but missed. She has the children and is under protective custody until we locate our suspect, C. Louis Herman. Can you add anything to that?"

"No, why should I?" I didn't like the way he said that, and Marlys could sense me getting defensive. I looked at her. "Are you okay, Sis?"

She was about to answer when a microphone was thrust in front of me. The press was on the scene, and I saw the camera rolling. "Can you shut that off please. I need to call my parents, and I don't want them to see this before I have a chance to talk to them." My request fell on deaf ears so I yelled, "We have no comment." I escorted my sister into the house. The detective and uniformed cop followed, shutting the door on the press.

I called Dad, told him that Marlys and I were fine, then filled him in on what I knew. He actually said he'd be home as soon as he could. I then got hold of Mom, whose boss volunteered to bring her home. I called Sherm, who agreed he should come over to help run interference and provide some objectivity to the scene. I called Mary, explained what was happening, and we decided for her to stay at home with her folks to see what unfolded.

My parents arrived about ten minutes apart, and we all gathered in the kitchen. Sherm came as Detective Wills started asking questions. Even though my dad was still angry with Sherm over interfering with me years ago, you could tell both my parents were glad to see him.

The detective said Sherm could stay and gave us an update. "Doctors believe your daughter-in-law has been stabilized and is out of immediate danger. She is in, and will remain in, ICU for the next twenty-four hours at least. She, her mother, and children are under protective custody although we think your son is on the run."

He let that sink in before continuing. "Rather than our suspect, may I call him Louis?" Mom said that was fine. "We are in the process of searching Louis's house looking for anything that may help us understand what triggered his behavior or where he might go. I'm sorry if I came across harsh at first, but the first hours count toward having a peaceful ending for Louis when we find and attempt to apprehend, and we will do so. I know you want that too, and we could use any help you could give us. Do any of you know where he might go?"

We all looked at each other, saying nothing. "He really doesn't have any friends to turn to," Mom finally said. "I am not and will not make excuses, Detective, but we can give you some background on his personal life—Lord knows it has been complicated—which may help. I think my brother would be best to do that. Would you please, Sherm?" Sherm gave his sister a hug, patted my dad's shoulder, and asked Detective Wills to join him in the living room. I tagged along.

Sherm gave a brief synopsis of Louie's life, from birth. Although he touched upon all the critical medical issues, he stressed what he thought was psychologically important for the police to know. He gave them his professional opinion on what triggered Louie and what could be expected once he was found. I was fascinated by what he said, and Detective Wills took it all in and seemed to ask very good questions.

"Bottom line, I believe," Sherm hesitated, "Louie will not be violent toward the police when found. He has vented his frustration on the one thing that he thought was being unfairly taken away from him, access to his children. I don't say not to be very cautious, but don't be trigger-happy either."

"Doctor," Detective Wills said, "in over thirty-five years of being a policeman, I have never had a family member be so open and forthright about what we are facing. You have made our job much easier; we have a lot we can work with to bring this to a peaceful conclusion. Here's my card with my home number," he wrote it on the back, "so call me anytime if you think of something else." They shook hands.

"I have one idea where he might go," I said. "Mom and Dad have a cabin on Pine River in Cross Lake, just outside Brainerd. It's secluded, and he may not think we'd look for him there."

They wrote down my information, and the police left with one bit of advice from Detective Wills. "Try not to watch the news, it won't help, and the press has a reputation for not getting their facts right." He also left all of us with a number to call if we heard from Louie.

It was decided an extra patrol car would be assigned to my parents' neighborhood that night, and we'd see what tomorrow brought. I went home to be with Mary.

The next day, Detective Wills informed us the Brainerd police and Minnesota state troopers had checked the cabin that morning and found Louie had been there earlier. One of the local residents said he had been out walking his dogs the night before and actually talked to my brother, down by the river. Louie seemed fine and said he was just checking out the cabin for his folks. The police likely had missed a chance to capture him by just a couple of hours. No one had any more ideas on where he might go. Back to square one.

A week passed with no sightings of Louie or his car. Mar and Jim returned to Michigan, Uncle Sherm was confident they were in no danger, and Mom, Dad, and I returned to work. My sister-in-law was home recovering, she wouldn't see me or return my calls, and the press was no longer covering the story. Mom was doing fine, only wanting her son back safely before anyone else got hurt. Dad was having a hard time accepting that his son actually committed such a crime. I just wanted Louie caught and locked up.

The night of July 17, ten days after the shooting, Mary and I were just getting ready to leave my parents' house when the phone rang. I answered; it was Aunt Irene, in Seattle.

"Aunt Irene, what a surprise," I said, then whispered to Mary to get my mom. "How are things in Seattle?"

"It's actually nice weather right now," she said. "And we're enjoying Louie's visit."

"That's great," I tried to remain calm. "Is he there now?" She said he was out at a local hangout with his cousins. "I know Mom would love to talk to you. I tell you what, she and Dad are visiting Sherman right now. Why don't I call over there and have them call you right back? Then you can talk to them both. Yes, yes, it'll take just a few minutes. Yes, okay, I love you too."

Mom, Dad, and Mary were staring at me. I thought fast. "I'm

going to call Sherm. He'll be the best one to talk to his sister, explain what is going on, and keep her calm. Then I'm going to call Detective Wills, interrupt his dinner if I have to, and tell him where Louie is. Mom, write down Sherm's and Irene's numbers so I can give them to the detective." As she was doing so, I called Sherm.

"Irene's house ... well, I'll be," Sherm said. "Good work, Rich. I'll call Detective Wills and tell him my opinion on how to proceed with the Seattle Police. I'll then call Irene and tell her what to do if Louie comes back before the police find him. I don't think he'll put up a fight, but everyone needs to be cautious. Stay with your mom and dad; I'll get back to you as soon as I can."

The next several hours seemed like an eternity. Finally, the phone rang close to midnight. No one was sleeping, and I answered on the first ring.

"Mr. Herman?" It was Detective Wills. "Your brother is in custody. He was at a local bar and did not resist." I was holding the phone so we all could hear. Mom and Dad actually hugged, then included Mary and me.

"In fact," he continued, "when the police approached his table, he looked up and told them it took long enough to find him and could he finish his drink? Of course, taking no chances, they took him down immediately, with no injuries. He's in the Seattle lockup and will be arraigned in the morning."

"Thank you, Detective," I said, "that's great news. My mom and dad are right here and heard you. Is my Aunt Irene okay?"

"She's fine. She certainly is your mother's sister. Even being told her nephew had a felony arrest warrant issued for assault with a deadly weapon, she asked if she could go in ahead of the police to talk him into surrendering. They denied her request, but she earned the respect of every cop, believe me." My mom had a big smile, no doubt thinking she'd expect nothing less from her big sister.

Louie accepted extradition and, because he traveled out of state, was flown back to Minneapolis under U.S. marshal guard the same afternoon. He was arraigned that evening and charged with aggravated assault, which was good enough to hold him over for a bail hearing. The following morning, Sunday, I went to visit him at the U.S. Federal Detention Center.

After passing through security, I was escorted to the visiting room where I sat on a steel stool looking through a glass or plexiglass partition. It was just like in the movies. A steel door opened. Louie, in an orange jumpsuit, walked in and took a seat opposite me. We picked up the phones. He was actually smiling.

"How can you smile?" I asked. "You almost killed your wife, in front of your girls. Thank goodness you're a bad shot."

He stopped smiling. "What do you mean, a bad shot? When you read the report, you'll find out it should have killed her. The bullet ricocheted off her breastbone and up her back. Should have gone through her heart." His smile returned.

"Well, you've screwed up your life for good now. Your past medical condition won't explain this away, and you must know you're going to pay, big time."

"Not really." He hesitated like he wasn't going to continue but couldn't help himself. "My lawyer said I may be out in a couple of years. Extenuating circumstances."

I tried not to show my disbelief and changed the subject. "Mom and Dad said they'll visit you when you get moved out of federal custody into the Hennepin County jail. I just came to see how you were doing and pass on their message. I'm a little surprised by your attitude. I was hoping you would be sorry for what you did and ask for help."

"I don't need help. I had every right to fight for the right to see my girls. I stopped by to see them, and she said she was filing for a divorce and a restriction order keeping me 100 yards from her and the girls. I told her I had gifts for the girls in the car, and when she came to the car, I pulled my rifle and shot her. It only seemed fair that if I wasn't going to see my girls anymore, then she wasn't either. Her mother shouldn't have tried to interfere."

I had heard enough. I didn't recognize my own brother. "Good luck with that story, Louie."

I stood up, told the guard I was ready to leave, and walked out of that depressing building thinking one thing. My brother was unstable and dangerous. For years he had been manipulating the system, using his medical condition as an excuse. I had tried, not hard enough obviously, to get my family to see this, but they refused to accept my concerns, even his trying to eliminate me. *He can't be allowed to be free until there has been a drastic change to his mental state,* I thought.

Mom and Dad saw Louie after he was transferred to the county jail and invited Mary and me over for dinner the next day. I hadn't talked to either of my parents since Louie was transported back, even avoiding Mom at work.

"Louie is in good spirits," Mom said. "We offered to get him a good lawyer, but he said that his public defender was good enough and already had pretty much come to an agreement with the district attorney on a plea and punishment. Isn't that great?"

That wasn't what I expected to hear. Mary's look showed I wasn't alone. "Do you know what the plea deal is, Mom?"

"Only that he'll be charged with the lesser charge, aggravated assault under extenuating circumstances. If your brother pleads no contest, meaning he isn't admitting guilt but does accept responsibility, the prosecution will recommend five years. By leaving the state, he made it a federal offense so will serve time in a federal penitentiary. Considering, your dad and I think that's reasonable."

I was stunned. "Reasonable? Reasonable?" My voice raised a bit, and my dad gave me a stern look. *Tough.* "Mom, Dad, he tried to kill his wife, his mother-in-law, and who knows who else if they had gotten in his way. And he doesn't have to admit guilt? I don't consider that reasonable."

Mom had teary eyes. "He's our son, your brother."

I thought back to the conversation Uncle Sherm had with me the day I collapsed in the ER and he took me in to recover. That day he had told me what to expect. Angeline Herman, my mother and the smartest in the family. My mother, the most practical and a fierce fighter for one's rights. My mother and father, both blinded by their love for their son, and unable to accept his flaws, or his guilt. *Maybe, Mom and Dad, it is your own guilt you can't accept.*

Leaving, I hugged Mom, but Dad had already left the room. "Mom, I respect you and love you more than you know." I hesitated, took a deep breath and found Mary's hand. "I'm going to see his lawyer and the prosecutor, Mom. This will be the only way I can accept what happens. Remaining silent would haunt me for the rest of my life."

The next day I called both lawyers' offices. The public defender said he had no reason to talk to me; a deal had been reached. The prosecutor, however, agreed to listen to what I had to say, and we met in his office his first available time, Sunday morning, July 26.

"It is a game of numbers and money, Mr. Herman," Hennepin County Prosecutor Evers said. "Although a federal case by definition, they have asked local authorities to dispose of the matter, and they will carry out the punishment. Standard procedure in a cut-and-dried case, and with your brother pleading out, it is just that. One-day trial, before a judge with no jury, pleas made, sentence imposed, and we all go home. Except, your brother," he broke into a smile, "he'll be going to Stillwater Federal Penitentiary for three to five years."

"How can you accept his plea in all good conscience?" I said. "He tried to murder his wife and mother-in-law, point-blank with a 22-caliber rifle. He shows no remorse, and, take this from someone who has lived with him for seventeen years, I have no doubt he is not only a menace, he is a danger to society. Isn't the purpose of our justice system to issue penalties within the parameters of the law that serve justice for its victims, as well as an opportunity for the accused to be rehabilitated while serving that just sentence? What you're doing is a travesty of our justice system."

"No, what I am doing is what's best for all concerned," he fired back. "Take a look at this." He walked over to his conference table and pushed three six-inch-thick binders my way. "The defense lawyer, the day I met with him, brought these to me to review. It is just a portion of your brother's medical history. He said, if forced to, he'd drag this case through a jury trial, go over section by section, piece by piece, and even find more. The jury would see your brother had a horrific childhood, and, through no fault of his own, was one of society's overlooked children."

I could only try and comprehend what he was saying.

He leaned over the table, not twelve inches from my face. "I promise you: a trial could go on for weeks, months, and your parents would be dragged through hell. I've met them and they are wonderful people. I believe they went above and beyond to help your brother his whole life, and, although your mother would have no problem handling the fight, your father wouldn't do well. In the end, the jury would feel so sorry for your brother he could possibly get off, be found innocent even, as insane at the moment. Is that justice? No, the plea deal is our one and only option."

Dejected, but satisfied I did everything I could, I headed home to the Ehlert family dinner, held my wife (of five weeks), and gave thanks for what we had. Tomorrow, I had a meeting to attend. I told Mary it had to do with veteran's benefits so I wanted to wear my suit; I told Mom the same thing, giving me a reason not to be at work in the morning.

Actually, I didn't know what the meeting was about; it was arranged during a mysterious phone call I had a couple of weeks back. I figured it didn't cost anything to listen.

CHAPTER 15

July 27, 1970, U.S. Federal Courthouse, Minneapolis

I CHECKED MY NOTES, AGAIN. I READ ROOM 126, again. The brass plate on the wall said Rooms 121-130 with an arrow pointing this way. I walked the marble hallway again. On my left were rooms 121, 123, 125, 127, and 129. On my right were 122, 124, 128, and 130. There was no room 126. *Okay, what do you do now? Could this have been a prank? Or a test?*

My notes came from a call I had received from a Mr. Jones. He said he worked for a newly formed branch of the Department of Veterans Affairs that was looking to help veterans reenter society after meeting their military obligations. He knew I was married, had completed a four-year enlistment in the Navy, and had been caught up in the shut-down of the country's colleges and universities following the Kent State fiasco. Mr. Jones said he thought his office might be of assistance to me. I decided it wouldn't hurt to listen to all options available.

"Can I help you?" a voice asked from behind. I turned and saw an elderly gentleman wearing a blue uniform with a patch on his sleeve and an emblem on his hat that said U.S. Courthouse.

"I was looking for a room," I said, "but I must have written it down wrong." Not wanting to say why I was there, I added with a smile, "I've been known to confuse my own numbers before." I started to walk away.

"Have a good day," he said, "but if you're looking for room 126, follow me." He started walking down the hallway. I followed. We came to a door with no name or number on it—I didn't even realize it was there before—that was nowhere near room 125 or 127. He knocked twice and walked off.

The door opened, and a woman in a brown skirt and jacket with white blouse, white hair pulled back, and dark-rimmed glasses stepped out and said, "Mr. Herman? Come in, take a seat." She walked over and sat at a desk that had a telephone, a pad of paper, and a pencil on it. She looked at me, expressionless. "Please, take a seat."

I took a seat at the only place available, a small wooden chair. There were no windows, no pictures, or any other furniture in the room. There was one other door near the woman's desk. I smiled at her, and she acted like I was invisible. After what seemed at least ten minutes, the other door opened, and a tall man entered. He had wavy brown hair, a small mustache, and the same style dark-rimmed glasses as the woman wore.

"Mr. Herman, join me, please," he said with a smile.

I entered another sparse room, no windows or pictures, and only a small wooden chair in front of a small metal desk, which held a telephone and pad of paper just like the outer office. One difference was a three-inch binder lying on top of the desk.

"Mr. Herman, I am not Mr. Jones of the VA department," he said. "Actually, I'm a personnel representative of the Central Intelligence Agency. At this point, my name is not important, and based on the talk we are about to have, this meeting either may or may not have occurred." He smiled. I didn't.

"You don't look too surprised," this big anonymous man said.

"Well, sir," I said, "as soon as room 126 didn't exist, I began to think I had been set up. I will admit, though, I never gave a thought it could be the CIA. Actually, I don't know what I thought." Now, I smiled. "But now I'm interested about why I am here."

In reality, I was getting nervous; all the crazy things, those near-international incidents I almost caused, the bizarre situations I was involved with during my enlistment ran through my mind. Sleeping on the wrong ship in a foreign port, causing a near riot in Turkey for staring at a belly dancer who happened to be married to a high-ranking Turkish official, being threatened with life imprisonment in

Malta for attacking an anti-American Communist sympathizer, just to name a few.

"First, let me put your mind at ease," he added, "you are not here for your involvement in any of the incidents you may think you are here for. In fact, in my office at the agency, you are a topic of conversation among many agents and thought quite highly of for your resourcefulness for keeping your record so clear." He was actually chuckling. "No, you're here for a much different reason."

He opened the large binder on the desk. "Did you know your grandfather attended a Communist meeting in the spring of 1929?" His look at me was dead serious.

"No, I never knew either one of my grandfathers. My father was adopted, and to this date I do not know who his real father is. My mother's father, who died before I got to know him, I have always been told was very smart and an inventor, so I wouldn't be surprised if he attended a meeting out of curiosity. Actually, if he did attend a meeting, I kind of admire him for at least checking out the competition." I don't know why I said that.

"We don't consider that a problem." he said. "Here is why the CIA has asked you here today. Mr. Herman, you have some attributes that we are interested in. You are an honorably discharged veteran, held a top security clearance, and have been trained in some specific areas of communications, which have given you skills, let's just say, that are very valuable commodities to the agency."

Mr. No-Name talked to me for the next hour and finally stood, came around to the front of the desk, and sat on the edge. "My name is Donnelly, we are interested in hiring you and are willing to make you an offer, starting at $6,321 annually, but I need your decision today."

I left the U.S. Courthouse after spending two more hours in one of the most significant and definitely most interesting meetings of my life. As I drove home, I thought back to the conversation my mother and I had the day I returned home just seven months ago. She was sure this day was in my future, maybe not this quickly, and I would be making a decision like she did so many years ago. And like her, I must make it alone, taking no one into confidence for advice.

Richard William Herman had come to the fork in the road at age twenty-four, just as his mother predicted. Unlike my mother, rather than choose a path, today I rejected the alternative. I felt good driving home, vowing never to look back.

"It was just someone trying to get me to sign up for some type of federal programs," I said to Mary at dinner when she asked how my meeting went. "I think he was trying to make some kind of quota, and it turned out there were thirty or forty people there. I left during a break."

The telephone rang, and it was Evers, the prosecutor. "I felt I owed it to you, Mr. Herman, to call myself. The judge finalized the sentencing in your brother's case today. He is officially sentenced to no less than three and no more than five years at a federal holding facility. There is an automatic thirty-day delay in starting his sentence to allow for appeals and the prison board to choose where the sentence will be carried out.

"He will most likely be transported after Labor Day to the Stillwater Federal Penitentiary. Prison rules state there are no visitors for the first thirty days, and then only those people on an approved list will be allowed. Louis said you will be on that list. Any questions?"

"No," I said, defeated. "The system has spoken, and I believe in the system. For the record once again, Mr. Evers, I disagree with this sentence but accept it. Thank you for your professionalism, sir. Goodbye."

Then I turned, pointing to the TV. "Listen."

"This just in," Gary Moore on WCCO News said. "It was announced today that colleges and universities will be reopening in time for fall semester."

The same day I learn my brother's future, I learn the country's schools are reopening in the fall. Suddenly, our future was clear.

"Mary, we need to talk."

CHAPTER 16

"WITH THAT ANNOUNCEMENT ABOUT THE SCHOOLS and that phone call about Louie, it's time for that serious discussion, honey." After dinner, I got a pen and legal pad. "Let's start a tradition. Any time we have a big decision to make, we'll make a list of pros and cons. After discussing both sides, we'll make a decision, together, and never look back. There will be no pointing a finger if something doesn't work out, because we will be equally responsible. Never will either of us say, 'I told you so.'"

"I like that." Mary drew a line down the center of the paper. "What's first?"

"Now that schools are opening up, what do we want to do? And where do we want to do it?" My wife looked confused. "I know, I already threw a curveball. Hear me out. First, I want to go to a smaller college, one not so political and one more interested in education. Second, I want to get out of Minneapolis."

"Wow, what a start. As I see it then, here are our two columns: Live in Minneapolis and attend the U of M; Move to another city with a smaller college." We agreed, and she wrote Pro/Con under each. "As Jackie Gleason would say, 'Away we go.'"

Several hours later we had eight pages of notes to consider, and we agreed it was enough to make our decision on. "I feel good," Mary said. "I think we both had a chance to say what we think and get all our concerns written down. Thank you for accepting my thoughts and opinions, honey, and I hope you feel the same way. I'll admit I didn't expect your wanting to change schools, but now I understand why."

"And I was surprised you brought up moving away from the families was a good idea," I said. "I thought for sure you'd fight me about being away from your mother."

"Nope. I love my parents, just like you do yours, but Mom and Dad have already shown they think they know what's best for us, and I need to get away from that. The quicker the better. Now let's summarize and see what our future, in the near term anyway, looks like."

It was almost midnight when we had everything down to one sheet of legal pad paper. We decided to sleep on it, review it again tomorrow, and then get our parents together to tell them all at one time what we planned to do.

Wednesday night, Mary cooked dinner. She had asked her brothers to have plans not to be home. We had a casserole with French bread and a tossed salad. Both sets of parents complimented the chef, and I had to agree it was delicious. We cleared the table, served coffee, and after some small talk, I explained why we had them over for dinner.

"Mary and I have put a lot of thought into our future and have come up with what we consider a plan that not only meets our needs, it's best for us. Please hear us out before saying anything. I contacted the school already and will be enrolling at Mankato State College to start with the fall semester. They've already approved accepting the G.I. Bill as well as my U of M grades transfer."

There wasn't a sound. "We will be giving notice at our jobs and working until the first week in September." Still not a sound.

"This weekend we will be taking a look at renting or buying a mobile home in Mankato. We think of it as being practical and, if we buy, it should be no problem selling to another young couple when we leave. A lot of details need to be worked out, but it's nothing we can't handle."

I looked at Mary, she nodded, and I ended, "The floor is yours." We had a bet on who would go first. Her domineering father or my forceful mother. Our answer came immediately.

"Don't even start, Bud," my mom said. "Kids, I think you've done a fantastic job thinking things through. What can Clayton and I do to help?" *Go, Mom!*

"Not so fast," Bud jumped in. "You're awfully young to move away from your mother, young lady."

"Don't you mean from you, Daddy?" Mary fired back. He wasn't ready for that and sat with his mouth open.

"Oh, Bud," my mom said. "She's twenty-one years old, Rich twenty-four and a veteran. They're married. Do you want to tell us what you and Margaret were doing at that age? I don't think so. How about you, Margaret?"

"I just want them happy," she said meekly.

The talk went on for another hour, we received all kinds of advice, some of it actually helpful, and when Mom and Dad left, everyone was in good spirits with the parents already planning their first trip down to see us.

We decided it was more cost effective to buy and became homeowners. Our new home was delivered and set up at a mobile home park not far from campus. We even had some say in the design, and our fourteen- by seventy-two-foot home, the largest single-wide made, was a fully furnished three-bedroom, bath and a half, with washer and dryer, a storage room, large living room, and a raised dining room/kitchen. At over 1,000 square feet, it was bigger than a lot of permanent dwellings.

We officially moved in on Saturday, July 19, and woke up Sunday morning to our parents knocking on our door. We couldn't believe it.

"We thought you would like some help setting up," my mother said. "Margaret and I brought a lot of groceries, and the boys want to get you set up to watch the Vikings opening game today."

There was a blackout rule in the National Football League; home games couldn't be shown within ninety miles of the home stadium. Bud had done his research, our home was just over 100 miles away, and games could be picked up on the relatively new system called cable TV.

"Dad, Bud," I called to them outside. "I don't have cable TV; I don't even know if it exists here, it's Sunday, and the game starts in four hours."

"I already called the cable company," Bud yelled back. "They're just starting up their company service, and the owner said for an extra hundred he'd come out himself. Your dad and I agree it costs that for tickets for the game so think it's a fair price. We'll pay your installation fee and first six months' bill. Deal?"

He found my dad under the house looking for a good place to put the junction box. I had no argument and, true to his word, the owner had us hooked up an hour before game time. He even stayed for a beer afterward to make sure his system worked and talked about his vision for future cable television. I was fascinated with his imagination.

The mothers were busy helping Mary put her kitchen together, and it was halftime when Bud called out from the guest bathroom, "Hey, Clayton, I'm on the pot, and there's no water in the tank to flush. And believe me, I need to flush."

"Hang on," Dad said, heading to check things out. Being a plumber, he found the problem immediately. "They didn't hook up the hoses to the guest bathroom yet, Bud. Give me a minute." He went to the car, came back with his tools, and after a couple of minutes shouted, "It should be good now."

In seconds, we heard Bud scream. "What did you do, Clay? I just burned my you-know-what! Marge, get in here."

Minutes later, they emerged from the bathroom, and Marge helped Bud gingerly sit on the couch. He was definitely finding it hard to find a comfortable position for his bottom and not very happy about it. Marge had obviously put her nurse's hat on and was very caring. Once her husband got settled, she headed to the kitchen and started laughing.

Embarrassed, my father entered the living room and sat next to Bud. "Sorry about that, I accidentally put the hot and cold hoses on the pipe backwards. All fixed now." Bud just glared at him, while everyone else tried not to laugh.

The Vikings beat the Kansas City Chiefs 27-20, getting the season off to a great start. Our parents left, and walking out the door, Bud said, "The Vikings play the New Orleans Saints next Sunday at home so we'll drive down in the morning."

"We need to redo our pros and con list, Rich," Mary said as we watched them drive away. "A hundred miles isn't far enough away, and they are going to drive me nuts."

"Be thankful half the games are away and they can watch from their own homes." We went into the house, Mary to start redoing the kitchen the way she wanted it, and I to get ready for school the next day. "On the positive side," I said, heading to one of the rooms we set up for me to study, "we have free cable for the rest of the year."

I made one trip in October to visit my brother, as Mary and I agreed it was good to stay in touch with him and keep tabs on his mental state.

"Open door one," a prison guard called out. I had already been interviewed, given strict verbal instructions on what was and wasn't allowed during visitation, patted down, and passed through a metal detector. The door opened, I stepped through, and it slammed shut. "Open door two." I stepped through and cringed when that door slammed shut. "Open door three," and I went through the final door into the passage leading to the visitors' room. It seemed like that last door closing was much louder than the first two.

A guard checked my pass and directed me to a table. Louie, in handcuffs, entered less than a minute later and sat across from me. It looked like he had gained twenty pounds, his face puffy, a little bruised. "Good to see you, Rich," he said smiling.

"How you doing, Louie? You look good, heavier, but considering, good."

"Yeah, they like to fatten you up in here. Have you talked to Mom and Dad? Or Marlys?"

"I've talked to them, yes. Mom said she hopes to get down to see you soon, but Dad, he's a little hesitant, so give him time. Marlys is busy teaching and raising her family in the Upper Peninsula so it'll be hard for her to get down here." I wanted to change the subject. "You know that Mom and Dad did all they could to help you on your case, don't you?"

"My lawyer told me," His smile left, and he almost scowled at me. "He also told me that you went to the prosecutor and tried to get him to charge me with attempted murder and put me away for a long time. Why did you do that?"

"Because I think you need help. Look, I believe you could have a good future but not without professional help, Louie. You told me yourself you meant to kill your wife, and to this day you don't think you did anything wrong. A couple years in here will be wasted if you don't get counseling. I'll concede, it may not be your fault, you were dealt a lousy hand of cards at birth, but deal with it." I stopped to make sure I worded this right.

"Please, your kids need their father, Mom and Dad their son, and I want a brother. Sherm has a lot of sway within the prison system. Ask to see him and see what he can do to help. Please, Louie."

He was silent for a minute. "I don't think I did anything wrong to fight for my kids; no father should be kept from seeing their children. As for Sherm, you mean the uncle that has tried to help you put me away with all his psychological wisdom? You both can go fly a kite." He called for the guard. "Thanks for coming. It was good to see you, and I hope you come again. But, for the record, I plan to be a model prisoner, do my time and get early release, then fight to see my children. It's the right thing to do." He walked away and didn't look back.

We spent Thanksgiving at the Ehlerts' home with Mary's family and my mom and dad. As it worked out, the Vikings were on the road the next Sunday so we were able to enjoy that day by ourselves. We spent Christmas Eve and morning by ourselves, enjoying our first Christmas as a married couple, but drove up early enough to join in the traditional Herman brunch.

Jackie and Gary, with four-year-old Sonya and two-year-old Wayne, and Marlys and Jim with Steve, were there and, later in the afternoon, we all went out for a holiday drink while the grandparents babysat. We confided in each other that it was nice to have Louie locked up and not a threat. We toasted to that and the holidays, Marlys having a soda and announcing she was pregnant and due in May. Mary and I got stares but had no such announcement.

With the holidays and football season over, our parents cut down their visiting, and we finally seemed to have some air to breathe, settling into a comfortable routine. We had made a few friends from school and Mary's work and, with everyone on a tight budget, socialized at each other's houses with everyone sharing the cost.

I was maintaining a B average but was thinking of changing my majors, which presently were math and physics. How would I apply that to what I wanted as a lifetime career? Time passed, and then one day, in late April, Mary said she needed to talk. Early on, we had agreed that any time one of us felt there was something they needed to say, we would ask for a talk. I grew up keeping too much inside, and, as I learned from Uncle Sherm, it was best to get things out in the open, the sooner the better. After dinner we cleared the kitchen table and sat down with our coffee.

"Rich," she started, "I'm having a hard time. It's nothing you did or are not doing, or what I am or am not doing. It's bad enough my mother has to constantly remind me on how to be a good wife, or your mom telling me what you like. I know they mean well, but give me a break. I think we can figure out what each of us needs and likes." She looked at me and all I did was give a sympathetic look; she was on a roll.

"I'm not happy at work, a monkey could be trained to do what I do. I may not be as smart as the Hermans, but I certainly can do something more challenging, and better paying." She paused, sighed.

"I can feel that you too seem less enthusiastic about school. Are we just spinning our wheels, honey?"

"I hadn't thought about it quite like that." I collected my thoughts. "First, you definitely know how to make me happy—remember, I am my mom's baby, and like your parents think of you, no one is good enough or knows what is best for us, but them. Second, you are just as smart as the Hermans, a lot smarter sometimes, as a matter of fact. Give me some credit." She smiled.

"I admit I'm at a loss right now about school. It's more obvious than I thought if you picked up on it so easily. I know I can get my degree, but so what? I don't see me as a teacher. I do know what to do though." I got up and left the room.

Returning with a legal pad and a pen, I handed them to Mary.

Soon, the paper had a line down the middle and the two columns: Stay Here, and Go Elsewhere. Under each were two more columns, labeled PROS and CONS. My wife, now refreshed, began. "I'll start. Pro: We have a nice home in a good town. Con: I'm not satisfied with my present job. Your turn."

Two hours later, we both sat back, exhausted. "Then we agree," I said. "The Cons outweigh the Pros for maintaining the status quo. The Pros outweigh the Cons for making a clean break from here and distancing ourselves even further from our families. You'll give a three-week notice to work, and I'll put college on hold after finishing out this semester, so we don't leave any burned bridges behind. We'll sell our mobile home and car, and continue our lives where we discussed."

"Yes," Mary agreed.

I had always talked fondly about Norfolk, Virginia, and we enjoyed our honeymoon visit there, especially with the Hills, so we decided to relocate there. That is, contingent on one phone call.

The next day I called Mark Newsom, now a Navy chief petty officer, my friend and mutually agreed-upon cousin, and told him about our wanting to make a fresh start and asking if we could stay with him and his wife, Patti, until we found a place of our own. Without hesitation, he said there was always a room available in their house.

We drove up to Minneapolis on Saturday and broke the news to our parents. We made a checklist of action items and assigned who was responsible for each. In three weeks, we had sold our mobile home for cash, even making a profit, to an older couple who gave it as a wedding present to their daughter and son-in-law, both starting at Mankato State next semester. A friend and fellow student bought our old Plymouth for his wife, who just started a new job.

With all our belongings in a small U-Haul truck, we departed Minnesota and arrived at our new home in Norfolk on May 22, 1971, the day before Mary's twenty-second birthday. We had $700 to our name.

CHAPTER 17

May 1971, Norfolk, Virginia

MARK AND PATTI WELCOMED US WITH OPEN ARMS and helped us get settled in. Space had been made in the garage for all our belongings, and Mark and I unloaded the U-Haul with no problem. By the time we got back from returning the truck, the girls had already set up the room we would be staying in. Our wives were about the same height, Patti fifteen years older and a little thinner, with short hair as black as Mary's was blonde. As fast as they were talking, it was obvious they were quickly becoming friends. We went downstairs and met the kids. The Newsoms now had five children, since Mark Jr. was born six months ago and joined Patti's four children from her first marriage.

We wasted little time, and our first morning with the Newsoms, a Sunday, we sat down and went over our list of action items. We included Mark and Patti as we wanted their thoughts and respected their opinions, plus they knew the ins and outs of Norfolk. At noon, Patti took a break to feed the baby, got him down for a nap, then she and Mary made sandwiches and we all took a break for lunch. The kids, Didi (thirteen), Donny (eleven), Frankie (eight), and Lily (five) joined us and peppered us with questions. Back to our list ...

About three o'clock, Patti slammed her hand on the table. "Enough!" She then went into the laundry room and returned, with all the kids, carrying a cake with burning candles. "Happy Birthday to Mary," everyone started to sing. With tears in her eyes and after giving everyone a hug, my wife was speechless. Yes, it was a good start.

That evening, I circled several job advertisements in the morning paper and was on the phone Monday morning applying for jobs. I got seven appointments lined up, including one at the Norfolk Social Service Bureau, to be followed by taking the Civil Service exam. Patti said she would help Mary look for a job too. Along with the family 1968 Pontiac station wagon, Mark had a 1965 red Opel he used to commute to work at the Naval Air Station. I was covered under his insurance, and we were given the use of the Opel until we settled. I started my interviews early Tuesday morning.

After two weeks, neither of us had any success finding a job, and we were getting discouraged. My interviews went well, but I was either not educated enough or too educated for the jobs I wanted. We did have one positive event when I received my Civil Service exam scores—scoring over ninety in every area. Being an honorably discharged veteran, I was given five bonus points for each part of the exam (math, English, clerical, mechanical, etc.) giving me scores of over 100 in several. Then I learned the process of actually getting hired as a civil servant took an average of six months. Our frustration mounted.

Mark and Patti knew we were trying hard and were very supportive. Even though we were living here rent free, they appreciated our helping with grocery expenses, household chores, and taking care of the kids when they went out. Any pressure we felt came from ourselves.

On Sunday, June 13, the Newsoms tried to cheer us up, and we had steaks and corn on the cob from the grill to celebrate our first anniversary. The kids helped, and the mood was lively when Patti asked Mary if her wine was bad; she hadn't tasted it.

That's when the announcement came nonchalantly, "I'm sure it's fine, it's just that I'm pregnant." After the shock and excitement wore off, we were ecstatic but also realistic. I had to find work, and fast.

On June 23, my twenty-fifth birthday, I interviewed at a local bread company and (I don't like to say I lied but will admit I misled) told the personnel manager that I was an uneducated, soon-to-be father, and desperate for work. Merita Bread Company hired me to drive a delivery truck, full-time with medical benefits after a ninety-day probation period. I was to start Monday.

The same afternoon, I received a phone call from the Norfolk Social Services Bureau director, Dr. Sheila Wade, herself. She had received a personal letter of introduction concerning me from the director, Minneapolis Department of Social Services, highly recommending me for the position of a social worker. She interviewed and hired me over the phone to start the following Monday. During my interview with her office manager several weeks earlier, I had been told I didn't meet their educational qualifications and thought that was the end of it. Dr. Wade, based on the letter and my interview, waived that requirement and hired me on a trial basis.

I hung up the phone, smiled, and said, "Thank you, Mom." I had no doubt she wrote that letter herself for her boss, held it before him, and he signed it. Angeline Herman strikes again! I called the Merita Bread Company.

Monday morning, I met with the Social Services personnel department, got a strange look from the office manager who had originally interviewed me, and did all the administrative paperwork. With my new picture ID, the manager took me in to meet the director. A tall, silver-haired woman, early sixties, slim, wearing wire-rimmed glasses, met us at the office door. As she introduced herself, I finally met Dr. Sheila Wade. She shook my hand, welcomed me, and led me down a hallway to a door with the sign, "Welfare Qualification Unit 1."

The room was divided into four cubicles. William Pratt, a retired Army major, who had been the unit supervisor the past twelve years, held out his hand and said, "Welcome, Richard." He was maybe five-eight, with a short brown crewcut and somewhat baggy pants and shirt. I liked him immediately.

He introduced me to Emily Banner, about thirty-five, my height, trim, with short blond hair. She never stopped smiling. Next, I met silver-haired Edith Tully, at least sixty. Standing maybe five-foot-two and heavyset, she made me think of Grandma, except she was black.

"Please, call me Rich," I said. Having no wardrobe to speak of, Mary and I had gone out and purchased three pairs of pants (two being bell-bottoms), three colorful shirts, and three wide painted ties. I stood out a little but not enough to be a spectacle, I hoped. "It's great to be here, and I honestly mean that."

"Call me Will," my new boss said. "I'm going to assign you to tag along with Emily to start. You have a lot to learn about Virginia welfare laws, but don't feel too overwhelmed, we all were a little lost to start. Emily will also show you the ropes for interviewing techniques and what you can expect from the individuals when they come in to apply for benefits."

As we walked over to her cubicle, Emily gave me a little wave. "Rich it will be," she said. "Before we get started, let's get a cup of coffee and get to know each other better. I find that makes it easier to work together. First, who picked out your clothes?" She gave me a wink, chuckled, and led me to the breakroom.

That night at dinner I probably talked too much, but no one stopped me. I think, now that Mary and I had an income and some breathing room, everyone was finally relaxing a bit. "I guess it's time for me to shut up," I finally said.

"We're happy for you guys," Mark said, still in his chief's uniform. "Take your time with your next steps. Actually, Patti and I are getting used to having you around. The kids will definitely miss you."

"No," Mary said, "we have what we need to make some plans for getting our own place and car. And, no offense, I'm anxious to get on our own. But not too much on our own." She reached over and squeezed Patti's hand. They had grown close in this short period of time.

As was becoming a custom, and a very successful one, we made a list of pros and cons on moving and what was required. First on the list, Mark offered to sell us the Opel, for a fair price, or we could look and buy a car on our own. We went from there. Mary took me to work the next few days, and she and Patti looked for a place for us to rent. By the end of the week, we had our plan, and, once again out of respect, asked the Newsoms for their comments and advice. The plan firmed up, and we made our list of action items with dates and responsibilities.

We bought the Opel and found a two-bedroom single-family home, with space for a washer/dryer, small kitchen and dinette, a fair-sized living room, and a covered carport. The rent fit our budget, and the house, only four blocks from the Newsoms, would be available to rent mid-July. Through one of Mark's retired Navy contacts, we got an extra good deal and were able to buy three rooms of inexpensive furniture. We arranged all the utilities to be turned on, the furniture delivered, and planned our move for Monday, July 19. We took possession on Friday, giving us the weekend to do some much-needed preparations.

The bedrooms needed some new wiring, light fixtures, and a fresh coat of paint. The living room had hundreds of Marlboro cigarette boxes thumbtacked to the ceiling, and one wall was decorated with worn-out, green-and-pink shag carpeting that absolutely had to go. Our landlord agreed to pay for the supplies and make our first month's rent free if we did all the work.

Luckily, Mark had a couple of sailors who owed him favors and readily agreed to help the chief. Mark's best friend and now a chief, Daro, who became a friend of mine when I was here before on active duty, was an electrician and took care of the wiring. Everyone helped move our belongings from storage, and the wives provided refreshments. Sunday night we were ready to move in.

I paid attention, listened to and watched Emily for several weeks before I started seeing clients on my own, getting her approval on all my paperwork. At the end of the month, Will spent two days with me and then signed off, recommending me to be qualified as a welfare recipient application specialist. Dr. Wade came to our unit's spaces and in front of my co-workers made it official, signing my Letter of Appointment and congratulating me. Tomorrow, I would be on my own to interview and approve welfare payments.

Mary had driven me to work that day, and I was looking for her outside when Will came up to say I just missed her call; she was running about a half-hour late. He invited me to join him for a quick celebration drink across the street at The Well, a local hangout for employees at the Social Service and Federal Buildings. When we arrived, I found out why Mary wanted the car. She was already there sitting at a table with the rest of our team and their spouses. I was introduced to Will's wife, Wanda; Emily's husband, Ed; and Edith's husband, Roger. The conversation flew, and Edith and Roger even hired Mary to clean their house, every Friday, for thirty dollars. These wonderful people soon became like family.

The beginning of August, now with thirty days on the job, my medical insurance became effective and, although it didn't cover family members for a year, as a state employee, Mutual of Omaha would provide that coverage at a reduced rate. I signed up for it and found it was effective immediately. Mary found an OB/GYN, Dr. Best, recommended by Emily. We both felt better when at her first appointment, she was found to be in good health and the baby fine. My wife also teased that she liked her young, very fit, and attractive doctor, who told her he was just starting his practice after serving four years in the Navy. Her due date was established as early next March, with the delivery at Norfolk General Hospital.

"It's been ten weeks since we left Minnesota, Mrs. Herman." Mary and I were relaxing on a lazy Saturday morning, sipping our coffee at the kitchen table. "Any regrets?"

"None, Mr. Herman." It was nice seeing her smiling and looking at magazines about babies and parenting. She was about to say something else when a loud racket started outside. Motorcycles?

I looked out the front door, and pulling into the driveway were five, six, I finally counted nine motorcycles parking or going around circles revving their engines. Along with the drivers, I counted seven female passengers. All were dressed in black, including leather jackets with "Hell's Angels" on the back. I wasn't positive but, besides several knives in plain view, I felt sure most of them were armed with handguns. I told Mary to go into the bedroom.

I decided the best course of action was to simply open the door and see what they wanted. It seemed obvious they were here for something, and refusing to answer and cooperate would not have a good ending, for the Hermans anyway. I opened the door an instant before one of the bikers was about to knock. "Good morning, can I help you?"

"Tell Jack he has company," the guy said. He stepped up to the top step.

"I don't know any Jack, sir," I answered right back without opening the screen door. "We just moved in recently, and maybe he was here before us."

"Kipper, you and Tony check the back," the guy yelled over his shoulder, "and Owen, get up here." One of the bikers carrying a leather case approached. I heard one of the girls yell to get on with it and she wanted a joint and a beer. "Shut up, Stacey, somebody get her a joint." He opened the bag Owen brought and pulled out an envelope, showing me the return address. It was mine. "You sure you want to stick with your story?"

"It's not a story, it's the truth. Look, I don't want any trouble so what's this all about?"

"He was holding something for me, a lot of something. If he's not here, maybe he left it for me. Let me and the boys in, we'll look around and be on our way." Three of the bikers approached, and I didn't like the way they looked, or trust what they would do once inside.

"My name is Rich ... Rich Herman." I didn't budge and looked directly at the leader. "I'll make a deal with you; it's obvious you are in charge." He nodded and put his hand up, stopping everyone in their tracks. "I see you have an American flag tattoo as well as an eagle. I will admit I am not a biker, but I do respect your freedom and right to your beliefs. At the University of Minnesota, I witnessed another chapter of the Hell's Angels stand up against protesters demeaning our Vietnam veterans.

"I am a four-year Navy veteran; honorably discharged and now social working, just trying to raise a family and do what I can for the less fortunate. How about you and one other member come in and search for what you want, meet my wife, and see for yourself we are hiding nothing."

He smiled and put his hand out to shake. "I'm Pete, and that sounds reasonable. Owen, you're with me, everyone else just chill and don't destroy anything." The two men came in and saw Mary, now back at the kitchen table. "Ma'am," Pete said, "we'll try not to disturb anything, we're just looking for something valuable to us."

It didn't take long to search our small place (including a quick look into the attic by Owen while Pete held him in the air) and realize we were hiding nothing. Owen left and Pete shook my hand again, saying, "Thank you for your service," before heading to the door.

Looking back through the open door, he added, "Sorry to have bothered you. Jack has ripped off a lot of medicine (*Marijuana? Heroin? Cocaine?* I wondered) from the brotherhood and is a wanted man. I'll put the word out that your place is clean. By the way, I like the way you've fixed up the place, especially getting rid of that awful shag carpet on the wall and Marlboro packs on the ceiling." He shut the door behind him.

Mary ran over and hugged me. "I was scared to death. How could you be so calm?"

"Remember, dear, I survived falling from a second-story window, a collision at sea, a beating for having black friends, a duel with sabers in Turkey ... need I go on? I must have a few lives left." I guess she didn't notice my knees still shaking.

"Now where were we? Right, we don't have much, but we have a roof over our heads, our friends, and our health. Yes, we are indeed happy here."

CHAPTER 18

September 13, 1971

I BEGAN PLAYING SOFTBALL ON A TEAM MARK managed, and we played once or twice a week in the Norfolk City Softball League. Mary and I budgeted enough so that after the games we could join Mark, Patti, the other players and significant others for beer and sodas at Buddy's Bar and Grill, our team sponsor.

I played catcher for our team, mainly because I was one of the younger players and still foolish enough to stand my ground blocking home plate. One player, Stu Block, who I had recruited to play with us, was the best outfielder I had ever seen. He hit over .700 and could throw a softball from the center field fence to home plate on the fly, not going over eight feet on his trajectory.

One game, toward the end of the season, we were the home team playing the Norfolk General Hospital team with the score tied 7-7 going into the last inning. We had played them earlier in the year, lost 11-9, and were tied for second place in the division. I don't know why, maybe it was just the competitiveness, but our teams didn't like each other much. You could feel the tension in the air, some taunting was definitely going down on both sides, and Mary, visibly pregnant, and Patti were two of the loudest.

The leadoff batter for the hospital doubled and went to third when the next batter grounded out to second. The next hitter hit a deep fly to center, and I knew the runner on third would tag up and try to score. But I also knew one thing the runner didn't—the center fielder. Stu Block caught the ball near the fence, and the runner tagged and took off for home. Taking only one step forward, Stu threw a bullet from his ear toward home. In all fairness, unless they had seen him before, no one would have believed it possible as they witnessed the ball reach my glove without touching the ground.

I got in position to block the plate, kneeling, bracing for the slide with my glove ready. What happened next was not expected. The runner didn't slide, he remained standing and decided instead to plow into me, hoping I would drop the ball. I didn't, and heard, "OUT!" Double-play, inning over.

I lay on the ground, the hit having propelled me almost to the backstop, and took inventory of my bones. Then I was being helped up by the runner, who had hit me like a bull, saying, "You okay, Rich?" *He knew me?* "No hard feelings, right?" *Huh, what?* "I promise to be gentler when the baby is born." *What is this guy talking about?*

We scored a run in the bottom of the inning and won the game. Later, at Buddy's, my teammates voted me player of the game, but all I could think about was my headache, so Mary took me home. I was having trouble keeping up a conversation. My head still hurt in the morning, and she took me to the ER at General Hospital instead of to work. I had a slight concussion, several bruised ribs, and a large contusion on my left thigh. Mary spoke to my boss, who said to have me rest for a few days. Later that night we had a good laugh—the man who ran me over was Dr. Best, her OB/GYN.

We spent several outings with my co-workers and enjoyed our get-togethers. One Saturday, Will and his wife, Wanda, had our unit over for a seafood cookout. Relaxing and enjoying a drink as we all watched a pot of large Maryland blue crabs cook over an open fire, I had the chance to ask Will how he was always able to stay so calm. He told us that in the Army he was a demolition technician, serving five tours in Vietnam, and when you're in a war zone trying to diffuse a bomb about to blow with dozens of lives at risk, you didn't have any choice. No argument there from me, just respect.

When the crabs were ready, Mary, who insisted on sitting next to Will, asked him for about the sixth time to show her how to properly crack and extract the meat from a crab. We found he did have a breaking point. "Look," a frustrated Will said, "Hold the claw like this." He put it in her hand. "Now, take the claw cracker." He never got a chance to go further.

"You mean like this?" Mary said. She picked up a whole crab, flipped it into position, cracked and pulled the entire meat sections out of the claws and body, dipped a large piece in butter, and held it out for Will to open up wide and try. All in fifteen seconds.

"Will Pratt," Wanda said, "are you actually speechless?" She started laughing.

"Will," Mary said, holding back her laughter, "I may be from Minnesota, but my father owned a grocery/meat store with seafood one of his specialties. I've been cracking crabs since I was three." Everyone was laughing now, including a red-faced Will, who knew he had been had. Then Mary added, "You're pretty good at it, by the way." Now everyone started clapping and cheering. I hadn't heard so much laughter since we told our group about our first date and the encounter with what Mary was certain were black bears.

With the baby due in a couple of months, we kept our first holiday season simple. Emily and her husband were Catholic, and we joined them Christmas Eve to celebrate midnight Mass. We slept late the next day and enjoyed a quiet morning, taking two calls from our parents wishing us good cheer. Later we joined the Newsoms, bringing a little something for each of the kids, enjoyed an afternoon dinner, and watched the Miami Dolphins defeat the Kansas City Chiefs 27-24 in the longest game played in NFL history.

———— 🌳 ————

On Friday, February 11, Patti took Mary, eight months pregnant, out to shop for a few items for the baby's room. "Hey," Patti said, leaving the second store, "since we're downtown, why don't we have lunch at that place you and Rich always say is so good? I'd like to splurge on us one more time. My treat."

As they entered The Well, they were met by Dr. Sheila Wade. "Hello, mother-to-be," she said, "and this must be Patti." She shook her hand. "Nice to meet you in person. I'm Sheila, a friend of the family, and Mary, this is your day. Come with me."

They walked down the hallway, Mary whispering to Patti, "This is Dr. Wade, the big boss. What's going on?" Patti just smiled. Instead of turning into the bar/lounge area they usually went to, they were led to a private room near the rear. Sheila rapped the door three times and it opened.

"Surprise," happy voices cheered, horns started blaring, and as Mary entered the room she saw Emily, Edith, Wanda, Daro's wife Betty, and the Newsom daughters, Didi and Lily. On the back wall was a banner, "Baby Herman's Shower," and Sheila ushered a blushing mother-to-be to her seat, sitting down next to her as the others all found their chairs. Two waiters came in with carts of fancy sandwiches, fruit and vegetable plates, and delicious-looking desserts. A beverage cart, fully stocked, appeared, and a bartender came to take each lady's order.

"Mary," Sheila started, "you have become like family to us—in fact, Edith and Roger want to adopt you guys." Edith stood and bowed, smiling. "We know a little of what you have been through starting out, and we just want to be a small part of your memories of your first-born. Enjoy this afternoon and know that we are *all* here to support you." Mary stood and they hugged, to clapping and an audience visibly showing tears.

After games were played and small prizes given, Mary opened gifts, each one thoughtful, needed, and much appreciated.

Mary called both our parents that evening and told them about the shower. After finishing talking to my mom, she joined me on the couch. "Wow," she said, "today was amazing." She curled up next to me and took my hand. "Those are some pretty good friends we have there, Mr. Herman."

"I can't argue with that, Mrs. Herman. But want to hear the kicker? Sheila Wade had one condition to approve today's baby shower. She picked up the entire tab."

Two weeks later, Monday, February 28, we were watching the evening news when I said, "Hey, let's get some exercise and maybe you can have a Leap Year Baby." We both laughed and went for a walk, Mary waddling, around the block until she had enough.

At five o'clock the next morning, I was shaken awake. Her water had broken. As she got dressed, I dressed and loaded our prepacked bag into the car. I called the number Dr. Best had given us for this occasion and was told to bring her in. I made one more call, this time to Patti, and then drove to Norfolk General.

"Where is she?" Patti asked, arriving in the emergency room shortly after they took Mary up for delivery. She gave me a hug and we sat down.

"They took her up immediately," I said. "I was with her until she went through those doors," I pointed, "and they told me that was as far as I could go and someone would update me shortly." I looked up to see Dr. Best wave as he went through the same doors. "Well, her doctor is here, that's a good sign."

A hospital representative came out and took our insurance information, and I signed the necessary forms for her to be admitted after the baby was born. Mary had already signed all the consent forms required for the delivery itself. All seemed on track. Patti found us two cups of coffee, and we were sipping on those when a nurse came out.

"Mr. Herman?" she asked. I stood and nodded yes. "Your wife is doing fine and in the early stages of labor. It'll be several hours at least before she delivers, but we are confident it will be today. I'm sorry you," she looked at Patti, "or family can't be with her until after she delivers. Either I or my relief, if it takes that long, will let you know when it's close."

"In that case, I'm going to go to work." I announced. "Nothing I can do sitting here. Let me give you my number to call when it's time, and I'll come back." Patti said she would go home, get the kids off to school, and be back in a couple hours. We both left. It turned out to be a good decision.

I got a call at noon from the nurse to give me an update. Mary was doing fine, still in the labor process and starting to dilate, slowly. They said Patti was there now and would give me the next update. That came just before four p.m. when Patti called to say we had a baby boy and get your butt to the hospital, *Dad!*

"Who said all babies are cute?" I said to Patti. We were looking through the nursery window at my son. "He's all crunched up, and kind of ugly."

Patti smacked my arm. "He's adorable, in fact, he is beautiful," she corrected me. "He's just born, give him a day or two." Then she gave me a big hug. "Good job, Rich."

"I didn't have that much to do with it, Patti." She pointed, and a nurse was headed our way to direct us to Mary's room.

"Hey, honey," I said, leaning over and kissing my wife on the top of the head. She was smiling but looked exhausted. "You did it, and he's beautiful." The nurse allowed Patti to come in, and she immediately sat on the bed and relived the day.

Mary said, "Well, Daddy got his wish." Patti looked at us, confused. "We have Christopher Charles Herman, Leap Year Baby."

While I was going over the house one more time to make sure everything was perfect for bringing my family home the next day, the phone rang. The hospital asked that I stop by the front office before going to my wife's room in the morning. I figured some paperwork had to be signed for my family's release.

"I'm sorry, Mr. Herman," the hospital administrator said, "your wife said you did not have the money, and your insurance has not come through for paying your bill; therefore, we can't release your baby until they do, or you pay $630."

"What? You're going to keep my son? That's the craziest thing I ever heard." It was like a bad joke.

"My hands are tied," he said defensively. "Your wife can go home today, and hopefully we'll have all this worked out with Mutual of Omaha by Monday and you can take your son."

It was hard to get me angry, but I was almost there. Still sitting,

I took a deep breath and decided to use a tactic out of my mother's handbook.

"I cannot accept that policy. If there is no way you can see around it," I started to stand, "I'll have no choice but to take this to the press. Great headline for Sunday's Star-Ledger, don't you think? 'Norfolk General Hospital Holding Newborns Hostage.'"

Mary and I were home early that afternoon, with our son. Before leaving the office earlier, the administrator asked me to wait an hour before doing anything. I agreed. In less than thirty minutes, I was informed the hospital would make an exception in this case, realizing it was in the best interest of the child. I thanked him for getting them to reconsider our case, and I thought the matter would be resolved to everyone's satisfaction soon. At least we now had the weekend.

Mary fed the baby and got him to bed for the first time in his new home, in his newly renovated room and his brand-new crib, thanks to Grandpas Clayton and Bud. Looking down at Christopher sleeping, I heard Mary whisper, "What would you have done if they called your bluff?"

"What bluff?" I came back with quickly. "I was all set to make a new friend in the newspaper business." I hoped that sounded confident because, in reality, I didn't have a Plan B!

On Tuesday, the following week, I came back from a client interview, and a note on my desk said Norfolk General had called, leaving a number. Before dialing, I rehearsed what I planned to say if I ended up responsible for the bill. I didn't have a great solution, but Mary and I had come up with what we could live with.

"Mr. Herman," the same administrator said, "thank you for returning my call so quickly. Good news. Mutual of Omaha has paid your bill, in full. I hope you and your wife are relieved now that we handled the situation as we did. If you agree, I think we can consider this issue resolved satisfactorily?"

"Absolutely, thank you and your staff for all your help, care, and consideration of what is best for the patient." I hung up, called Mary, and said to myself, *Thanks, Mom, for your guidance: accept the win, do not gloat, and never burn bridges behind you.* Yes, I learned from the best.

CHAPTER 19

March 20, 1972

CHRISTOPHER CHARLES WAS A GREAT BABY, AND Patti couldn't tell us enough how lucky we were. Being first-time parents, we accepted what came and tried not to panic over little things, like a toy stuck in his nose. I also think it helped that the grandparents were so far away. Both grandmothers gave lots of advice over the phone, and Mary always thanked them and said it was great having them to provide such guidance. Of course, she did what she wanted, which was what was best for her and her son. I just enjoyed being a father.

I liked my job and knew I was good at it. Will and the team were first-rate, but they seemed to just do the interviews and paperwork and go home. I knew they were well qualified; the office manager always made a point of letting me know Will and Edith had master's degrees and Emily was in graduate school at night. Emily seemed motivated, maybe because she was young, but Will and Edith didn't seem too concerned whether a client was qualified, and each case was either just a yes or no. When I was the new guy, I never challenged them and concentrated on what I could control, my interpretation of my clients' cases.

As I gained experience, if I thought a case needed to apply a loose interpretation of a rule to help an applicant, I would go to Will to get his opinion. Maybe it was having been raised by a fighter-of-individual-rights mother; anyway, I tried to look for ways to get a client qualified and approved for assistance, not unqualified and rejected. It didn't take long before, hearing that I shouldn't try to manipulate the system, I stopped asking his opinion.

Some guidance seemed unfair, if not downright illogical. Under Virginia law, if an applicant for welfare had a car or even a telephone, they could not receive benefits. To get most benefits, they had to try and find work and provide proof of their trying by having possible employers sign that they were interviewed, although not hired. How did the state think they were going to call these people for an interview and then get there if they got an appointment? And who were they to contact in an emergency without a phone?

Constrained by such rules, actually less than sixty percent of those applying qualified for full benefits. These two rules alone upset me, and I looked for what assistance, partial benefits with food stamps and hopefully Medicaid, I could approve.

I was doing home interviews (part of our job description but I was actually the only one who volunteered) for applicants who found it too difficult to come to the office. It was never easy entering a residence, because I wouldn't be there unless there were problems, and I never found anyone who was comfortable opening up about their personal issues and lives. What I found, almost every visit, was good, honest people trying their best, many just to survive.

It was difficult to tell someone they didn't qualify for any benefits, and often I would be asked to leave under less than friendly circumstances, being cussed at and occasionally physically pushed out the door. I tried to be understanding, and even when physically abused, I never reported it to the authorities. These people had enough to deal with. At work, I would share some of my stories with my peers, not realizing they would ever make it to the front office and Dr. Wade.

I made it my mission to research and become an expert on the Virginia State Welfare System Manual, in particular the qualification rules and regulations. I wrote down the categories of welfare assistance (for instance, Aid for Dependent Children, Temporary Aid for Disability, Food Stamps, Medicaid) and what could disqualify applicants (such as having a car or telephone, owning a home). I kept this to myself and, for the next several months, tracked the approvals/rejections of all applications in our unit. I wasn't sure what I was going to do with the data but felt someone had to do something, and if the time ever came, I wanted to be prepared with facts, not just my opinion.

One afternoon, in early May, there was a scream from the hallway and, as I headed that way, a very distraught Edith came running out of an interview room, visibly shaken. Will took Edith away from the scene, and I opened the door cautiously. Sitting at the table was a man with worn, heavily soiled clothes, a straggly beard, and unkempt long hair. The odor he gave off was terrible, but I didn't smell alcohol or smoke.

"Hello, sir," I said, sitting across from him, never taking my eyes off his. He just stared straight ahead with his hands folded before him. "Are you, okay?" Silence. "Are you hurt?" Silence. "I'm Mr. Herman, you can call me Rich." Silence. The phone on the desk rang.

The man jumped up and with balled-up fists, took a wild swing that, luckily, I ducked. He started dancing around the room throwing his arms out and back, wiping his nose after every swing. I gave him room and stayed out of his reach. The phone rang a second time, and he got even more animated and started moving and swinging faster.

I unplugged the phone from the wall. I thought he was sparring or shadow-boxing or whatever you call it and said, "Okay, good practice round, you can sit back down." He smiled and sat.

There was a knock at the door, which the boxer didn't seem to notice. Opening the door slightly, I looked out and saw Dr. Wade standing there. "Come out of there, the police and medics will be here shortly; they can take over," she said. "We're familiar with Mr. Smith, and he is probably off his meds."

"Can I have a minute?" I asked. "He's calm now and I think will listen to me."

"No," she fired back immediately. I didn't move and tilted my head, silently mouthing please. "Five minutes, no more. And don't put yourself in danger."

"Good round, Mr. Smith," I said, sitting back down. "Can I get you some water?"

"No," he finally spoke, "it's not good to drink until after the fight." He smiled and started to relax.

"You look like a good fighter. Have you had many fights?"

He sat up and looked completely different. "Yeah, quite a few. I almost got a shot at a championship bout once, light-heavy, but started getting headaches." He looked at his hands and then around the room. "I'm sorry, did I cause a fuss again? I just wanted to stop to see if I could get some help with my medicine. My head is killing me." He shut his eyes and held his head.

"No problem, sir, you've done the right thing, and I can help you. Give me a minute. How about that water now?" He agreed.

It took me a few minutes but, with the medics' concurrence, I convinced Dr. Wade and the police to let the medical professionals take over and take him to the hospital. Mr. Smith had calmed and liked that idea, asking if I would go to keep him safe; he didn't trust the cops. Dr. Wade told me to see her as soon as I got back. From the look on Will's and Edith's faces, I was about to see the big boss's wrath.

"Mr. Herman," Dr. Wade started. She usually called me Rich so I knew it was not good. "Do you have any idea how stupid that was of you to enter that room in the first place? Did you think Edith screamed and ran out for nothing? I have never lost a social worker— are you trying to be the first?" I started to say something.

"Quiet, I'm talking. I also have reports, although unofficial, that it is not unusual for you to be in the middle of some tough situations. We are not law enforcement, and we are not equipped or trained to handle dangerous situations. You have, in the past, and I witnessed today, put yourself in danger. Mr. Smith, for all you know, could have been armed. Did that ever cross your mind? You could have become a hostage, if not killed. Or both. And you're a father now." She sat back heavily in her chair. "Well, what have you got to say?"

I admired Dr. Wade, and after sitting for a moment, I decided to go for it. Choosing my words carefully, I said, "I've been raised to help people. There was a reason Edith came out of that room screaming, and when I saw she was physically unharmed and safe with Will, I reacted by going to see what made her scream and if I could help.

"I am a veteran and, although I've never been in combat, I have on many occasions been in the position to have to make a decision, not in a minute or two but now, instantly. I have experience and I think do very well when required. If I didn't follow procedure then," I hesitated to see how she was reacting, "either we change the procedure or I find a different position to fill, hopefully here."

I don't know what I was expecting, but she got up from her chair and walked over to look out a large window, the view being the Elizabeth River and waterfront. "Look out over this city, Rich." I joined her.

"You are looking out at Norfolk, Virginia. I'm a sixty-four-year-old black woman, earned my bachelor of science degree at the University of Virginia and my master's and doctorate at Columbia University." She turned, with a big smile, and looked at me. "I was still young in graduate school so I studied and got both my DSW (doctorate of social work), allowing me to be in the field and make policy like now, and also my Ph.D., which means I am further qualified to teach social work at the highest level.

"Norfolk is my home, always has been, and I choose to live here because I feel a responsibility to its citizens." I'd forgotten how tall, stately, and imposing she could be as she looked me right in the eye. "Come see me in the morning. We're going to have a talk."

Later that evening, I told Mary about my day.

"What an accomplished woman," she said. "What do you think she wants? Maybe you shouldn't have given her an ultimatum. Do you think she'll fire you?"

"She could," I said. "She would be justified; I definitely gave her cause."

We sat quietly on the couch. She started giggling. I gave her a strange look. "The phone rang and he started shadow-boxing?" Now, I was laughing.

At nine the next morning, I was sitting once again across from Dr. Wade. Pointing at her bay window, she asked if I remembered her telling me yesterday how deeply she feels about this city. I smiled and told her I would never forget her words. She smiled back and I relaxed, just a little bit.

"Rich," she started, calling me by my first name, which I took as a good sign, "I understand you have difficulty accepting some of the eligibility parameters used to determine qualification to receive benefits." I nodded my head yes but didn't think she was done with her opening so said nothing. "Would you be surprised if I told you I do too? Now, first I want you to know your job is not in jeopardy." I couldn't help but show my relief and she smiled. "That said, in a nutshell, tell me your concerns."

For the next fifteen minutes, I covered as much as I could. I told her how, over the course of several months, I studied the cases denied assistance and reasons why. She seldom interrupted, but when she did her questions were right on, and we had a great discussion. She finally stopped me, not because she had heard enough, but because she had heard enough for now.

"Good input." She took off her glasses and rubbed her eyes. "I'd like you to put all this into a report. You can start it by saying, 'As requested by Director Wade, I have looked into your concerns, etc., etc.' This will make it look like you did this from the start because of my direction and keep you in the good graces of your peers, as well as those who wrote these rules. I can't make any promises that change will be forthcoming soon, but it will get my personal attention. Especially that telephone rule. If you can, without interfering with a case, I want you to come back at two o'clock to listen to an idea I have."

At two, I was back in my seat. Emily was covering my only appointment that afternoon. No one asked, and I didn't offer, why I had another meeting with the boss. Dr. Wade entered with another woman whom she introduced as Bernice Long, her legal consultant. I just nodded, hoping the lawyer wasn't for me.

"Rich," Dr. Wade started, "Norfolk has a population of 300,000 people, give or take. About twenty percent, almost 60,000 people, can be labeled in the welfare eligibility zone and eligible for food stamps at least. I throw out these numbers because it accurately describes how many citizens could apply for assistance and what numbers our Bureau of Social Services is responsible for." Statistics don't lie, and these were staggering.

"Many factors come into play, and this morning we discussed areas to look into where we can possibly make changes that will help ease the process and lessen disqualification factors. Want to know why you and Bernice are really here?" I knew she was going to tell me and didn't respond.

"Yesterday, we had a situation that pointed out something I have given much thought to the past year. There is another percentage I think we need to consider when discussing the system and what, who, and why of social services needs. And that percentage, although very small, has been neglected far too long. I'm talking about the individuals no one in our field wants to—or admits they aren't qualified to—accept as our responsibility. I'm talking about the mentally challenged, homeless we've lost track of, and angry people who think they have been wronged. This group is often considered unsociable, untreatable, and possibly violent." She paused and took a drink of water.

"All too easily, we label them as a criminal matter and turn them over to the judicial system, getting rid of them as no longer our problem. The system is set up to put Mr. Smith in that category. But you didn't. You saw an individual in need. Whether you realize it or not, I think you learned this compassion from living with your uncle, Dr. Nelson, and seeing how he sought to better the client, not plug them into a set system."

The mention of Uncle Sherm surprised me into a smile, but I kept quiet.

"You immediately got Mr. Smith out of the justice system and into the medical system to be treated and then followed up by social services to try and help, even rehabilitate. You made no friends with the police yesterday. And why? Because through our ignorance, we have made them feel that only they can help, and you took that away from them," she said.

"Until now, I saw no solution or way to address this issue. Now, I see hope we can actually start addressing the behavior for what it is. In the judicial system, these individuals have no future; in ours, they might. I needed to find the right people to accept this role and the challenge. I see that in you. You may not have a master's or doctorate degree, but you understand the streets and the need."

Believe me, this was getting more and more interesting as she went on!

"I want to start a new unit, under the Bureau of Social Services umbrella, to take on those cases no one else will touch because it's a square peg not fitting into a round hole or could involve violence so it's easier to justify it as a police matter. We, I, have to get rid of this out-of-sight, out-of-mind, attitude and instead, do as you do, Rich, see a problem, deal with it, and force the system to change if we have to, but get it done."

I thought she was ready for some feedback. "You know I've studied our State Social Service Manual in depth, so let me go out on a limb here, ma'am. I think your idea is great and may not be as hard as you think to implement. The rules already exist, we just need to change our mindset on how to interpret them." I stopped with that.

"Exactly," she jumped in. "Bernice, that is why I wanted you here. We need to apply the rules not only properly, but legally. Rich, I want you to head this unit. I will give you four qualified social workers to take on cases which I personally assign you. I will give you the leeway to run your unit as you see fit in order to get these square pegs to fit into our round holes."

She instructed the lawyer to get back to her in two days if her plan was solid, legally. Dr. Wade added that she would tell Will that she was assigning me to a special project. "I have several people in mind for your unit, once Bernice gives us the go-ahead, so let me know if there is anyone you would like in particular," she concluded. "Let's make it happen."

Ten days later, my team had been chosen. Dr. Wade selected three individuals, and I chose one, all having master's degrees and at least five years' experience. Each had their own area of expertise that the director thought was necessary; however, how I used them in the field was up to me. After one-on-one meetings, followed by two group sessions, I felt comfortable with our composition and ability to be successful at our tasking.

Dr. Wade and I reviewed dozens of cases and designated twenty-four of them for my team's initial handling. With Bernice signing off, Dr. Wade gave the green light and, to make sure we got the support we needed, scheduled a rare all-staff briefing.

On May 23, everyone crowded into our largest conference room. Dr. Wade stood at a podium and to her left, at a table, were my staff and I. Doug Bingham and Cheryl Hoover sat on my left, and to my right were Phyllis Nuberg and Emily, my first mentor, beside me. "Good afternoon," Dr. Wade started, "thank you for attending. For several years now I have seen a need for a unit to handle difficult cases, cases turned over to legal authorities because we chose not to be burdened with them. No more." She let that sink in.

"Today, under the supervision of Mr. Herman, I will be assigning these cases for his team's review. From now on, only he can recommend and I can approve denial of assistance and closure of a case. If you have a case that you think may fall into this category, refer it to me. Everyone, Rich Herman, head of The Red Tag Squad."

Red Tag Squad. I liked that and took over at the podium.

That evening, I drove home, elated, and surprised Mary by taking her to Victoria Station, a fine dining steak restaurant located inside three renovated railroad cars. The Newsoms readily volunteered to babysit their godson.

"Happy twenty-third birthday, honey," I said as we clinked wine glasses. For this special occasion we went outside our budget, but I already had a plan to supplement our income. We enjoyed a London-broil steak for two as she listened to me tell her about my day and the Red Tag Squad. She was glad to know I had hand-picked Emily and that people didn't resent my promotion.

"I actually got a lot of congratulations, and several said 'better you than me.' It was like they were relieved they wouldn't have to get involved themselves anymore; if a case was hard, just transfer it to Herman."

CHAPTER 20

May 24, Norfolk Bureau of Social Services, Red Tag Squad Office

"GOOD MORNING," I SAID TO MY TEAM, GATHERED IN my cubicle in the back of our new office. It was decided to give the Red Tag Squad (now being referred to as RTS) our own space because of our clients' reputation as possibly disruptive. "I have numbered and divided our caseload into two areas, eleven old cases needing another look at, and thirteen new cases to be reviewed and action determined. Each of you has a copy of the inventory including case number, nature of the case, status, and action required." I gave them a minute to look over their sheets.

"Phyllis is our official record keeper and the only one who can sign these records in and out, and then, only to one of us five or Dr. Wade and Bernice, her legal consultant. These records are *confidential* and for *RTS eyes only*. We need this stringent control to protect the privacy of our clients and to ensure the integrity of RTS. Make sure all your notes are maintained securely and not shared outside the confines of the case itself. I cannot and will not bend this policy." Everyone was nodding that they understood.

"As a reminder, we go into the field in twos, preferably with Cheryl or me being one of them. There will always be one of us, usually Phyllis, here in the office to answer phones, keeping the burners going and tabs on our whereabouts in the field. If someone needs to locate you, I expect the person manning the office to know where you are and how to reach you. I was able to get us all pagers, so make sure you keep them turned on and have everyone's numbers. Mine will be on 24/7, feel free to call."

"How about when we take breaks in the field?" Doug asked.

Doug Bingham, single, thirty-two years old, six-foot-three, with a large Afro, was a George Washington University graduate with six years' social work behind him in D.C. Although six years older than me, he was the youngest member of my team, and I was sure, our weakest link. Dr. Wade said he was brilliant and, having come from a poor neighborhood and family, was driven with loads of potential to help those in need. She said he reminded her of herself when she started out, idealistic about making a difference and very naïve. I appreciated her honesty, and he would be my work in progress.

"I think you'll do what you're comfortable with, Doug." I smiled, the others looked away grinning, and we continued. I told them I would hand out their first assignments to review the cases, prioritize their needs, and start making appointments. "Cheryl and Doug, you'll be together, with Cheryl lead agent," I said. "Phyllis, you'll begin recording and start our status board."

I stood and removed a covering from the side wall to reveal a six-by-twelve-foot whiteboard I had installed. Using black grease pen, I had divided the board into twenty-four columns across the top and entered our first case numbers. "Phyllis, I started it. There are eleven more colored pens. You can develop your own system for tracking cases. Just make sure we can understand it when you're done." Everyone laughed, and Phyllis jumped up to get started.

Phyllis Nuberg, black, sixty years young, tall and trim, had white hair, half-lens glasses on a neck cord, and a master's degree from Norfolk State University. A widow with five children and three grandchildren, she had thirty-five years on the job. Some might see her as old and movement restricted, needing a cane. I saw experience with a proven track record that could not be overlooked, and watching her, I could tell she would be the person my team members went to. Priceless.

I handed Cheryl ten cases, and Doug moved over next to her. Cheryl Hoover was my pick for second in command. Age forty-four, black, master's degree from Howard University, married to a fireman, two children, five-three and stocky, she had sixteen years' hands-on social work in Richmond, before moving here when her husband became Norfolk assistant fire chief. She was outgoing and told Dr. Wade she needed a challenge like this job offered. She said we should be helping people to get welfare and the help they need so they would no longer need welfare and the help we give. *Yes!*

And that left two of us. "Emily and I will take these remaining cases," I said, taking a batch from Phyllis. "I know it's going to take a while to get your caseload organized. We're on no timetable—take advantage of her experience and expertise and feel free to ask Phyllis to assist." That got a big smile from her.

"You may all know that there was a case not long ago that prompted Dr. Wade into getting RTS off the ground. That case, number 22, went cold, and I am reopening it now as our first official case. Emily and I will be on our pagers." Phyllis annotated the board and we walked out.

"And where are we going?" Emily asked. I handed her the case and she smiled. "Well, I'll be! Mr. Smith, our boxer." We headed to Norfolk General Hospital, the last place I'd seen him. There was an administrator there I thought would be able to help.

A month later, Dr Wade brought me in to give an update on the RTS caseload. From the start, it was determined my squad would always have twenty-four cases ongoing; as one was closed, Phyllis would activate a new one from hundreds that were pending. Of the twenty-four initial cases, twenty-one cases had been resolved. The other three cases were officially closed, one because of a death of the applicant and two because the applicants were incarcerated. Twenty-four new cold cases had been activated.

"Not one has been turned back to the judicial system," Dr. Wade stated as a fact. "That's fantastic news. And how is our boxing friend?"

I knew she was aware of his status and was looking for how Emily and I handled it. Mr. Smith had become our pet project, and we had grown quite fond of him. Norfolk General was able to give me an old address, and as we drove there, Emily saw him, only a block away from the address, picking up cans.

"Mr. Smith," I said, approaching slowly, "Remember me? Rich Herman?"

"Of course, I do." He pretended to throw a punch and laughed, showing the few teeth he had left. "I'm on my meds now." He reached in his coat and handed Emily a bottle. She wrote down the doctor's name and prescription information and handed it back.

"How would you like some lunch?" I asked. "Our treat, and you can tell us about your boxing career." He liked that idea and got in the back seat of our car, cans and all.

There was a diner nearby, and over hamburgers, fries, and a vanilla shake we got the life story of Mr. Reggie Smith, Army veteran and one-time golden gloves boxing champ who almost had a shot in the pros. That was before he received a beating he never recovered from. He had never married and thought he might have a sister in Oklahoma, but his parents were dead. When he went to the bathroom, I discussed a plan with Emily. We took the old man back to the building where he was staying and called it a day. Baby steps, I told Emily.

Taking the information we had, Emily and Phyllis were able to establish a little background on Reggie Smith. He had served a tour in Korea, been honorably discharged from the Army, and first sought help from the Veterans Affairs Agency after being picked up for vagrancy in Portsmouth, Virginia, several years earlier. He was diagnosed with chronic depression and delusional episodes, often found blacked out in the streets. When on his medications, he seemed capable of functioning and taking care of himself. Two days later, Emily and I went for another visit.

"Hi, Reggie," I said, as Emily and I got out of the car. "Ready for another talk?"

The following Tuesday, we met with a VA representative and discussed Reggie Smith's case. They had a file on him and contacted his old doctor while we waited. It was agreed upon that Reggie appeared to be eligible to reenter the VA system as an active patient, and an appointment was made for further evaluation. One week later, after his initial screening, he was accepted for VA assistance, including medical and psychological evaluation at a live-in VA facility.

Emily had tears in her eyes when we dropped Reggie off, without his cans, and saw him escorted to his new home. Of course, it didn't affect me.

My squad's first official case was temporarily closed, and Phyllis would earmark it for a six-month follow-up by the RTS. We knew this was a huge success for establishing our credibility and looked favorable for our existence. Of course, my entire team, maybe idealistic, was not unaware that reality would also bring failures. We may not have expected just how.

"That was good work with Mr. Smith, thanks for the details." Dr. Wade reached into her middle drawer, pulled out and handed me a case file with our newly created RTS red tag attached. "You are holding a special case, one that is personal to me and could affect the reputation of this office. It must be handled discreetly and, whatever the outcome, must be able to withstand scrutiny from any state evaluation. What I am about to tell you stays within this office for now."

"I've made confidentiality a priority with RTS. You'll never hear of a leak from my people, I bet my career on that." I sat back, confidently.

"I appreciate that, I really do." She went over to the window and looked out, a common habit, I found. "An elderly Jewish couple has filed an appeal to this office claiming, of all things, discrimination regarding their not being eligible for welfare assistance. The husband was forced to retire for medical and mental reasons and filed to receive disability to help pay huge medical expenses. They were turned down benefits for numerous reasons; income, owned property, two cars, you get the picture. The man is a well-known lawyer; in fact, he was the mayor's attorney. He said the caseworkers assigned have no empathy for anyone's rights and were anti-Jewish. Like all applicants, he has a right to appeal and he did.

"His wife has never worked and has found herself being his caregiver and wants to support her husband of over fifty years. In truth, she is embarrassed about all the fuss her husband is raising. To make matters worse, and sensitive for me, is I approved the finding of not eligible, and they are long-time dear friends of mine."

"You can assure them that I will be fair, open-minded, and both sympathetic and empathetic as I reexamine their case, Dr. Wade." I stood to leave.

"As I said, this is sensitive and has political pressure being applied too, so tread softly. Bottom line, I want you to make this go away quietly, while showing my friends the respect they deserve. Now, let me give you a few tips about the Greensteins." A half-hour later, walking me to the door, she said, "If it helps, I have complete faith in you."

I smiled, walked out, and couldn't help thinking—*no pressure, Rich, just do your thing.*

The Greensteins lived in a beautiful home on the Elizabeth River near downtown. I studied their entire case file including the initial application for assistance based on disability, the social worker notes from background checks and two interviews, medical records, financial sheets, and whatever else seemed important to the case worker. On top of the file was the two-page letter outlining the reason for denial, signed by the case worker and approved by Dr. Sheila Wade.

On purpose, I left the file in the car. Hugh Greenstein might be physically disabled and not of sound mind, but he was still a lawyer, one of the best, and he could take me to school if I let him see the file. With the file fresh in my mind and Dr. Wade's inside information about the couple, I had a plan in mind and now hoped it would work.

Mrs. Greenstein greeted me at the door, shaking my hand with a firm grip and asking me to call her Stella. Near eighty, she was petite, very alert, lively, and impressive in every way. "Before we go further," she said, "I want you to know that Hugh is a great man who, unfortunately, is in the decline. He's normally friendly, but since he was forced to retire and is bedridden, he has on occasion gotten a little violent." I said I understood. "Right this way, Mr. Herman," she said.

We walked down a long, wide hallway, filled with paintings and sculptures beneath its twenty-foot ceiling, to a large, dark wood double-door. "We had my husband's bed moved into the study when it became too difficult to go up and down the stairs, even with the elevator. He is having a good day, and he's anxious to talk to you." She knocked lightly and a young nurse, in uniform, opened the door and motioned us in. "Mr. Herman is here, Hugh," Stella said.

"Did he bring us any money?" were the first words I heard Hugh Greenstein speak. He was sitting up in a king-sized bed with several pillows behind him. He wore a silk jacket with a velvet collar and lapel. At age seventy-nine, he was down to 130 pounds (I got that from the medical record) from his normal 175 and had oxygen available next to his bed if needed. His wavy white hair was neatly combed, and he appeared alert as he stuck out his hand to shake. Very professional.

"Well, Mr. Herman. Did you?" You could tell he liked being direct and he wanted an answer.

"Nice to meet you, Mr. Greenstein, and your appeal is what I am here to talk about. First of all, Sheila Wade," (I had been told to drop the *doctor* with him) "asked me to extend her regards and hopes you're feeling better." He actually smiled a little and nodded, then told me to call him Hugh. A man appeared out of nowhere and put a chair out for me to sit.

"She also said to extend her thanks for following procedure and filing your appeal, as every applicant has the right to do, through the proper channels. This way, she was able to look into your case personally, assign me directly, and avoid looking like favoritism, because of your close friendship, which could be misconstrued."

"She's a smart woman," Hugh said with a chuckle. "Would you like a drink?"

"A plain water would be nice. Thank you, sir." He appeared coherent and well aware of why we were meeting. The man who brought the chair now handed him what looked like a scotch on the rocks and me a glass of ice water. I don't think it was eleven in the morning yet, but it was his house and he surely wasn't driving. *Hail to the Queen*, I thought. I noticed Stella remained in the room, although on the other side, barely in listening distance, but the nurse and, I assumed, butler had left.

Hugh took a sip of his drink, seemed relaxed, and smiled at me. My cue.

"Hugh and Stella," she nodded she could hear, "First, let's get the facts out there and be done with that. I thoroughly reviewed your initial case, reason for denial and your appeal. Denial was based on your income, which is substantial, your property owned, which is also substantial, and your access to numerous other assets." I saw Hugh wanting to say something.

"Give me one minute, Hugh, to finish the facts and then we can open up discussion." Surprisingly, he accepted that. "You said you accept the denial reasoning but filed the appeal based on your now having no incoming income and no health or medical insurance. As your bills continue, you eventually will lose everything and want the state to help prevent that. Is that about it?"

Stella joined Hugh and sat next to him on the bed. She looked at her husband and he nodded.

"My husband, and I too, I guess," she started, "don't think it's right that just because we're well off, we don't need help. Hugh worked hard his whole life and now is being told, thank you for all you've done over the past fifty-five years, and as soon as you are dirt poor, have lost your house, cars, and everything else we will be happy to assist you. Why do we, why does anyone have to go through such a demeaning process to be helped? This is the United States after all; we should take care of our own. Our citizens, including us Jewish ones, deserve better."

How do you argue that, especially when that's one of the reasons I am a social worker and how I got here in the first place? I asked to use the restroom; we all could use a break. The butler showed me the bathroom, and the nurse tended to Hugh. I put cold water on my face and went back to do what I had to do. No one ever said the system was fair.

When I reentered the study, Hugh was eating an apple and looked refreshed, still sitting up. Stella had moved to a chair near the bed. The nurse and butler were nowhere to be seen.

"Fresh fruit here, Rich," Stella said, pointing to a bowl on the table. "Help yourself." As tempting as it was, I declined and picked up where we left off.

"Hugh, did you ever have a case that you knew had to go to court but, deep inside, you knew you couldn't win? Not because your client wasn't deserving of their day in court and had every right to be there, but you knew the law was cut and dried, and your/their case didn't meet the minimum threshold of credibility to be ruled any way but against them?" I thought that was enough of an opening.

I was being stared at. Thirty seconds. No movement. A minute. No movement. Two minutes. "A few," Hugh said, finally. He took a sip of his drink. "Go ahead, Rich, I'm sure you have a point here." He sat back against his pillows looking directly at me again. But it was a look more of interest than anger, I hoped.

"Yes, sir, thank you. I ask you to think of yourself in that position again, only this time you are the client, Sheila Wade is your lawyer, and I am the appeals court. You lost your original case, turned to your lawyer, a good friend, and asked to appeal. Although she knew it would be a baseless appeal, you had every right to do so. Your lawyer, a very smart woman and knowing the law, tried everything in her power to win your case, to the point she called in a few favors and got me assigned as her 'appeals court judge.'

"And why did she do that? Not just because I know the rules, a lot of people do, it's because I care about justice and, if at all possible, will not look for a way to deny a client, but a way to approve a client. We let the process work, and it did. So, I ask you, client Greenstein, what do you think was not only the only possible, but the right outcome?"

This time it was over five minutes before the silence was broken. Then, "Do you know what they call a closing argument in court that convinces a jury, Mr. Herman?" I could see that once again he was expecting a response.

"No, sir, I do not."

"A lawyer's dream. A blessing from the court above. I had a few of those in my day." Hugh Greenstein, a proud man, was talking to me like a junior colleague. "Today, Rich, you can say that. I may not like the result, but you certainly have explained to me why it was made. I'll sign that affidavit and drop the appeal. Stella was right all along." Stella came and kissed his hand. I gave him the forms, and he and Stella signed them.

"For what it's worth," I said, "with Sheila's encouragement, I have been looking into ways to improve our state's manual on how we look at qualification criteria. I think it's terrible that we force people, like yourselves, into a position of possible poverty before reaching out to help. It's not only embarrassing, it's inhumane. I intend to use cases like yours to justify the changes we recommend. I wish you all the best."

Stella was walking me to the door when we heard Hugh yell out, "Stella, is that Mr. Herman here?" We walked back to the study.

"Yes, Hugh, I'm still here," I said, approaching his bed.

"You Herman?" He was looking at me very confused. "Did you bring me my money?" Stella went to his side. "Well?" he shouted.

"Not today, sir." I was trying to think. I never expected what happened next.

Hugh Greenstein, old and frail, picked up his bedpan and threw it at me. It was full. "I want our money!" he screamed. The nurse and butler got to him and started to calm him down.

The butler provided me several towels, and I cleaned up the best I could in the bathroom before departing. I soon realized I couldn't get rid of the urine and feces smell. Stella couldn't apologize enough, but what was done was done. I told her I had experienced much worse and left it at that. I drove home, with the windows open. A motorcycle cop pulled alongside me at a stoplight on Tidewater

Drive, slowly looked my way, took a whiff, and closed his visor, making a quick getaway when the light turned green.

Mary met me at the door and opened it slightly, saying, "Go around back and strip. Don't pass go, and head to the shower. Don't you dare pick up Chris." I handed her my clothes as I entered the back door. "Dr. Wade called and told me what happened. She wants you to call as soon as you can." I realized she was laughing.

Fresh from the shower and sipping on what I thought was a well-deserved beer, while Mary was doing a special load of laundry, I spoke with Dr. Wade. "Yes, ma'am," I said. "Understand, and thank you. Yes, I'll see you first thing Monday morning."

I hung up, leaned back, and shook my head. "Can you believe that, honey?" I yelled. "My distinguished, well-respected, and usually poised boss is laughing. So much for discreet."

Mary came out holding Chris, almost four months old, and carrying a cupcake with a lighted candle. "Happy birthday, Daddy!" All the thoughts went out of my head except enjoying my family. For one thing, I'll never forget my twenty-sixth birthday.

CHAPTER 21

June 26

WHEN I WALKED INTO MY CUBICLE MONDAY morning, I was surprised to see my whole team already there. Usually I was the second one in the office, after Phyllis, who thought it was her duty to have coffee ready for everyone's arrival. They were all just standing and silent, highly unusual. I turned and Dr. Wade came in holding a package.

"Happy belated birthday, Rich," she said. "Just a little something from all of us," handing me the package.

I'm sure the laughter from the RTS office was heard throughout the entire floor, if not building, as my team retold over and over my "discreet" interview last Friday. Even Doug, who had a hard time grasping humor, got a chuckle once the meaning of my gift was explained to him. In fact, because of his height, Doug had the honor of mounting my gift on the wall behind my desk so all who entered my space could enjoy my trophy. Mounted on a piece of plywood was a shiny metal bedpan with an engraved plaque underneath: "HE TOOK ONE FOR THE TEAM."

That afternoon, Dr. Wade told me that Stella Greenstein had called and given her a recap of my visit, including being hit with the fully loaded bedpan. "She offered to pay for your dry cleaning, by the way. She also said that Hugh didn't remember any of that part but he did remember the young man who treated him with respect and so eloquently explained their application denial, appeal process rights, and final decision. Stella said what upset Hugh now was he should have known better but felt he had to go down with a fight, and Mr.

Herman understood and admired him for it. Although the outcome didn't go his way, he was very satisfied with the right decision being made and was willing to put that in writing if it would help."

Dr. Wade called for another review at the two-month mark. In addition to the caseloads, she wanted me to be prepared to give an assessment, unofficial this time, of my team. She gave me enough notice so that we had the entire morning, July 21, blocked off for RTS review. She even had two pots of coffee on and told the office manager not to disturb, short of war.

"I know you're aware of this," she started out, "but to make sure we are on the same page I'll mention it anyway. Your group has cleared seventy percent of the cold cases and almost sixty percent of the new ones I provided from my two-year study prior to the team's existence. More importantly, RTS has quickly established a reputation as a no-nonsense, action-oriented, and highly efficient team. Agree?" I did. "Phyllis also made a separate sheet, she said at your direction, to separately track all reasons for denial, and this was an unofficial report only to me. Great idea, and I'll use it in my argument for manual qualification changes."

"I knew you'd figure that out," I said, smiling. "Phyllis is a wealth of knowledge and really good at separating facts from opinion. We're lucky to have her." We spent the next two hours going over active cases, and I made a lot of notes from the remarks and suggestions my boss made. "I think that wraps up my caseload, ma'am."

"Yes, and I see your unit is busy, but I think they can be pushed a little more. I'd like to double your active caseload to forty-eight. Any problem with that?"

"None. I think each day we get a little better. Part of it is understanding our role and how far we can push ourselves. I have a feeling that's what you want to discuss next?"

"Yes. Let's put these aside." She pushed all the active cases, now twice as many, to the side of the table. "It's only two months, but I would like your honest opinion on your team, one by one. We can't afford any dead weight if we want to maintain an elite status. Start wherever you like."

I was prepared. "Emily Banner: I feel my pick of her has been justified. She was not happy in our old unit, and it wasn't because of her ability, it was, at age thirty-five, not being confident and aggressive enough. She felt restrained by the system, and each case she couldn't approve, she got more frustrated. In this short time, Emily has stepped up to the plate and I think has the potential to be the leader, not the follower." Dr. Wade asked two questions, annotated her file, and set it aside.

"Phyllis Nuberg: backbone of our unit. She has found her niche, and the team loves her. She knows when to speak, and when she does, you better take note because she is always right. After you appointed her and I welcomed her aboard, she said she would give me two good years before she retires; now she says that every day she feels we are making a difference and she has at least five years left in her. We can only hope." Dr. Wade smiled, made a note and set it aside.

"Cheryl Hoover: born leader. What she lacks in stature she makes up for with smarts, tenacity, and confidence in her abilities. She also has an amazing trait not many like her have—no ego. She cares only for outcome, not blame and credit. More than once, she has helped Emily and Doug overcome a misstep, and when it needed my intervention, she took the blame, but when things worked out, she gave them all the credit. This is something I learned early in my Navy tour by the way. I call it leadership. Honestly, she could take over for me tomorrow." More smiles from Dr. Wade, more annotations, and another record set aside.

"Doug Bingham: From day one, I knew he would be the weak link and made it my mission to give him opportunity to grow. Doug is a good guy and does his job, but he just isn't aggressive, and he often wants to look past the needs of the client and go off on a tangent on how the system works against minorities and how they never have a chance to succeed.

"I haven't given up, but he is still a work in progress. I may be forced to tell him at his ninety-day evaluation that his time here, with this unit anyway, may be coming to an end." This time Dr. Wade wrote in his record and didn't put it aside.

"I knew he would be a wildcard, Rich. I think you and your team have done wonders with him, and he's just reached that point where he has hit Peter's Principle. He's gone as high as he can in field work, it's just not for him, and it's time to rethink his future." She went out and returned a few minutes later, with Doug in tow, asking him to take a seat next to me.

"Mr. Bingham," she began calmly and professionally, "Mr. Herman and I have been going over his team's progress, and I'd like to know how you think you are doing? Be honest, please."

Doug sat up a little taller in the chair. "Dr. Wade, first of all, Mr. Herman has been a good boss, and all the team members are great, especially Mrs. Hoover. On the other hand, I'll admit I have a hard time dealing with all the people who come to us. I studied all this, and our job isn't what I expected. People should be able to manage their own lives, independently, a part of society, being safe and well. I don't think they should come see me to get what they deserve, instead they need to be taught they already deserve it."

"Doug," she said, "herein is the problem. You approach social work as empowering the people with their God-given rights and leading them to see what their needs are. What we need to do is get these people, through our programs, to the point they can first function as individuals and then as family units. Then it'll be time for you to take over."

"Exactly, Dr. Wade." Doug relaxed, with a big smile. "I guess we both know that isn't what I'm doing. What I need to do is go back to school, get my Ph.D. to teach and start mentoring students who care about social justice. You guys get them on their feet, and I'll lead them from there." Now he was really smiling, as was Dr. Wade. Yeah, okay, me too. He thanked us both and said he would submit his notice to leave the end of August. He planned to apply for a doctoral grant at his alma mater, George Washington University.

After Doug left, we sat back down. "I'll have someone to replace

Doug by mid-August. I think you'll like who I send. Okay, Rich, now your turn."

"I'm one of those that likes to let my record speak for itself. I will say that I love my job and totally agree when I hear that we are making a difference. I've also painted you a good picture of the RTS team, their strengths and weaknesses, and what they are capable of. I now owe you the facts of my personal situation.

"Frankly, Director, we are living paycheck to paycheck. In fact, Mary asked how I paid for her birthday dinner last month. I didn't tell her I was selling my blood, which is O negative and paying fifteen dollars a pint, to have a little spending money. I'm ... we're ... not complaining, just realistic that I need to look out for my family's future."

"I appreciate that, and I wish I could do more for you. That small one-year and supervisor rating pay increase was all I could do. You're not only the youngest supervisor we've ever had, you're the only one without a degree. Have you thought of night school to finish your bachelor's? I know you're not far away."

"We've discussed it, but even with that, my pay wouldn't increase that much. No offense, Director, but if I get a doctorate, gain experience, and get the top job in social services, I'd still have a difficult time raising a family. Maybe someday society will wake up and pay our teachers, firefighters, law enforcement, nurses, and so on what they deserve. Until then, it'll be huge egos and little pay for some of our most needed and important citizens.

"Anyway, I just wanted you to know my thoughts. After all you've done for us, I'd never leave you high and dry. And on the positive side, Cheryl could step up and do my job. She is more than qualified, and the team not only loves her, they trust her." We shook hands; meeting adjourned.

That night after dinner, I said, "Time for a talk." We got Chris bathed and down for the night, a family affair, before taking our spots on the couch.

I told Mary about my day, leaving out the personal information about my RTS staff. I even confessed about giving blood. She wasn't upset that I gave the blood, she thought that was thoughtful and unselfish; she was upset I didn't tell her. Feeling guilty, I told her I found another blood bank and planned to give every two weeks. This time, she just shook her head. I then told her we needed to look at our future.

Without another word, she got up and returned with a legal pad. Making a better future: Pros and Cons. Nothing was off the table whenever we started this process, and Mary showed just how well she knew me by jumping right in, "Rich, you enjoyed your time in the Navy, right?"

I nodded yes and let her run with it. "Let's start by making going back into the Navy option one; followed by going back to school full-time to get a degree, second; looking at another job that pays better without more school, third; and stick with what we've got for a while and ride it out, fourth and last."

It was one a.m. before we got to bed, but we had an exhaustive list compiled, discussed, and a plan of action made. I was smiling as I dozed off and slept like a baby. I'm pretty sure my wife did too.

The next night we had the Newsoms over to play cards. Mark had taught Patti how to play Spades, and she was convinced she and Mary could take the guys down, no problem. With Mark Jr. and Chris in a playpen (I thought this must be what it was like with Punky and me, years ago) the first Spades game began. Into the second game, after the men won the first, I casually asked Mark, "How is the Navy doing with recruiting now, with Vietnam supposedly drawing down?"

"You always hear that about Vietnam," Mark answered. "Remember Dave Gant?" Dave was Mark's roommate when I first came to Norfolk in 1966. A good guy, he made chief petty officer, got married, and settled down.

"He's a career counselor now and tells me many rates are still getting big bonuses to reenlist because they're needed just for the buildup still in Southeast Asia. In fact, I bet your old rate, radioman, is on that list. Want to go back in?" He laughed and so did Patti. I looked at Mary, who winked, saying nothing.

After the Newsoms left, games tied at three to three, we put a sleeping Chris down and broke out the legal pad. "Under Pros, possible in demand Navy with bonus," Mary said, writing it down. "Got Dave's number?"

CHAPTER 22

WHEN I CAME BACK FROM LUNCH, DR. WADE ASKED me into her office. "Mr. Herman, meet Gilliam Talbot, your new team member."

I had already seen his application and been briefed on his incoming interview with the boss, who had known him since his birth. Very impressive. Also, the grandson of our previous director. Doug would still be with the agency for the rest of the month, but Dr. Wade had him reassigned to another unit for his transition. In other words, he was out of our way.

I introduced Gill, as he preferred to be called, to the team and they were open and warm in their greeting as always. Like me, they were very impressed by him. Our newest member, only twenty-seven years old, standing six-one, about 200 pounds, graduated from Georgetown University and played linebacker on their last football team, including their last game on Thanksgiving Day, 1966. He then served in the Marines, including a tour leading a Military Police unit in Vietnam where he received Bronze Star and Purple Heart medals, before returning to get his master's in social work last June.

Cheryl took him under her wing immediately, and his training began. I couldn't help but smile at the difference from Doug.

That night, Mary and I had invited Dave Gant for dinner, and he explained to us what the Navy might be able to offer me, based on what I could offer the Navy. I gave him the go-ahead to contact the detailer who would handle my case and get back to me on just what could be offered. He assured us he would keep our meeting confidential until I told him otherwise. We had a lot to think about.

On August 16, Dr. Wade and I met for our official three-month review of the caseload; I would also present my input for my team's official quarterly evaluations. Although no one questioned my being head of the unit, I recommended that the director sign and deliver all official evaluations; her signature and personal attention would go a long way with their egos and giving them one-on-one recognition from the boss. Of course, I wrote the evals and, as it turned out, after Dr. Wade met to discuss their reviews, Edith, Cheryl, and Phyllis all came and gave me a hug. After what I wrote, they should have. Then it was my turn.

"Rich, do you want me to repeat what's already officially written down, or can we just move on?" Dr. Wade couldn't help laughing as she spoke.

I read my review, signed it, and, looking as serious as I could, said, "I was actually hoping for a little better narrative, Director. I guess I have no choice but to file a rebuttal." Her laugh was gone, and her look was nothing but shock and confusion. It was my turn.

"Gotcha, Boss." I started chuckling, and once it sank in, she joined me. "Thank you for your kind words. I wish we could convert that into pay, which brings me to what I've been holding back on telling you," I said. "As much as I love it here, as much as I think I can be making a difference, I can't raise a family with no future ahead of me—even if I could go back and get my doctorate. I've been looking at options and, although I haven't made a commitment to anything, I could be giving you notice to leave between Labor Day and mid-September."

"I fully understand where you're coming from, Rich," she said softly. "I think we both knew this day was coming, and I respect you being up front from day one. Tell you what I can do. For now, keep this between us. I'll accept today as your official notice but won't initiate any paperwork until you tell me. Like you said, we have Cheryl, and you have groomed her well to replace you, so it's not like I'll be left hanging. Good luck on whatever you decide, and remember, your job here is ready now, or any time in the future." She came around her desk, shook my hand, looked out her office windows, and gave me a quick hug. It was going to be hard to leave this great lady.

The following Monday, Dave called and gave me the word on what we could expect if I were to reenlist for six years. I would have to go back to a sea duty tour first, but, for a case of scotch, the detailer would get me homeported in Norfolk. I would keep my rank of E-5 (second class petty officer) but would lose my longevity from the time I was out—yet would be credited with the four years I did serve.

Knowing my rank and time of duty, we were now able to determine my pay that would be effective the day I signed up. *Impressive, almost $150 a month increase from what I make now.* Of course, all benefits of medical, housing, insurances, commissary/exchange, and base privileges would be effective immediately. I promised to call back shortly.

An hour later, after a conversation with Mary, I called Dave back, and we agreed to meet the next afternoon following work. I walked in, and Dave introduced me to Master Chief Johnson, the local recruiter. Two hours later, I left the recruiting office with all the paperwork filled out, approved, and needing only two things before I would make the ultimate decision of, once again, serving my country: First, I was scheduled for and must pass a physical on September 4 in Richmond; the last thing would be my calling the master chief to tell him to schedule my reenlistment day.

Master Chief Johnson called me September 4 saying I passed the examination with flying colors. He understood my wife and I still had a big decision to make and said just to give notice one day before, if I decide to reenlist. I told him I would get back to him one way or the other within two weeks.

It was a half-hour before Dr. Wade usually went home. "Dr. Wade," I said, having opened her door a little after knocking, "got a minute?"

"Always, Rich," she said. "However, I have a feeling I'm not going to like what you're here to tell me." She smiled and pointed for me to sit down.

Dr. Wade asked if I would work through Tuesday, September 12, in order to do a proper turnover with Cheryl. I agreed, and we decided the unit would be told tomorrow morning.

I think Cheryl was nervous when she was asked to see Dr. Wade. I was already in the director's office when she came in and took the seat next to me. "I feel like I've been called to the principal's office," she said nervously.

"You can relax, Cheryl," Dr. Wade said, smiling. "In fact, I've called you in here because we want you to be the first to know, Rich is leaving us." Cheryl was genuinely surprised and reached for my arm. "He has strongly recommended to me that you be his immediate replacement and promoted to Red Tag Squad leader. I agree 100 percent and would like to make the announcement right now if you have no objections."

Cheryl opened her mouth and nothing came out. She swallowed and tried again. "I don't know what to say. I never, in my wildest dreams, expected to head this unit. Oh my, what will the team think?"

"How lucky they are to have you replacing me," I said. "You're a natural, Cheryl, and if I hadn't been here first, you would have been the perfect person to have started the boss's dream unit and get it established. Congratulations." We stood and hugged.

The team was asked to join us in the director's office, and Dr. Wade made the announcement official. I told the team that it would be difficult leaving, but Mary and I were looking at growing our family and exploring other job opportunities. No one questioned me beyond that, and Cheryl took the limelight and accepted congratulations. I looked at Dr. Wade, and we both knew the squad was in good hands.

Arriving at work for my final day, I took a seat alongside what was now Cheryl's desk. I had brought an empty box for my trophy, the now infamous bedpan, and a few personal items from my desk. I noticed Edith wasn't at work today and hoped she was okay as this was the first day she ever missed. The mood was light and I mostly drank coffee and talked to all my fellow workers from the past sixteen months. Then the place was like a ghost town, with just Cheryl and me.

Cheryl answered the ringing phone and after a minute said, "I'll be right down. Mr. Herman is here; he can help me." She said maintenance had two new chairs for her cubicle and asked me to help her get them.

She led me into the conference room, and I had been set up, again. Most, if not all, of the staff had gathered, and up front at the podium stood Dr. Wade with Mary holding Chris. Looking at who else was next to her, I now knew why Edith wasn't at work; she was responsible for getting my family there.

Dr. Wade spoke a few words and ended with, "I want to share something with Rich and have chosen to do that now, with everyone here. Before accepting leadership of the RTS, he did a study for me on all welfare claim applications and, if denied, the reason why. Two of these reasons, he made perfectly clear, bothered him and needed something done to correct them. I took that onboard as my personal project.

"I am proud to announce, the Virginia state legislature is going to make your request an action item for the upcoming legislature. No promises—government works in strange and usually slow ways, but owning a telephone is being looked at as a safety and health issue and a necessity for all citizens to have access to. If this happens, having a phone will no longer be a disqualifying factor for benefits. It's a good start." She opened the podium to the floor.

Will, my first boss, told the story about Mary and the crab dinner he hosted. I think he added a few things, and everyone had a good laugh. Phyllis told how she agreed to come here to work for Dr. Wade for two years before retiring and now, would stay until they threw her out. Everyone cheered at that. Cheryl got up, saying she had followed her husband to Norfolk and was fortunate to be given a chance by Dr. Wade in the RTS. She now thanked me for giving her the opportunity to spread her wings, and said she would not let us down.

Then, to my surprise, Gill said he had something to say.

"I know I've only been here a month, so you're wondering what could I possibly add. Well," he looked at Dr. Wade, who nodded, "for those of you that didn't know, I'm the grandson of our last director. I'm also Dr. Wade's godson." I didn't know that, and there were a few murmurs.

"I came here because I was expected, or thought I was expected, to come here. The first day, I'm introduced to my new boss, and I find someone younger than me in charge of the prestigious RTS team. I knew this was not going to work out, not with my background, graduating top of my class at Georgetown and a Marine officer who had served in Vietnam. Guess what?" Gilliam paused, knowing everyone was thinking the same as me. *What?*

"I'm assigned to Mrs. Hoover and learn she not only loves her job, but the cases Mr. Herman trusts her with and the freedom she's given to work them. Emily tells me how she was Mr. Herman's first mentor here, before RTS, and that he immediately showed he was destined for bigger and better things. I learn from Phyllis that she has never felt so satisfied with what she personally, as well as the unit, has accomplished not only in helping people but also giving them hope, always with dignity. I then personally got some hands-on guidance and soon came to accept that this guy is really good. And then today, to top all things off, like this guy couldn't be more of a saint, I meet his wife and son and take a good look at him and realize, he's not black."

It took quite a while for the laughter to subside. For me, it was one of the greatest compliments I could ever receive. I stepped up to the podium. "I can't top that, Gill. And I want you to know, Dr.

Wade," I looked her way, "I think I misjudged your godson after all, he does have a future. Not sure if here, but a future." Now I got the laughs.

As I started to say something else, Edith and Emily approached carrying what turned out to be a money tree. "This is too much," I continued. "Honey, take it and Chris and run before they change their minds." I was on a roll but out of humor. "Seriously, Dr. Wade, thank you for the great news on my telephone issue. To you all, Mary and I do think of this as home and you as our family. We will never forget you."

I reenlisted Friday morning, September 15, 1972, at 0830. I was wearing my newly purchased dress blue uniform with a second class petty officer radioman insignia on the left sleeve. Mary and I started our new adventure; together, this time with an infant son, a new career opportunity ahead, and like the last time, broke. No, wait ... thanks to our newfound family and friends ... yes, $437 attached to the money tree.

As we lay in bed that first night back on active duty, we were happy with our decision and would never look back. And as I looked at my wife sleeping, I thought, *I hope I live up to your trust, Mary, and our future will be as successful as we envision.*

We were about to make a lifetime of memories and, hopefully, a legacy to proudly pass on. As with everything, time would be the judge.

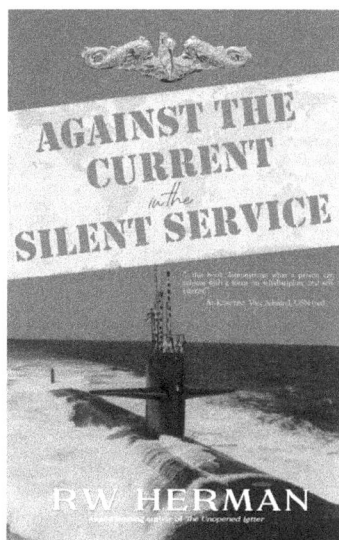

Author's Note

Finishing my first book, I thought I had done what my mother asked, leaving something tangible for my descendants; it would be an accurate history of my life in those important years. Winning a gold medal for the book gave credence to my thoughts. *One and done.*

But I had left many unanswered questions. After much thought, a year later I wrote my second book, which also won a gold medal.

In it, you learn how and why I returned to the Navy and ultimately achieved my goal of becoming an officer—but with a huge, possibly career-ending twist. I was commissioned as an officer in the *submarine* force, presenting one major problem: I was not qualified in submarines and would not be a welcome addition among this small, close-knit professional group known as submariners.

As Vice Admiral Al Konetzni remarked, "This book demonstrates what a person can achieve with a focus on self-discipline and self-esteem!"

Now, turn the page to read about my life after retirement.

RETIREMENT YEARS

July 1997 – September 2010

"I looked at the speedometer, 135 mph. I slowed Bigg Redd down to take Exit 29 ... and sped up again en route to the hospital ... Shirley cried out in pain and was struggling to catch her breath."

CHAPTER 23

July 24, 1997, Officer's Quarters, Kings Bay Submarine Base, Georgia

"I DON'T THINK THIS ROOM HAS CHANGED SINCE WE were here five years ago," I said, following Shirley into what would be our home the next forty days.

My wife and I had stayed here in 1992 when, still on active duty, I reported to Commander, Submarine Group Ten as the Assistant Chief of Staff for Communications. Later we had bought a home, affectionately referred to as the "Little Yellow House," rented it out while stationed in Hawaii, and our tenants' lease wouldn't expire for another month.

"Rich," Shirley said, sprawling out on the couch exhausted, "after this past week, I just look forward to doing nothing for a couple of days. Don't you agree, ah, do I call you Mr. Herman now?"

I was reentering the room from a trip to the car, getting the last of our luggage and joined her. "Agree, Mrs. Herman." She was already asleep. I was too keyed up to take a nap so put the six-pack of beer I bought into the refrigerator, opened one and stepped out onto the balcony off the bedroom. Yes, it had been a whirlwind week.

Last Friday, on a beautiful afternoon at the Submarine Memorial Park on the submarine base in Pearl Harbor, I unofficially retired, as a commander, after a Navy career spanning over thirty years. My official retirement date would be November 1, following an extended leave period. It's mind-boggling when I think of all the different changes my life and career took. More than ten years enlisted in the surface Navy, married with two sons, and then having my dream come true, commissioned an Ensign (Limited Duty Officer, or LDO) and becoming a submarine communications specialist.

I had been in my second year as an officer when my wife, Mary, and I decided to go our separate ways. After eleven years of marriage, she had found she could not adapt to her new role as an officer's wife. She raised our two boys, in Minnesota for the most part, although we made major decisions together and both sons followed in my footsteps, joining the Navy. In fact, Chris, eighteen months older than brother Scott, was still on active duty as a submariner, stationed in Hawaii.

———✦———🌳———✦———

In the fall of 1981, I became a member of the American Legion in Norfolk, Virginia, and met Shirley Stephenson, a divorced mother of three and the club's bartender. Originally from West Virginia, she was self-confident, bright, and attractive, about five-foot-four with long, jet-black hair. After an unplanned dinner one evening, a whirlwind three-week courtship began, and we married on April 16, 1982.

We lived on islands—from Sardinia, Italy, to Hawaii—for most of our marriage until now. With her at my side I rose to my current rank and retired as the senior submarine communications officer in the Navy and head of Submarine Force C4I (Command, Control, Communications, Computers and Intelligence). As I told Admiral Staten, my final boss and our friend, when I asked to retire, I had accomplished what I could, it was time for the next Rich Herman to come on the scene, and I wanted to leave while at the top.

Our last weekend in Hawaii, we relaxed at the Hale Koa Hotel on Waikiki Beach. We stayed an extra day, to celebrate Shirley's birthday and have one more opportunity to say farewell to our closest friends before flying to Orlando, Florida. We picked up Bigg Redd, our Chevy Camaro, at Port Canaveral earlier today and drove up to the Georgia coast.

"I'm awake," Shirley called out. "Just needed a cat nap. Let me take a shower, and we'll go check out Camden County and see how much has changed in St. Marys and Kingsland since we've been gone. Then, I'll let you buy me dinner to celebrate our return and start of our life as civilians." She patted me on top of my head on her way to the bathroom. "By the way, I don't like calling you Mr. Herman so I'm still going to call you 'The Commander.'"

I called our tenants to let them know we were in town, and they asked us to meet with them. It turned out that their new home being built was completed early and ready to move in. We told them we would let them out of their lease and not to worry about the last month's rent.

We were settled back into our home within a week. One evening, just before sunset, we were on the lanai when we heard, "Hello, neighbors. Like some company?" It was Reverend Tobias, founder of the First African Missionary Baptist Church in Kingsland, with his wife, Crystal, and Mr. Henry, who lived side by side in houses across the street. Shirley quickly served refreshments, sweet tea for the three of them and lemonade for us.

"We certainly missed you from the cul-de-sac," the Rev (he liked being called that) said, sipping his tea. "Are you fully retired now or do you have plans to try another career?"

"For now, we're retired, Rev," I said, "but we want to keep active. We're in no rush, and want to make sure whatever we do is worthwhile. Want me to come preach at your church?"

Mr. Henry couldn't contain himself. He slapped his knee and sprang to his feet shouting, "Hallelujah, hallelujah, Mr. Rich is going to speak the word to the folk in the congregation. Lord, help us!" He started laughing so hard he opened the screen door, lay down in the grass, and shouted, "Praise the Lord, Mr. Rich is going to lead the way!" Now Miss Crystal joined in, and I wished I'd kept my mouth shut.

Suddenly, the Rev stood and said, "Now, there's a thought. It would keep everyone awake for sure." Then he joined in with everyone else and laughed. It was a nice welcome back on our neighbors' part, and after a little more catching up, or gossip from Miss Crystal, they left after more welcome-home hugs and kind words.

"Well," Shirley said, "that was interesting. I can't believe you said that." Then looking at me, "You were kidding, right? Preach?"

"Maybe it's my true calling," I said with my most serious voice before adding, "Not on your life. I enjoyed the time we attended one of the Rev's services, but I couldn't handle all that standing and moaning, swaying with arms in the air. Hmmm, I don't think I could anyway."

"Let's leave it at that," Shirley said. "We do want to get involved with something, though. Of course, we need to make a plan to see our families. Let's go to the Pub tomorrow to see how many of our friends are still there and find out what's happening."

We entered the Pub and, after two-and-a-half-years, it was like we had never left. We were still the only car parked out front, and we sat in our normal seats at the nearest end of the bar. Even the bartender was the same.

When we were here in 1992, we were watching the local news one night when a story caught our attention. The TV show "Cheers" had run a contest to find which bar in the United States most resembled their Boston neighborhood bar and patrons. The winner was The Olde Town Pub in St. Marys, Georgia. Shirley and I frequented most of the drinking establishments in Camden County (cities of St. Marys and Kingsland) and had never heard of it. We watched the reporter at the Pub interviewing the owner and some of the patrons and decided we had to check it out.

We drove by the Pub twice before Shirley said, "There it is." A small, old, brown log cabin building set back about thirty feet off the street, it had a gravel drive-through area out front and no cars or vehicles of any kind in sight. A little neon sign declared it was open. "This has to be it, let's go in and see," Shirley said. We parked and entered, not knowing what to expect. There were three people at a twelve- to fifteen-foot-long bar with six stools, who looked up at us.

"Close the door," one of them yelled, "the light is bad for my eyes."

We entered, stood for a minute to let our eyes adjust to the darkness and found two empty stools at the closest end of the bar. To the right of the bar were two pool tables and a jukebox, and past the bar toward the rear was a spacious room with tables and seating for about forty people. The place was huge inside. The bartender, mid-thirties, came over and asked what we'd like.

"I'd like a draft beer and a Dewar's and water for my wife," I said. He went to the tap, poured a ten-ounce glass of beer, returned, and set it in front of me.

"Here's your beer," he said, "but in case you didn't notice, this is a pub, not the Ritz-Carlton. We got no Dewar's or any other expensive drinks. I got well scotch, MacGregor's, and that's it."

"That would be great," Shirley said immediately. "When I bartended, that was the well scotch I liked to have on hand, it's good and it's affordable." Immediately, the bartender smiled, made her drink and returned it, on a napkin yet.

"I'm Denny," he said. "So you were a bartender." He looked at me. "And you?"

I told him I was in the Navy and stationed at Submarine Group Ten. "Hey, gang," he yelled out to everyone there, "these people are going to fit in just fine. The gent's a sailor, and his wife a bartender."

"The next drink is on them," one of the men on a stool at the end of the bar said without even looking up. He had long, shaggy hair, a scruffy beard (or maybe just in need of a shave) and three Miller High Life beer cans in front of him.

Wanting to get off to a good start, I motioned to Denny that I would pay for the next round. We introduced ourselves as Rich and Shirley, loud enough so everyone could hear, and they all yelled back different greetings. "Denny," I said, "we saw your place on the local news as winning the 'Cheers' TV contest. We didn't even know you were here. There are about ten people in here ... where are they parked?"

He laughed. "Out back. You don't think anyone wants their vehicle seen out front, do you? Some don't want their spouse to know they're here, and none of them want the police to know. And yeah, Sandy, who's one of our regulars, sent a video of us into the show and they sent a camera crew down here one night, unannounced, and filmed us. This is a great hangout for people who like privacy and just want to enjoy friends without being judged. We were a good pick, but my mother, who owns the place, refuses to change the name to 'Cheers of the South.'"

We soon were regulars at the Pub, known as the Red Camaro couple, and close friends with several folks there—including Sandy Alben, the base security manager, who actually had worked for me; Dusty, the man who volunteered us to buy a round our first day here; and Jack Tempe, a shipmate and friend from Hawaii who did his last tour in the Navy and retired here.

"Nothing has changed," I said as we came in this evening. Along with Denny still here, there was Dusty, like a fixture in his seat at the other end, who hadn't changed a bit, with empty Miller High Life cans in front of him. Jack sat next to him with a pitcher of beer and a glass with his name on it.

"I got the next round for the bar," I announced, and Denny put empty shot glasses in front of Dusty and Jack. "Five years ago, Dusty, you said those same words for us when we came here for the first time." Dusty raised his can, took a sip, and never took his eyes off the TV which was still on CNN Headline News.

"Rich and Shirley," Jack said, "welcome back. Still parking in front with the red Camaro?" I saluted him. "Join Dusty and me. I have something I want to discuss with you, and Dusty wants to talk to your better half."

We picked up our drinks, and Jack moved down so I could sit

next to him and Shirley next to Dusty. I wasn't too sure how long she would last, Dusty always looked in need of a shower.

On the ride home, Shirley said, "Well, that certainly was interesting. Dusty is actually looking at moving out of his trailer and buying a condo. He said he knows he's a mess and wants to know if I'd be willing to talk to him about changing his lifestyle. How can I say no to that?"

"That's great, honey. Dusty reaching out to anyone is a shocker. You know, we don't even know his name? All these years, and all we know is he's retired Navy, drinks Miller High Life, spends his days at the pub watching CNN and sometimes talking to Jack, Denny, or a few select others. So private."

"I think that is about to change, I really think he's serious. I gave him a few ideas, and he said he had a lot to think about but would get back to me. By the way, he was offended when I mentioned his personal hygiene, and said he bathes when he needs to. He did add he will try to wear cleaner clothes. How did your chat with Jack go?"

"Jack is now the director/manager of the St. Marys Submarine Museum. He actually helped establish it on the waterfront, leads fund-raising, and has put tons of work toward the goal of making it the best submarine museum there is. He asked if I'd be interested in doing some volunteering. I said I was and would get back to him. I don't want to commit to a lot until we find out what else we might get involved with."

"Hi, Rose," I said as she answered the phone. It was Halloween night, and I was fulfilling a promise.

Rose Emon and I had met when she was fresh out of college and hired by a Navy research command, as an analyst studying future submarine communications. I was a young Navy ensign, submarine communicator, sent to listen to a briefing on proposed systems to bring the submarine force into the twenty-first century. My actual orders were to listen, take notes, and commit to nothing. In other words, be seen, not heard. What happened was, after that meeting, with only three (Rose, her boss, and me) in attendance, the foundation of the submarine force's future communication was, in fact, established.

Rose and I would work together many times over the next eighteen years, and as she advanced in the submarine community as one of the leading experts of research, development and installation of state-of-the-art communication systems, I advanced to the rank of Commander. As the U.S. Submarine Force spearheaded the military's worldwide dominance in communication capabilities, there is no doubt our working together led to the success of both our careers. More importantly, Rose and I became great friends.

Just before my retirement, Rose had come to Hawaii and taken Shirley and me to dinner. Overlooking Honolulu Bay and with after-dinner drinks in hand, our conversation got down to her underlying reason for the visit. Driving home, we discussed the very generous offer my friend made for me to go to work for her. In fact, it gave us a lot to think about, and I had told Rose I would give her my answer before I officially retired.

"Rich," Rose said, with that distinct Boston accent. "I see you're keeping your word, it's not the first of November until tomorrow."

"I figured I'd call a day early to show my respect for you, great lady." We both chuckled. After a minute of catching up on our personal lives, I got down to business. "Rose, I've given your offer a lot of thought, and I want you to understand my thought process."

"Thank you, Rich, I appreciate that, go ahead."

"Do you remember my telling you how nice it was going to be not having a secure phone next to our bed, getting calls every night and weekend to handle a crisis or be informed of a potential one? Well, guess what? Since retiring, I haven't had a single call." No reply, so I continued.

"Remember my telling you how nice it was going to be not to have to get on a plane Saturday night to make a meeting thousands of miles away Monday morning, and then turn right around and fly back because I had to oversee a project the admiral made a priority of his? Well, guess what, I haven't seen a plane, or admiral, since returning from Hawaii and don't intend to for a while."

"I understand, but you'll be well paid for the inconvenience, Rich."

"Yes, the pay and incentives are great. Shirley and I thought about that too. You said I would need to work out of San Diego or Washington, D.C. With the cost of living in those two cities, compared to Kingsland, Georgia, even with that great salary, I can live here, not work, not travel, not tied to a phone while maintaining the same lifestyle and, believe it or not, save money."

"I offered you the most I could, Rich, but I don't think that would matter. I respect your decision, just want you to know you're highly regarded and we'll miss you, especially the submarine force. You were always the one senior military officer the civilian industry could count on to be forward-thinking and willing to stick your neck out. I'm not sure if another Rich Herman is out there right now."

"There's always someone waiting in the wings, my friend. You worked with my predecessor, Commander Mike McCann, who retired but I think is still active in the community. My right-hand man, and still one of the smartest communicators we ever had, Jason Townsend, lives in Texas somewhere now, look him up. And, Rose, my whole philosophy of leadership was to train our reliefs, and I think you need to look no further than Lieutenant Damien Spanos. Get your admiral to have him located and see if he wouldn't want to be your active-duty contact. I trust him with my life."

"I remember Spanos," Rose said. "Good idea. Thanks, Rich. If you're out my way, a room is always ready. Say hi to Shirley, call anytime."

"Will do, girl. Stay safe." I hung up the phone and smiled. *Rose Emon, you'll always be a part of my life.*

"I'm turning off the lights," I announced. It was almost nine p.m., and after 100 or more trick-or-treaters, I called it quits. "I'll make us a drink and then tell you about my call with Rose."

"She's right about one thing," Shirley stated matter-of-factly. "You'll be missed, but more important than that is the reverse, how much will you miss them?"

"Yeah, good point." I thought a moment. "I think it's okay to miss it. After all, I had a successful career that I thoroughly enjoyed, as long as I don't dwell on it and look back at it like I made a mistake retiring from it all. We just need to find something to get involved with, stay active, and not become a statistic of retirees who go stagnant and die within five years."

"That's a morbid thought, ugh!" Shirley took a drink and sat up straight. "Tomorrow is your first official day of retirement and being a full-time civilian. For the next two months, let's take some trips to visit friends and families over the holiday season and start 1998 with a new fresh look. In fact, how about starting with a new Redd?"

That last comment came out of the blue, but I liked it. "Let's go see our friends tomorrow."

We had bought our third red Camaro, a 1992 RS two-door coupe, from Calvin's Chevrolet here in Kingsland after learning the dealership had a five-star rating and was pro-military. That car we traded in Hawaii for our present red 1995 Camaro LT. I kidded Shirley that she must be anti-oil change because we always seemed to buy a new car before our current car needed one.

* * *

"Jerry," I said, walking into the dealership, "glad to see you're still here."

"The Hermans," he said, heading our way with a big smile. "Nice to see you back in town, retired now I guess."

"Yes, and we'd like a new Camaro," Shirley said, shaking his hand. "Same rules as the last time, Jerry. No sales pitch, no gimmicks, and no pressure. You give us a fair market price for our trade-in, and bottom-line the cost of a new 1998 Bigg Redd, black or grey interior, V-6 fully loaded, and we'll sign the papers. We'll pay cash and bring a certified check with us when you call that the car is ready. Deal?"

Jerry just stared at her. So did two other salesmen along with a tall, silver-haired distinguished man behind them, who I recognized. "Why don't you get to the point, Shirley?" Jerry said, laughing. "I think we can handle that. Follow me."

"Jerry," the older man said, stepping forward. "Why don't we do this in my office." He looked at us and continued, "Rich and Shirley Herman, right? The red Camaro?"

"Mr. Calvin." I shook his hand, smiling. "I'm surprised you remember us. Yes, that's us, the 'living out their mid-life crisis' couple. It's nice to see you again, sir." Charles Calvin owned this business, as well as three other dealerships in southeast Georgia. We had met him in 1992, when I was here in uniform, and found him to be a military history buff and big supporter of the armed forces.

In his office today, coffee and sodas were offered. "Jerry," he said, "I think Shirley was pretty precise so why don't you get the paperwork pushed through, tell the office it's for one of my VIP customers and to add an extra $1,000 to their trade-in." Jerry ran off and Charles continued, "Now, tell me all about your last tour in Hawaii."

We drove our fifth Bigg Redd off the lot three days later.

CHAPTER 24

January 5, 1998, U. S. Naval Hospital, Naval Air Station, Jacksonville, Florida

"AND HERE WE ARE AGAIN," I SAID AS WE SAT DOWN IN the Ear, Nose, Throat (ENT) Clinic. "All checked in and they said it should be less than fifteen minutes. I'm just glad Dr. Bannon is still on active duty and willing to take me on again as his patient."

"I'm not surprised he did. You two got along so good, it's amazing you don't trade Christmas cards." Shirley wasn't a big fan of my doctor—his ego and personality did leave a lot to be desired—but I liked his confidence and, even she had to agree, he did help save my life. They could make a documentary about the day we met.

On December 2, 1993, I was having my routine dental cleaning when the hygienist asked, "Lieutenant Commander Herman, have you always had that little white spot beneath your tongue?" I told her I never noticed, thinking to myself, *How many people look under their tongues?* "I'm going to ask the dentist to take a look at it," she added and left the room.

"Mr. Herman, I'm Dr. Flutie," a tall, thin man said as he sat down beside me. "Let me have a look." He had me stick out my tongue, and he pulled on it.

I couldn't help but think of my father telling me, when I was small and thought it was cute to stick my tongue out, that if you stick your tongue out too far, it will fall off its roll and may not be able to be put on again. I never stuck my tongue out again.

"Normally," the doctor went on, "I would add this to your chart and have it reexamined after six months, but to be on the safe side, let's take a biopsy. I'll cut enough away so that I leave clean margins, just in case." He cut out what he needed and cauterized the spot.

Two weeks passed before I got a call from the dental clinic; Dr. Flutie wanted to see me, during his lunch hour if possible. There was no way to think anything other than this was not good news, or a dental tech would have just called and said my test was negative. I was at his office at noon.

As soon as I sat down, Dr. Flutie said, "Commander, there is no easy way to say this. Your biopsy came back positive for cancer." He gave me a minute, I tried to stay composed but all kinds of things, all bad, ran through my mind. "On the positive side, if there is one, it appears to be a floor of the mouth cancer and may not have spread yet. I took the liberty of making you an appointment at the Naval Hospital in Jacksonville to see an ENT specialist, Dr. Haight. I already talked to him and faxed your information. He said his schedule is full the next month but, seeing as cancer has already been confirmed, will fit you in at 0700 tomorrow. I wrote down all the information for you."

I took the paperwork, thanked him, and told him to thank his hygienist. It wasn't good news, but now I knew and hopefully could get ahead of it.

A short, thin young man met me and Shirley the next morning outside Room 1107. He opened the door and asked us to follow him into what I assumed was his office. "I'm Dr. Haight and will be looking into your case. First of all, sir, are you a smoker?" When I said yes, he smiled and said, "My father was chief petty officer in the Navy and a smoker. Got mouth cancer and died less than a year after his diagnosis. This after losing half his jaw, a third of his tongue, and all of his teeth. Not saying this will happen to you, but it's not going to be easy for you, either of you."

Getting the diagnosis was hard enough; I didn't think we deserved this. "Excuse me, Doctor," I responded, "don't you think you should examine me and look at all the facts before scaring my wife, and me, to death?" I was on the verge of walking out. "I'm sorry about your father, but I am not him."

Outside we could hear footsteps. Heavy footsteps like a soldier marching. There was a rap on the door, and another doctor walked in. "Dr. Haight, what are you doing?" He walked over to the desk, picked up my file, took a brief look at it and, with it in hand, headed to the door. "Lieutenant Commander Herman is now my patient. I'll talk to you later." Opening the door, he looked at Shirley and me and said calmly, "Please follow me."

I had never seen anything like it. Dr. Haight never stood up, just sat there like a scolded little boy and said, "Yes, sir."

We quickly followed this new doctor into the passageway and found it hard to keep up as he literally marched, long, heavy-sounding strides, down to another wing of the hospital. He walked right past the front desk, ignoring the staff request to sign in, and led us to his office where we read the door nameplate: LCDR Jeffrey Bannon, MD. Otolaryngologist, ENT Department Head.

"I am Dr. Jeffrey Bannon, and I run this department and patient assignments. Forget everything Dr. Haight told you. He has a tendency to tell patients the worst possible scenarios before having all the facts. He can be over-dramatic and has never forgiven his father for being a smoker. I've tried to tell him that in the sixties and seventies, smoking was not yet proven to be harmful to our health and, in fact, was made out to be good for you; people were encouraged to do so." He never looked up from reviewing my record.

"Mrs. Herman, please step into the waiting room while I examine your husband." He still hadn't looked up, and surprisingly, Shirley gripped my hand, smiled, and left the room. Finally looking up, Dr. Bannon gave me a little smile and asked me to get onto an examination table. He examined my mouth and ears, felt my throat and neck, asking a few questions. He sat back down.

He wrote a few notes and then called for a corpsman. They conversed a minute before Dr. Bannon said, "I'm going to do a nasal endoscopy. I'll numb your nasal passage and throat with this spray, it tastes like lemon, and afterward you won't feel a thing." I found this to be famous last words as it wasn't tasty—and not only was it uncomfortable, it hurt. When he finished, he sent the corpsman to get Shirley. After she was seated, the corpsman was asked to leave.

"I wanted you together when I discuss my findings and the course of action. If you have any questions, feel free to ask, but wait until I'm finished. First of all, if you expect me to apologize for any discomfort during the exam, you're not going to get one. It is necessary for me to get a good picture of what we are facing so if it is a little uncomfortable, so be it. I always say, if you don't choke and gag a little, I'm not doing my job." I had to admit his bedside manner was different and I found kind of refreshing. I could sense Shirley didn't share my opinion.

"To put your mind at ease, I am the expert for cases such as these, and I don't see any reason you can't overcome this cancer and lead a normal life. A few changes, but nothing you can't handle. Officially, you have floor-of-the-mouth cancer, which has a high survival rate. If you had cancer of the upper mouth, we would be talking a whole different story with life expectancy very low. I feel confident saying the cancer has not spread into the nearby glands or lymph nodes.

"Your dentist, Dr. Flutie, should be commended, and I will be calling your clinic commanding officer to pass that on, for doing a biopsy immediately and not waiting six months as dentists are prone to do." I told him about the dental hygienist; he wrote that down, saying that was where the credit would go as well.

Then he added, "However, when you do a biopsy, you remove a portion around the cancerous area so that what we call good clear margins are left. Dentists are not trained ENT surgeons, and as good a dentist as yours is, I'm afraid he may not have taken enough of the area out." He paused.

"I'm going to rectify that today and remove what I think necessary. Let's suffice it to say your hygienist and dentist probably saved your life by getting you here, and now, I am going to ensure they did. This new removal will be biopsied and, if negative, which I'll bet my career on it, I will recommend three-month follow-ups the next year with no further surgery, chemotherapy, or radiation."

"I could tell you didn't think much of Dr. Bannon," I said, driving home, holding an icepack to my throat when I could. The doctor had said my recovery from the minor surgery just performed would take up to two weeks. I could tell Shirley was worried about me, and I wanted to let her know I was okay.

"He's egotistical, cold, and comes across as a jerk," she said. "His own staff seemed uneasy around him."

"Maybe so, but I like him being straightforward, and I can handle the ego, if he deserves it—even you have to admit, the two corpsman/nurses you talked to at the desk said he was the best doctor they'd ever seen. Just different."

"I'll give you that, and I am glad you got him for your doctor. That Dr. Haight was about to cut your tongue and jaw out, without even examining you. That's scary. I still don't have to like him though." I gave her that last word.

My second biopsy returned just as Dr. Bannon predicted, clean. He scheduled me for once-a-month check-ups for three months, and then follow-ups every three months for the next year, and I never had a recurrence. I was one more success story for Dr. Jeffrey Bannon, and I was not only his fan, I became his friend. Of course, as he said, I had to make a change.

On January 2, 1994, after twenty-nine years, I quit smoking; cold turkey.

"Rich," Dr. Bannon said now with a smile, handshake and big hug. "And Shirley," he shook her hand and clasped it with both of his. "You retired on me. Sorry I couldn't make the ceremony, especially in Hawaii, but my wife and I appreciated the invitation. Where have you decided to make home?"

We filled him in on being in Kingsland and recapped our retirement ceremony. Shirley was actually relaxed, and I think her opinion of him had changed over the years, or maybe she just accepted him the way he was. It didn't matter, it was nice to see.

"Your annual check-up, I see. And you never had another cigarette?" I told him no, but I still wanted one every time I golfed. "I hear that a lot from my patients that quit. There's always somewhere, usually after dinner but some when they have a drink, go fishing, or are just bored. I want you to know though, you're the only patient I ever had who quit cold turkey and never started again, at least once. You have more discipline than anyone I've ever met. How did you do it?"

I didn't mind telling him my theory of success, maybe it would help someone else. "You always had my follow-up exams scheduled the same date and time as dozens of others. We all were given an appointment time of one p.m. but, of course, we were only seen one at a time, so we all sat in the waiting room with nothing to do but read old magazines and stare at one another. After several hours sitting with people with no chins, half a face, and throat devices to allow them to speak, I never wanted to see a cigarette again. Every time I would want a cigarette, I would just think back to those afternoons and those people, and it was a no-brainer—*don't do it, stupid*."

He performed his exam, forced me to gag, and all three of us laughed as he shouted, "Success," before giving me a clean bill of health. "I want you to know, Rich, and Shirley, one more year and you'll be what I call smoke-free. I have written articles on the subject, and in my professional opinion if you go seven years without smoking, I will declare you a non-smoker, even for insurance policy examinations."

We left his office, this time both of us getting a hug, and he said as long as he stayed in practice, even if after his Navy retirement, I could always be his patient. He even gave me his card with personal phone number.

Driving home, Shirley asked, "Do you think he knows I smoke?" I looked at her and didn't say a word. "Yeah, I know, dumb question.

Well, if I ever need a doctor like you did, give him a call. Just don't tell him I asked you to." I smiled to myself. Yes, she certainly had been won over.

———————————

"I found everything," I said triumphantly, as I walked into the living room a few weeks later and put two cardboard boxes, marked NASCAR, on the floor next to our oval-topped coffee table. Actually, it wasn't too difficult finding what I was looking for as we had our third bedroom dedicated to Rusty Wallace and the #2 Miller Lite Ford. The day before, qualifying finished for the 1998 Daytona 500, which was scheduled for the next Sunday, February 15, and it was time to get our house ready.

Shirley had already cleared and polished the tabletop and was sitting in her recliner with the qualifying sheet results. "Let me know when you're ready." She sounded excited. I opened the first box and found the collection. We had all sixty-two Authentic NASCAR active car models in 1/64" scale, and I placed them carefully on the table. I nodded I was ready.

We lined up all forty-three starting cars by their qualifying positions—twenty-two on the right (front) side of the oval racetrack and twenty-one on the left side of the table. All the cars not active, or those that tried but didn't qualify, went into the middle of the table, which we called the pits.

Placing a note from Rusty Wallace on top of the TV, Shirley said, "This will sit here for every race." I had sent Rusty an invitation to my retirement, and he sent back the RSVP, in his own handwriting, with apologies that other commitments kept him from attending. Shirley then added a plaque with a picture and personal letter from him, which was read at my retirement. Everyone who was a NASCAR fan was in awe of this gift. I thought it now was one of my wife's prized possessions and how I'd love to figure out a way for her to meet the great race driver some day.

On race day, Shirley wore a large Rusty Wallace T-shirt with a Miller Lite #2 blanket wrapped around her while I wore a Rusty shirt and ball cap. As the cars took the one-to-go sign, I went to the kitchen and returned with two ice-cold Miller Lites, opened them, and handed one to Shirley. She didn't like beer, just the tradition.

As the green flag flew and the cars crossed the start/finish line, we yelled, "Go, Rusty, stay safe," and we toasted the #2 car. Shirley then would give me back the beer to put on ice until I was ready for it, and I brought her a Dewar's and water.

This Daytona 500 proved rather boring until the last few laps when Rusty and Dale Earnhardt still had a good chance to win. Either love them or hate them, Rusty and Dale were fierce competitors on the track and their fans, like Shirley and me, were just as competitive if not fiercer. To add to the drama, Earnhardt had led the most laps and was the dominant car but, after nineteen previous tries, had never won this race. That ended today when he held on to win, on his twentieth attempt, what he called his greatest ever victory. Rusty finished fifth but was gracious enough to congratulate and hug his friend in the winner's circle after the race.

Shirley and I, exhausted after an over three-hour race and more drinks than we would normally consume, called it a day and took a nap. Tomorrow was soon enough to put the cars away. Next Sunday's race would be in North Carolina, and we would be ready. Thirty-two more races this year. Yay, NASCAR.

CHAPTER 25

April 14, 1998, Little Yellow House, Kingsland

"MOM, DAD," I SAID, "CAN WE GET YOU ANYTHING TO drink?"

"Lemonade would be nice," Mom said, stepping out onto our lanai and finding a seat. Dad sat in the chair next to her. Shirley went to get refreshments and I joined my parents.

We'd seen them a few times over the years, twice in Hawaii, and this was their second visit here. I had just picked them up from the Jacksonville airport, where they flew in from Las Vegas, Nevada. For the last dozen or so years, once the Minnesota winters got to be too much for them, they had made Lake Havasu, Arizona, not far from Vegas, their winter home. One time, after they told us about living six months here and six months there, Shirley and I had suggested they relocate by us. We offered to help purchase the house next to the Reverend and thought it would solve a lot of their concerns. They didn't see it that way and were so adamant I never raised the subject again.

"We didn't plan anything for today," Shirley said, entering the lanai with glasses. "We figure you'd like to just chat and rest. We have plenty of time to make our tours and visits." My parents, now in their eighties, were slowing down a bit as Mom was experiencing some heart issues and Dad with chronic obstructive pulmonary disease (COPD).

"First thing, son," Dad said, "I'd like to find a meeting either tonight or tomorrow." He picked up his lemonade, sat back, adjusted his turquoise bolo tie, and nodded like that was an order. I smiled and nodded that I understood. Then winked at Mom.

I thought back to when Mom took me out for a mother/son talk over lunch after I returned from my first enlistment in 1970. She shared with me, and I don't think ever told anyone else, that she would confront my father about his drinking before they retired.

True to her word, she had that talk and called me afterward to tell me what took place. In August of 1978, Mom sat Dad down and said, "Clayton, you are not going to get up and walk away this time. Sit there and listen. We've been married almost forty years, have three children, five grandsons, and two granddaughters together and have endured many ups and downs over the years. We plan on retiring soon, with a home in the city and a lake home we can live in year-round. We've made tentative plans about our future, based on our retirement and savings. Do you agree we've done well to get to this point?"

"Yes, I do," Dad replied.

"Well, there is one hitch." She took his hand. "I am not going on that retirement journey if you don't stop drinking. I will not watch you drink away our future." My father tried to get up.

"No! You stay there. We are ending this today. Clayton, your family loves you, but they are hurting, like me, as they see you continuously in the bottle. You're not fooling anyone, except maybe yourself. I am here to help, and I want that—but it can't be for me, or anyone else. You have to want this. Take responsibility for yourself, admit you need help, or else retire on your own. I'll be fair and give you half the assets, but I never want to see you again. Your choice." She walked out of the room.

The next morning, Marge, my ex-mother-in-law and now a nurse on the substance abuse ward of Fairview Hospital, came to the house. Mom was surprised to see her, until Dad came into the room. "I called her, Ange. Thanks for coming, Margaret." My father spoke softly and humbly. "I have a drinking problem. I trust you and would like your help."

He and Marge went into the kitchen and my mom to the bedroom, after hugging my dad and thanking Marge. After three hours, Marge knocked on the door and asked Mom to join them. Dad was at the kitchen table. "Angie," Marge said, "Clayton has told me a lot of things, many personal, that will go no further than to my boss, with Clayton's approval. He has asked me if I would accompany him and help him get settled into our Dependency Ward. Now, today."

"Before I chicken out," Dad said, smiling. He was visibly shaking.

"I've already called the head of the program; he said he will accept Clayton as a patient based on my recommendation, which I gave. Once he enters the program, he will not be allowed any visitors the first two weeks. It is not easy, in fact it's very difficult, but Clayton has taken the most important step. He has admitted he needs help."

That afternoon, almost twenty years ago, my father entered treatment for dependency, suffered all the emotional and physical hardships of the program, and after three months as an in-patient, left the hospital a member of Alcoholic Anonymous (AA) and a changed man. During those three months, as part of the program, he had to face us one-on-one and admit his dependency and ask that we forgive him.

As I was in Italy and we couldn't meet face to face, my visit was by a letter. He not only apologized, he also included one comment that stuck with me: "Rich, truthfully, you have never seen me sober. I have been drunk every day since you were born, what they call a functioning alcoholic. I am deeply sorry and would like your forgiveness." I not only forgave him that day, I realized my father, for the first time, was sober. I'd always loved my father ... now I liked him.

"I already checked on meeting sites, Dad," I was happy to answer, "and there is one at eleven in the morning on the submarine base.

They're expecting you." All of us were proud of his accomplishment, but not as proud as he was of himself. He smiled at me, and I changed the subject to their winter stay in Arizona.

"I think we're done spending our winters in Arizona, or anywhere besides Minnesota," Mom said. "Our primary doctors are there, and being realistic, we're going to need them and good health care nearby. We already have plans to move into an assisted living place when we get back to Brainerd."

"Did the couple who bought the cabin and river property change it much?" I was taking a chance that Dad was over having to give up owning his own home.

"Actually," it was my dad answering, "the Palmers did a beautiful job with the place. They added another bedroom upstairs, a bigger den, new siding and roof, and paved a circular driveway around a twenty-five-foot flagpole. In fact, you'd feel like saluting it. They also told us we could visit the river any time and, if they weren't there, just go on in and make ourselves at home. You know, I met the husband, Harry, at AA and became his sponsor."

I didn't know that, but now I knew why he and his family were accepted so well as the new property owners. Marlys had told me another fact—that they gave my folks more than the asking price because they didn't want to cheat such good people out of the fair value. I'd like to shake their hands; not many people exist in this world like that anymore.

My parents hadn't made it to my retirement ceremony because they felt the trip would be too much for Dad, and they didn't want to be a distraction to our last week's events. Many people, our Hawaiian friends and military who had met them from previous visits, were disappointed because they loved my dad's storytelling (mainly fish tales) and my mother's spunk and humor. In truth, I was sure those who knew Mom were hoping she would roast me, either at the farewell party or the ceremony itself.

I dropped the girls off at the Navy Exchange to shop and took Dad to the chapel where his meeting was scheduled. An hour passed and I saw Dad come out, shaking a young sailor's hand before getting in the car.

"Only one other member today," he said. I must have looked disappointed as he quickly followed with, "But that's fine because it just takes two for a meeting. He was a nice young man, seven months sober and trying to get a group started on base. Can you bring me back again Friday? I'd like to meet again, hopefully others will come and I'll help him get his program started."

I was incredibly proud of my dad just then. Confident, outgoing, and most importantly, happy. "Sure, Dad, no problem, now let's get the wives and I have a special treat for you."

I drove my parents and Shirley to downtown St. Marys, only two miles from base, and parked on the waterfront of the St. Marys River. On the other side of the river, you could see Fernandina Beach, Florida. Getting out of the car, we walked across the street and I introduced my friend. "Mom, Dad, meet Jack Tempe, director of the St. Marys Submarine Museum."

Jack, Shirley, and I originally became friends when we were stationed in Hawaii. Then, he was the "Bull Nuke" (most senior nuclear-trained enlisted person) on the USS Buffalo. Not tall, barrel-chested and built like a bull, he had to fight his weight and had a hard time meeting the Navy's physical standards. With the help of his fellow shipmates, we managed to help him pass his annual physical training (PT) exam. We had met again when we were here in 1992 and ran into each other at the Pub.

He gave Shirley a hug, then turned toward my parents. "Nice to meet you, Mr. and Mrs. Herman. Rich called to say you were coming. Let me give you a personal tour." We entered the converted movie theater that now was home to the museum. "Rear Admiral Eugene Fluckey, submariner and Medal of Honor recipient, who the three of us got to meet in Hawaii, dedicated this museum on March 30, 1996. We know Rich served, Mr. Herman; did you also serve?"

"I was in the Minnesota National Guard two years," Dad said, "and was drafted into World War II, but D-Day happened and, although I got my uniforms and orders to report, I never had to see combat. My wife and I have a lot of respect for the military, sir."

"Thank you for your service," Jack said, and my dad stood a little taller. "I think you're going to find the tour interesting." For the next hour, Jack had my parents listening to every word, and they asked a lot of questions.

As the tour ended, Mom wrote a check and handed it to Jack. He took a quick look at it, broke into a big smile, and gave her a hug. "Rich's words about you two aren't nearly enough to express just how wonderful you are."

He walked us to the car and held the doors for Mom and Dad. Jack may be a bit rough around the edges, but he was sure learning how to win people over and it was obvious: The St. Marys Submarine Museum was in great hands.

The next morning, just after seven a.m., I found Mom already on the lanai enjoying a cup of coffee. "You're up early, Mom," I said. "Did you sleep okay?"

"I slept great, thank you," she said. "I was hoping you would get up, son, so we could have a chat with your dad sleeping. He won't be up for a while."

"I'm not sure I like the sound of that. Well, Shirley is still asleep too. What do we need to talk about?"

"I've always been more open with you than anyone else, and we share a special bond that way. I also think, except on how I handled Louie's situation and let myself be blinded by love over reason, that we're very much alike. That's why I want to share something with you that others don't need to know at this point. We didn't come here for a week just to see you and Shirley; in fact, your father wanted to go straight home. No, we're here because I insisted." She lifted her cup and I went for refills.

"This was our last trip to Arizona because I don't think your father has any more in him. I'm not saying he is near death, just that the travel is too much for him and takes away what I consider would be a better quality of life if we stayed in Minnesota. He won't admit it, of course. I don't think it'll be long before he is on oxygen 24/7, and that alone is going to limit some movement.

"Also, at home in Brainerd, he loves going to his AA meetings and being a sponsor to others. He enjoys seeing his friends when he wants and reliving old stories. He is just much happier and younger at home. Also, Rich, I admit I'm aging a bit too, and my heart is eventually going to lead to other problems. Just a fact of life. Anyway, I wanted you to know our true situation."

"Thanks, Mom." I grasped her hand and we just looked out at the sky for a minute, listening to the birds.

I knew she hadn't gotten over—and never would—the one thing in our lives that she realized I saw as a dent in her armor: my brother's treatment of me and how she let it happen. I had forgiven her seventeen years ago, after Louie died just before his fortieth birthday, and I don't regret leaving his funeral feeling the world was better off with him gone. That wouldn't be the case with my parents, and I was glad she shared her feelings once again. Of course, I never kept anything from Shirley and would tell her later.

Friday morning, we dropped Dad off for his eleven o'clock AA meeting at the base chapel and I drove to the Kings Bay Village Shopping Center. Mom had mentioned she'd like to pick up some postcards, and I could think of no better place than Shelly's Card Shop.

Shirley and I had met Shelly, the owner, at an open house at the Sub Museum. A very impressive woman, Shelly not only owned this successful shop, she and her husband, Bert, had been strong supporters of the Naval Submarine Base Kings Bay since its inception in 1979, and she was the commissioning president of the St. Marys Submarine Museum. I knew my mother would enjoy meeting her.

"You must be Mrs. Herman," Shelly said as we entered her store. Mom was surprised by the greeting. "I'm Shelly, owner of this store. I know Rich and Shirley through the museum. I also understand you and your husband have become lifelong members. Thank you for the donation."

"So much for anonymous donations," Mom said. I could tell she liked Shelly immediately. "Are you involved with the museum, Shelly?"

"Mom," I said quickly, "Shelly is president of the museum board of directors and also one of the reasons the submarine base is here in the first place. She and her husband are two of the most well-known and respected citizens of Camden County."

"I'm sure you're not here to talk about me," Shelly said, leading Mom down an aisle. "What brought you here today?" Forty-five minutes later, Shirley and I left to get Dad, while Mom stayed to have coffee with her new friend. When we returned, we had lunch, and after a wonderful meal, we said our goodbyes. A great day.

When I took Mom and Dad to the airport the next Wednesday, I could tell they were ready to go home. I was glad they came, and seeing them a little older and struggling was a wake-up call. We needed to make a point to talk regularly and plan a trip to see them not too far in the future.

CHAPTER 26

May 11, 1998, The Pub, St. Marys, Georgia

"HI, GUYS," DENNY SAID AS WE SAT ON OUR USUAL
stools at the end of the bar. "I want you to meet Lily." A young lady,
maybe twenty-five, about five-foot and 100 pounds, with long black
hair and cute as a button, stepped out from behind him and shook
our hands.

"My mom finally said I could hire someone to work the bar,"
Denny said, "so I can have a break once in a while. Lily, Rich drinks
Miller Lite drafts and Shirley has MacGregor's and water." She went
off to get our drinks. Denny watched her go, looked at us, crossed his
fingers, and walked off.

"Hey, Shirley," Dusty called out from his normal spot. "When
you get your drink, will you join me, please?"

"Lily," Shirley said, "put my drink next to Dusty's. On my way."
She got off her stool and whispered to me, "This might be interesting.
See ya later, miss me."

"So, Lily," I said, "are you new in town?"

"My husband is on the USS Tennessee," she said, "and we just
got here last week. I need something to keep me busy while he's at sea
so here I am. Slinging beers and making simple drinks is something
I can do." She had a big smile. "We found an apartment just down
the block so I can walk to work, and Denny said my hours will be
flexible, especially when my husband is in port. Win, win for us all."
Someone yelled from the back for a beer and she was off.

I nursed my beer and found myself staring at CNN Headline
News. *How does Dusty do this every day?* About a half-hour passed

when Shirley called me to join them. "Rich, meet Milton Banks." Dusty told her not so loud. He didn't like people to know his real name.

We shook hands like we had just met and, in a way, we had. "Dusty is thinking of buying this." She handed me a brochure with the heading "Pine Lakes" and showing a townhome on its cover. I opened it up and saw pictures of bedrooms, baths, kitchens, living rooms, and garages all in different layout styles. Very impressive.

"Nice, Dusty," I said honestly. "When do you move in?" I thought I was being facetious and gave a little laugh. Bad mistake.

"Next month, I think," he said seriously, "at least your wife thinks I should."

I was speechless but Shirley wasn't. "Dusty and I talked a little about this before and now that he's done his research and gotten the Navy Federal Credit Union to say they'll back the mortgage, it's time to make a decision." She looked at Dusty, "Is it okay to share with Rich what we talked about?" He nodded.

She told me Dusty's home was a run-down trailer on Highway 17, where he and his fiancé had lived since he retired eleven years ago. "Stop me if I get this wrong, Dusty," Shirley went on.

"Jennie died unexpectedly seven years ago, at forty-three years old, and Dusty has been in a downward spiral, off and on, since. He held a job on base for a couple years, then found himself showing up for work less and here at the Pub more. Making matters worse, over time he stopped really caring. Then he met us, and he thinks it's time he stops feeling sorry for himself and changes his ways. Is that about it, Dusty?"

"Yes, ma'am." Dusty said, this time actually looking up and smiling a little. "Actually, I am a brilliant man masquerading as a bum."

He has a sense of humor? "I bet," I jumped into the conversation, "you are speaking words not too far from the truth, Dusty. I have a deal for you. My wife here, Shirley," I put my arm around her shoulders, "is the best judge of character I have ever seen. She obviously sees something in you. Why don't you, if you can fit it into your social calendar, join us for dinner tomorrow night and we'll continue this conversation?"

———————✧———————

"I'll get it," I yelled to Shirley in the kitchen as the doorbell rang. I opened the door, expecting Dusty but was met by another man who I assumed was selling something. Nicely dressed, he was a little older than me and had graying brown hair. "Can I help you?"

"It's me, Milton," the man said.

I couldn't believe my eyes. Our friend Dusty, long, shaggy, dirty hair, scraggly beard, and usually in a soiled plaid shirt and dirty jeans, had obviously gotten a haircut, shave, and new wardrobe. "Come on in," I said, recovering from the initial shock, "Honey, our guest is here."

She came into the living room, and I only wished I had a camera to capture the look on her face. "My, my, Milton Banks, come here." As Dusty, or Milton, held out his hand, Shirley knocked it away and gave him a hug. He seemed uncomfortable being embraced. "Nice to meet you, the real you, sir."

When I first met Shirley, she was bartending at an American Legion club in Norfolk, Virginia. She was known for her lasagna, which she served every Thursday night. It was as good as everyone had said it would be, but after we married and were stationed in Sardinia, Italy, our landlord's wife took her in and taught her how to make it from scratch. Now, the lasagna was to kill for, and she served it to our new friend, Milton Banks.

"That is the best Italian meal I've ever had, outside of Italy," Milton said as he sat back from the table. "Actually, I may even include Italy." He chuckled a little, and it seemed to be the first time either of us had seen him relaxed and looking happy.

During dinner, we learned that Milton retired after twenty-two years' active duty as a submarine senior chief sonar technician. When he was on patrol early in his career, he used to fuss about the sonar equipment being dirty and always needing cleaning. Like most submariners, he was given a nickname that stuck, Dusty, and he preferred to be called that. (He thought it was great our son Chris was also a submarine sonar technician. Chris's nickname was Waldo.) Dusty was originally from Illinois but, like me, left home in his late teens after joining the Navy and liked this area so retired here. He never married, although he and Jennie were together for five years.

We moved to the lanai and enjoyed freshly made cannoli and coffee for dessert. I poured everyone a snifter of Drambuie, and it was time to get down to a more serious conversation. "You sure clean up well," Shirley started.

"Yeah, I even amazed myself," Dusty said. "I can't believe I was letting myself go like that, and I know this is just one day but I think my future is suddenly looking bright. I wouldn't tell anyone else this and you better not either, I have an appointment tomorrow for a manicure and pedicure." He lifted his hands and feet as if to show us what that meant.

"A new you," I said. "What have you decided about your living conditions? Or is that just between you and your confidant for now?"

"No, Rich," he said, "Shirley made it clear that from now on you had to be in on everything we're doing; she doesn't like keeping secrets from you. I respect that and thank you for letting me have her ear to bend the last couple of weeks. There're not many people I trust." He pulled an envelope out from under his shirt and handed it to me.

"This is what I'm going to do. I'm buying the condo you see there," Shirley came to stand behind my chair and look at the paperwork, "which is the same one I showed you before. Shirley gave me some tips on things I should ask for, like backsplash above the counters, upgraded appliances, all sorts of things. I couldn't believe it, but they approved every request. At the time, I didn't realize it was over a $10,000 upgrade."

"I didn't dare have you ask for more," Shirley said, "for fear they might shut down the whole deal. And it was a good deal in the first place, so you did great to get all the upgrades, Dusty."

"I close next week and hope to arrange for the movers to come on Friday, May 22, so I can be completely settled before Memorial Day.

The owner of my trailer park offered me a fair price, considering the dump I let it become, for my trailer, so that's off my back." We gave our congratulations, and he beamed.

"What can we do to help?" I asked.

"I'm on a golf course, Pine Lakes Country Club," Dusty said quickly. "I play for free my first year as part of my homeowner's package, and I thought I'd take up the game again. I'd like you to join me if you play, Rich."

"I'd love to, but let's get you settled first, Tiger." Shirley looked at me and I mouthed "Tiger Woods."

"Right, first things first. I'd really appreciate if one of you would go to the closing with me. And, so you aren't surprised when I sign the paperwork, I came into some money a while back and have decided to pay cash for the house."

We tried not to be surprised at that revelation and agreed we'd both go with him to the closing, but only Shirley would go in for the proceedings and be the official witness. After all, this was her project with Dusty, let her reap the glory. I was so proud of her and thought back to my social work days. Dusty would have been a Red Tag Squad client at first glance, and after reviewing his case, he would hopefully have been helped and found a similar outcome.

"You're sure you can drive?" Shirley asked Dusty as we walked out to his Ford Bronco. For the fifth time, he said yes and headed home. Waving to him as he drove away, I felt my hand being squeezed. "What an evening. I'm happy for him. He's like a new person."

"He is the same person," I answered reflectively, "with a new attitude, and I give him a lot of credit to admit how far he had fallen and be willing to make changes in his life. You can thank yourself for a lot of that success, honey. He reached out to you, and where many would have ignored him, you accepted the challenge. I couldn't be prouder of you than right now."

While helping to clean up the kitchen, I had an idea. "Maybe this is something we can do for others. Let's look into ways to reach others in need, maybe behind the scenes. I don't want people thinking they can take advantage of us. Just a thought."

"I like that idea. Before we go further, though, you need to know I am a little concerned." Shirley suddenly had a serious look. "Dusty's getting a manicure and pedicure and isn't quite satisfied with the haircut he got, so he's going to find a stylist? Did you also sense that he is very smart, and, in this short visit, could even be self-centered and egotistical? Maybe I'm just reading into it but, what have we done? Will we be able to handle the real Milton Banks?"

I looked at her, gave her comments a moment to sink in, and realized she could be right. "How casually he said he had come into some money and would be paying cash. Is this a 'rags to riches' story?" I turned off the lights, and we headed to bed. "You're right, instead of one step at a time, we'll go one person at a time, following through with Milton Banks. Heaven help us."

I would keep close watch, but I had complete confidence in Shirley. Always in the background, never looking for any sort of recognition, she consistently helped people. I was sure her upbringing, dirt poor, with a strong faith and a close-knit family, instilled in her the compassion for others, and she was now helping those who faced the same challenges. In the back of my head, her one comment came back ... *and yes, indeed, what have we done?*

CHAPTER 27

June 1998, Little Yellow House

"I'M FEELING KIND OF GUILTY," SHIRLEY SAID, SITTING at the kitchen table. "Mid-June, we've been back and settled nine months and still haven't found the time to visit family, other than Mom and Dad being here in April. Sure, we've taken a lot of little trips—to the Okefenokee Swamp, Busch Gardens, Daytona Raceway to tour in the off-season, and a few other places that were fun but they were only for us. And I know you feel good about your work with Jack at the museum, but it's time to get some quality time with family."

"Can't argue with that," I said, taking a seat. Before going off traveling for a few weeks, there were a couple of things I wanted to do, both sore subjects with Shirley, and I figured now was as good a time as any to bring it up again.

"Honey, we need to get you on the base medical list so when the time comes, and I'm sure it will, you'll be in their system as my spouse. And for me, I need to find a dentist. Second, can we discuss doing some investments in the near future?" I could see her tense. It reminded me of when my mother would tell my dad, on the first Saturday of each month, it was time to balance the checkbook. He would scurry away and try to hide. I think Shirley wanted to do the same thing.

When we met, between us there had been very little in assets and a lot in debt, mostly mine. We discussed this, before she agreed to marry me and head off to the Island of Sardinia as a Navy officer's wife. We promised we would always be open about our money situation and that she would run the family finances.

It worked out great, and at one point, when I was contemplating retiring, she said if I gave her three more years on active duty, she would have us to a point the only work I'd need to do after calling it quits was volunteer work. We wouldn't be wealthy by any means, but comfortable for our lifestyle. I did four more years, thirty years in total, made commander, and here we were. However, to this date, she did not like to discuss putting our money anywhere other than savings and checking accounts.

"Remember what Lori said to us the last time we met with her?" Lori Wallace, easy name to remember because of Rusty, had been our financial advisor at the Navy Federal Credit Union (NFCU) since 1992. When we first decided to look into buying a home, she took us under her wing, and we've never gone to anyone else since. All of five-foot-one, a marathon runner with long blonde hair, she'd call me when she thought there was an investment that would be good for us to consider. I've never said anything other than I'd get back to her.

"I like Lori," Shirley said, "and she's obviously good at her job. She gave us great advice when we bought the house. You know I'm gun-shy when it comes to investing." As always, she was up front and to the point. It was also hard for her to admit she admired another woman; Shirley usually found it easier to trust men. I found it just the opposite. "I take it she called with an opportunity?"

"It never hurts to listen, honey." She didn't say a flat no at least. "If nothing else, let's review what we have and listen to what Lori has to say. You have done so well getting us to where we are, and I think we owe it to ourselves to look at options available. You can always veto."

"All right," a now laughing wife said. "You know how to compliment me at the right time, go ahead and call her. Now, can we discuss family?"

Shirley was right when she said we hadn't seen our families for a long time. Of course, when you marry and spend the next ten years outside the continental U.S., it does present a challenge to everyone's travel. We made a list of family members to visit and dates to find out if they would be able to see us. We decided to start with the Herman side of the family.

As Mom and Dad were just here in April, we checked them off as recently seen. Marlys and Jim still lived in the Upper Peninsula of Michigan, as did their three grown sons, and we put them down for August as a possibility. We decided when we planned a trip to Minnesota, we'd also see Margy and Irv and other family, especially Gary and Jackie. Chris was still in Hawaii and would see us when he could. Scott, honorably discharged, had returned to Minnesota and was finding his way so we'd let him reach out to us. The family had lost touch with my brother's two daughters.

We made a note to call Marlys, who did visit us in Hawaii just before I retired, although Jim hadn't wanted to leave the Upper Peninsula. She had also driven down to Kingsland in 1993 when we first bought our house. It was time we went to them.

Next, Shirley got out our address book, and we took a look at her family. Daughter Kim, John, and Katy (twelve) lived in Kentucky, an easy drive, so she'd give her a call and work out a visit. As far as we knew, her eldest son, Tony, wanted no family contact so we would honor his wish. Youngest son, Jeff, and his children Heather (ten), Ashleigh (seven) and Christopher (four) lived in Virginia, so a trip to see them in the near future was realistic. Shirley would give Jeff a call.

Everyone else that mattered, fourteen of Shirley's seventeen siblings, were still living in Summersville, West Virginia. Every year on Father's Day, the Stephenson clan gathered for a family reunion; we had been to two before, and we planned to go next year.

"I feel better now," Shirley said, putting away the address book. "I'm putting a list on the refrigerator of each of our action items to accomplish for our visits. Let's set two weeks to have them planned or, at least, in the discussion mode. Go ahead and call base medical, and also get yourself a dentist.

"Then, to appease you, call Lori and set up a time to see her, but not today," she said. "Remember, Lily asked us to stop by the

Pub this afternoon. I think she wants to talk to us about something private."

"What have you done with Dusty?" Lily said, running down to see us when we took our usual seats in the Pub a little after noon. "He's disappeared and some new guy, who owns a new house on a ritzy golf course, has taken over his seat."

"Knock it off," Dusty said from his normal seat. "Can't a guy get a haircut without making a fuss?" Trying to change the subject, he called out, "Hey, Rich, we still on for golf next week?" I gave him a thumb's up and he went back to staring at the TV. This early, it was only the five of us here, and we all were laughing, except Dusty.

Shirley walked down and patted a hatless Dusty on the head. "I think he cleans up quite nicely." Dusty pushed her hand aside but couldn't help smiling. She came back to her seat, our drinks were served, and she asked, "You wanted to see us, young lady?"

Lily made sure Denny was down by Dusty and out of hearing range. "Yes," she said softly. "I know from Jack that you volunteer, Rich, and Denny tells everyone how you have changed Dusty's life, Shirley, maybe even saved it, so I figured you may want to know about a new bar and grill, CAMS, that just opened.

"Michael Duffy, a thirty-six-year Navy veteran, is the owner. He's also founded the Civilian and Military Society, or CAMS—which he also named his new place—and filed to be a community non-profit organization. He's looking to bring together retired and active-duty military and civilians who would like to volunteer for projects that improve the life of residents in Camden County. Just thought you may want to check it out."

On the drive home, Shirley said, "I can see why Lily is keeping that quiet. Denny's mother would fire her if she knew she frequented another establishment serving drinks, no matter what good they were doing. I say let's give CAMS a try. The concept sounds good, and maybe this Michael Duffy could use our help."

I found it much easier than anticipated at base medical. They verified I was in the system, and Shirley automatically came up as an approved spouse. We were both assigned to the Gold Medical Team—with three doctors, designated to help patients in their group, who were assigned when we called for an appointment. In less than twenty minutes, I was done.

I then looked in the phone book and found a new dental practice, Camden Smiles. Lo and behold, Dr. Flutie, who had discovered my cancer, was the dentist. I called, found out he was retired from the military, starting his own private practice, and would gladly accept me as a patient. I was given an appointment the following month.

We kept our appointment with Lori at the credit union, and she was friendly as ever. "Rich, you actually got her to come in and see me. I don't see too many drag marks or bruises, so I'm assuming you are here of your own free will, Shirley?" We all took a seat in her assistant manager's office.

"Don't push your luck, young lady," Shirley said playfully. "I only came to listen because I always tell others to be open-minded. So I am listening, don't expect me to throw confetti."

"Fair enough," Lori said. "Remember, here at the credit union, I work for you and our employees don't make or lose anything off what our clients do or don't invest. That said, here is what is being offered right now that I think you should take a serious look at." She laid out several financial programs and explained the pros and cons, as she saw them. I liked two in particular but said nothing.

"Now," she said, "let's look at your assets and what I think is reasonable to consider putting into either long- or short-term investment." She excused herself and left to let us think about that.

Shirley was really studying the information before her. Then she took a pen that was lying on Lori's desk and started doing some figuring. I was impressed and let her go. She stopped, put the pen down, and smiled at me. "Maybe I've just been too nervous about losing our money. I grew up being taught the value of the dollar and not to be foolish and let another person talk me into losing it, especially when they have no money in the game. I trust her—what do you think?"

"I think we can tell her to stop looking out that window and come back to talk some more." Shirley looked over her shoulder and indeed, Lori was just standing there, daydreaming and waiting for the right time to return. When I waved, she immediately came back.

A half-hour later, we had three forms in front of us to sign, and with our signatures we would not only be Navy Federal Credit Union members, we would be investors in its future. I signed and pushed the papers before Shirley. Her hand was shaking and each signature took a little longer to produce.

When finished, she put the pen down, quickly stood and said, "I need a drink," then left the room. Lori and I laughed, I thanked her, gave a big hug, and hurried to catch my wife. Yes, a drink was very appropriate right now.

The newly opened CAMS Bar and Grill was located only three blocks from the Pub and just outside the gate of the St. Marys airport. There was ample parking out front, where a twenty-five-foot flagpole had the American and POW-MIA flags flying proudly. Entering, we found a larger room than expected; three eight-foot-long folding tables were placed end-to-end to the left of the entrance. This apparently served as the bar, and there were ten separate four-seat folding tables and chairs for dining. Nothing fancy but still warm and welcoming.

"Welcome," said a short, smiling man. "I'm Duff, come have a seat. What can I get you?" We immediately liked Michael Duffy, who was about five-foot-three, with long reddish-white hair and a neatly trimmed beard.

"I'll have a Miller Lite and my wife a scotch and water, please," I said as we took seats at the bar. There was no one else here. Several beach coolers were behind the bar, and Duff got out my beer and placed it before me. He opened another cooler, took a glass, dipped it in, and filled it with ice. Then he came down and stood in front of us.

"Would you prefer Dewar's scotch, Shirley?" he said. She snapped her head up when she heard her name, and Duff started to laugh.

"Lily, bless her heart, said she had two regular customers at the Pub, and if a nicely dressed couple came in and ordered beer and a scotch it would probably be Rich and Shirley. Am I right? I hope so because I invested in a bottle of Dewar's to have on hand just in case."

"You are correct," Shirley said. "Very impressive, and I'll have to talk to Lily about spreading our name around." We all shared big smiles. "So, Duff, tell us about your place and what you're trying to do."

For the next half-hour we heard how Duff came here five years ago as a master chief boatswain's mate assigned to the Submarine Base Kingsland. He and his wife, Lottie, fell in love with the area, the people in Camden County, and the cost of living so they bought their retirement home in downtown St. Marys, and when he retired, they stayed. We told him how we ended up here, our stories very similar.

"I don't do well with nothing to do," Duff said. "I got involved some, helping at the Salvation Army, Goodwill, and local community projects like cleaning up the waterfront. It was okay, but I told Lottie that, unlike anywhere we had been stationed, the military and civilian people really got along well here, and I think this community could benefit by bringing them together and providing services that aren't presently being offered. So I founded CAMS."

"Sounds reasonable," I said. "What services are you looking at providing and how many members/volunteers do you have so far?" I looked around and added, "You advertise being a grill too—who does the cooking and what's on the menu?"

"Here's the menu," Duff said, handing us two laminated menus handwritten on legal sized paper. "And," he reached behind him and produced a chef's hat he placed on his head, "I am the chef. What can I get you?"

Over cheeseburgers and fries, we discussed where the CAMS organization stood so far. Duff had done the background on what it would take to start this group and how to make it official as a non-profit business.

The leaders of St. Marys were very open to his idea and willing to help any way they could. With city council guidance, he was able to get a license for this building to be operated as a food and drink establishment. He applied for a liquor license, which the council approved. A non-profit license was applied for but required state approval; it wouldn't be on their agenda for six months, or until next January. The club had no official members as Duff wanted to make sure all his T's were crossed and I's dotted before he formed a board of directors and independent financial accounts in the name of the organization. He wanted to make sure his vision could be a reality before asking others to join and share in the costs.

We discussed some projects: repairing steps and porches; free transportation to medical/dental appointments for veterans and civilians who otherwise couldn't get there; basic shopping for necessities, and so on. We talked about getting local businesses involved to provide supplies at free or reduced prices, the need for someone to find, organize, and follow through on projects, and how to get people involved.

We left knowing we had just made a new friend and found a place we thought we could make a difference. We agreed to meet the following week with Duff and a few others who had shown interest in helping get it all off the ground. It was a good feeling. Oh, and I did donate some funds, anonymously and over Duff's objection, to help keep the doors open and to show that we would be proud to be called members.

CHAPTER 28

July 1998, Jacksonville, Florida

I PUNCHED IN THE CODE DUSTY GAVE ME, AND THE gate to Pine Lakes Estates and Golf Community swung open. Driving through, I took a left on the first street and there, four houses down, I saw Dusty sitting in a golf cart. He motioned for me to pull into his driveway and got out to greet me. His light brown brick condo was the end unit in a series of five homes. I was anxious to get a tour.

"Welcome," he said, "welcome to Casa Banks." He had on a Pine Lakes monogrammed golf shirt, shorts, new golf shoes, and wore a Scottish tam, which actually looked fitting on his head. I knew we were playing at a private golf course so had dressed in a nice golf shirt, with a collar, and shorts myself. However, my hat was a Miller Lite ball cap.

"The clubhouse called, and our tee time is moved up forty minutes so we better get going. Put your clubs on the cart, and you can change your shoes along the way." *Dusty moving fast?*

I always like to be early, and now I was being rushed. "I guess the tour will have to wait," I said, loaded my clubs and jumped in the passenger seat. He didn't answer. "I didn't know you had a fancy golf cart, Dusty, very nice."

"Soon after I moved in, I realized a golf cart was a good investment. My green fees are free my first year, part of my house purchase, but I would still be charged a cart fee. This way, I play for free and pay a small annual fee to drive my own cart. I also like to bird-watch, so I can just hop in the cart and drive to all the different water spots. I enjoy sitting and logging in all the different bird species."

I rode along, enjoying all the different home styles, some condos but mostly single-family houses, and how the streets curved around and over the lakes to follow the golf course layout. Beautiful, absolutely beautiful. At the clubhouse, a young man came out when we pulled up. "Good morning, Mr. Banks," he said, rushing to greet Dusty, "I'll bring the cart around to the first tee and make sure your clubs are clean before you start."

Mr. Banks? Clean our clubs? What has Dusty gotten into? Whatever it is, he sure is enjoying it, and I wish Shirley could see him. What an unbelievable turnaround. I followed him into the pro shop.

"Morning, Mr. Banks," the man behind the counter said with a big smile. "Thank you for teeing off earlier. I have three foursomes that want to be together, and I thought you'd rather be ahead of them than behind and waiting every hole to tee it up." He flashed that big smile again.

"Thank you, Rob," Dusty said, "and please, call me Milton." *Milton? You have to be kidding me.* "This is Rich Herman; he and his wife live in Kingsland and are friends of mine, so please extend to them all the same courtesies as you do me."

I signed in and paid my green fee, fifty-six dollars for weekday rate, which was comparable to those in Hawaii for active-duty military. I bought a new glove, some tees, and three sleeves of balls because I wasn't sure what was in my bag and didn't want to embarrass myself by running out on the course. I hadn't looked in my bag, or swung a club, since a month before my retirement. Even living in Hawaii, and enjoying the game, I didn't play often, or very well.

As I grew up, I was a fairly good athlete. I excelled at bowling, was an above average baseball and softball player, made it to state wrestling championships, held my own at ice-hockey, and didn't even try (at five-feet and 100 pounds) football and basketball. Then there was golf. From the very first time I teed up; I knew I would never be a good golfer. I was a decent putter, but I could never perfect a good backswing, always feeling uncomfortable, so had no distance on my drives or fairway shots. I accepted my limitations and played the best I could, always enjoying my round, no matter the score, and liked the camaraderie and competition. I had asked Dusty how he played but never got a direct answer, and still had no idea. TEE it up!

The course was difficult (of course, they all are to me) but laid out beautifully among lots of water and trees with challenging greens. I didn't make a fool out of myself and, even after not playing for over a year, managed to break a hundred with a solid ninety-eight. Dusty, whose ability was about the same as mine, managed to shoot ninety-three and seemed satisfied.

The same young man from earlier met us as we pulled up to the clubhouse after our round. "Change your shoes, Mr. Banks, and I'll clean them and your clubs while you enjoy the nineteenth hole. Cart will be out front when you're done." Dusty thanked him and gave him a tip. I did the same and noticed something odd. When I handed the young man a ten-dollar bill, he only had a quarter in his hand. *Are you kidding me, Dusty?*

We ordered burgers and fries and while waiting, enjoying cold beers, I said quietly, "I take it you don't want to be known as Dusty here?"

"Right. I'm Dusty up at the Pub and to you guys up there, but I want to be Milton Banks down here." I nodded okay, although I really wanted to ask why. "Okay, your house, your rules, Milton. You know, now that you told me you're nine months older than me, how about I call you the ol' guy?" I smiled, he didn't. So much for that idea.

The food was very good, and as the waitress came with the bill, Dusty excused himself and went to the bathroom. When he returned, I said, "I took care of the tab so we can go any time." He didn't say a word and we left. I loaded my clubs into Bigg Redd and asked, "How about a tour of your new home?"

"I'd rather not today," Dusty said. "I have somewhere I have to go and need to clean up first. Let's make it a time when both you and Shirley can come down."

I didn't push it. "Sounds like a plan, she'd like that. We'll probably see you at the Pub soon and talk about it. Thanks for today, my friend." He nodded and headed to his golf cart. At least I got a wave from him as I was driving away. *Yes, Dusty, or Milton or Milton Banks, you are a mystery for sure.*

"We said it would be interesting to see who we created," Shirley said as I told her about my golf outing. "It doesn't surprise me about the tab and his being—let's be kind and say frugal. Lily told me that no matter how many beers he owes for, he always tips a quarter."

"That's not frugal, that's downright cheap and a slap in the face to a bartender," I said quickly. "All I could think of was my father and the stories about how he always headed for the bathroom when the dinner tab came, and Uncle Irving or someone else had to pay. I swore then that would never be me. And you told me, when you bartended, a small tip was a sign you provided bad service and you'd rather have gotten nothing. Anyway, the rest of the day was good. Not sure when, if ever, we'll see his place."

"Up to him now," Shirley said. "We've helped him get to this point; the rest is on him. New subject—Sandy Alben called and said it was important she talk to you soon. She left her work number and home number so it must be serious. Why would the base security manager need to talk to you?"

"One way to find out." I picked up the phone and dialed the number she handed me. "Hi, Sandy, it's Rich Herman. I understand you want to speak to me?"

She certainly did. I was given a brief overview of what prompted the call and agreed to meet with her and the senior agent in charge (SAIC) of the Naval Criminal Investigative Service (NCIS) Kingsland, the next morning at NCIS headquarters.

Arriving a few minutes early, I was met at the door by the SAIC, Ralph Teeter, who I knew well. We had worked together several times on cases involving my sailors when I was on active duty. In fact, I met him working on a case involving Sandy, so, small world. Ralph was a field agent back then, had served eight years in the Marines, and I liked him because he was straightforward, made you think every case we were involved with was his top priority, and always showed respect to those being investigated. I was happy to see him promoted to Top Cop.

Sandy arrived a few minutes later and we all went to Ralph's office. After we had coffee and exchanged pleasantries, I found out more about why I was here. "Rich," Ralph started, "do you remember a Joyce Ashford?"

"No, but I think I had a Johnny Ashford who was a civilian and worked in my department as a watch officer."

"That's her husband," Sandy interjected. "Ralph, let me take it for a minute." Ralph nodded and she had the floor. "Johnny Ashford retired six months ago after thirty years civil service and has filed for disability. Or, I should say, his wife had him file.

"They—in this case it's really her pushing it—claim mental anguish and suffering from Commander Submarine Group Ten having forced his job reassignment when the base communications were downsized, forcing civilians into other jobs. Apparently, Johnny has never fully recovered from the stress this put on him and wants compensation."

"I don't get it ... why does that affect me?" I was puzzled as it sounded like a Civil Service matter, and I didn't have anything to do with their retirement system.

"Two things," Sandy said. "One, you were the one who brought up consolidation, you wrote the plan, and you headed the transformation. In the claim, you are one of those who they want brought in to testify on their behalf. But you're right that it is a Civil Service matter and will be handled through their channels. That's not the real reason you are here, though. While investigating the appeal, something arose that got me involved from a security standpoint. After seeing the initial report, I immediately got hold of Ralph and in turn, you."

Then it was Ralph's turn. "During one of the interviews," he said, "Joyce Ashford alluded to her husband possibly being unstable and that he had mentioned getting even. It's you he is mad at. I take this seriously, and you know me well enough to realize if I'm concerned, you need to be too. Thank Sandy here, as soon as she saw this a red flag was raised, and here we are. I just wanted you, and Shirley, to be aware, and I'm taking it on personally. No one under my umbrella of responsibility, especially a friend, is going to get harmed on my watch. Period."

"Ralph, remember the case of my lieutenant we thought was being abusive to his wife?" He nodded and smiled. I looked at Sandy. "Ralph investigated my concerns, and when we went to the house of this couple, thinking of possibly charging my lieutenant, we found the wife beating him with brass knuckles. For over a year, he had been the one abused and taking the blame because he loved her so much. I think maybe it's Joyce I better beware of. However, I don't think they know I'm back here, and if they do, they don't know where I live." Sandy and Ralph both gave me an *are-you-kidding-me* look.

"I didn't know either," Sandy said quickly, "and I found you in less than five minutes." I let that sink in and realized she was right. She patted my hand. "I got ya covered too, little buddy." Sandy was over six feet tall, and as she stood to walk out with me, I did like having her nearby. Of course, having Ralph and his agents involved helped too.

"Try not to worry, and you made a good point so we'll be watching both the Ashfords until this case is over," Ralph said. "I'll be in touch."

When I told Shirley the situation that afternoon, she was glad Sandy got Ralph involved. "It's amazing how people need to find someone to blame for their own self-induced problems," she said. "If I remember right, all the military personnel found equal jobs here in the area or received orders to commands they worked out with their detailers to go to. And, correct me if I'm wrong, every civilian affected by the consolidation found an equivalent or better position right here. How could they be upset now?"

"Sandy thinks the wife, who thinks she knows the system better than anyone, is trying to exploit the disability section of the retirement code in order to get seventy-five percent of her husband's retirement tax free," I said. "I was surprised when Sandy said many people who apply get thirty percent; she thinks that's just to end the red tape and money it costs to fight. No wonder the government is going broke."

Two weeks later, we pulled into our driveway, where a car I didn't recognize sat. It was Ralph Teeter with a woman I assumed was one of his field agents. "I thought you'd like to know we have closed the case on the Ashfords," he said as we walked up to greet them. "Rich, Shirley, this is Carolyn, my newest agent." We shook hands and invited them in. Surprisingly, they accepted.

"It's after five, Ralph, you out here on your off time?" I said with a smile. "Can I get you and your partner a drink?" I knew he would decline, but it was the friendly thing to do.

"We're never off, Rich," Ralph said. He looked at Carolyn and shrugged. "I am out here off the clock, however, and in my own vehicle, so yeah, a beer sounds good for me." Carolyn looked very hesitant before realizing it was okay and she accepted a cold Miller Lite too. I made Shirley a drink and we all went out to the lanai.

"Sandy called me earlier, and we were in the area so decided to just drop by," Ralph started. "First, good news, you both are safe and you won't be called in to testify at the Ashford hearing about the disability claim." We all clinked glasses. "Apparently, Joyce Ashford cut off more than she reckoned for. Once she made known there was a possibility of a crime, their case got security involved. The day after we met with you, Sandy called me and suggested a plan of action that I agreed to. I want to believe she would have done this for any base personnel involved, but your being her friend didn't help the Ashfords."

As Ralph explained it, an official Civil Service Administrative meeting had been called, as the Ashfords expected, to hear their claim. What they didn't expect was the meeting would be headed by the base security manager, Sandy Alben—and attended by the base judge advocate general (JAG) who swore everyone in and read the Ashfords their rights.

"Two armed Military Police also stood at the door," he said. "How familiar are you with the JAG, Rich?"

I almost spat out my beer and Shirley laughed. The NCIS agents had no idea what just happened. "Let's just say," I said, chuckling, "I have a deep respect for the Navy legal system. You see, Ralph, Carolyn, when I was enlisted, I was known as a captain's 'poster boy,' which meant that while I worked hard and was an outstanding sailor, I also played hard and had a tendency to get in difficult situations, some on the edge of causing international incidents.

"I won't go into detail, but … a JAG in Malta saved me from a possible life sentence in a Maltese prison; another JAG in Turkey saved the day when I allegedly attacked a Turkish national; in Italy, a doctor was persuaded by a JAG who believed in me, and I can thank her for being allowed to stay on active duty. You get the idea."

"I'd love to hear more," Ralph said, "but, another day. Continuing why we're here, after the Ashfords had their rights read, Johnny got really nervous, and Joyce made the mistake of asking why the security manager and JAG were holding the hearing. That gave Sandy all she needed, and she pounced. This is what she told us happened at the meeting."

Sandy had addressed the Ashfords very seriously, saying, "During the processing of your claim for disability, a statement was made of possible retaliation against a naval officer if it didn't go your way. That is a threat made, and we take threats very seriously. Before any decision is made on your claim, which on face value appears to possibly be made under fraudulent circumstances, we need to address this possible felony."

"No, wait a minute," Johnny Ashford had said immediately. "I'm not threatening anybody and want no part of fraud. Joyce, what have you done?" The meeting went into recess.

The JAG had a heart to heart with the couple, and when the meeting was called back to order, they dropped the disability claim and apologized for the misunderstanding about what some thought were threats made toward Commander Richard Herman. In fact, both said they thought Mr. Herman had been a great boss and did a good job with the consolidation.

"The JAG and Sandy agree that they are no threat to you anymore," Ralph said. He stood and walked with Carolyn to the door. As she stepped out, he turned and shook our hands. "I really would like to hear those stories, Rich. You ever thought of writing a book?" We all laughed as we walked him to his car.

As the car faded from sight, I remarked, "Well, another bullet dodged, Mrs. Herman. I just love the JAG corps and, in this case, Sandy Alben, watching over me. You know, if I ever do write a book, like Mom wants me to, I'll make sure those folks are part of the story." Shirley rolled her eyes, and her beautiful smile said it all: *Sure, you will!*

CHAPTER 29

January 5, 1999, St. Marys

"CONGRATULATIONS, MICHAEL DUFFY," I SHOUTED, "Civilian and Military Society (CAMS) is now officially a registered non-profit organization fully licensed and insured." The cheers went up from about twenty people, who would make up our initial membership, standing around the bar in our new and improved headquarters building.

"Thanks, Rich," Duff said. "It's been a long six months, but we did it and even have a few dollars to put into our new bank account. Before anyone has any more to drink, let's formally vote our board of directors into office and have our first meeting. First, for president, who do you nominate?" It was unanimous, and Duff took that role and was handed the gavel by his wife, Lottie. "Next, vice president?" Twenty minutes later, we had our board of directors.

Duff wasn't wrong when he said it had been a tough six months. With no official status, no non-profit status, no license to advertise and promote functions or ability to get insurance during this formulating period, it was difficult to fund the few events we did hold. We did some home improvements, which Duff and several other volunteers, along with myself, considered emergency help to neighbors. All the funding was anonymous, mainly three of us. We did, with Shirley and Lottie spearheading, pull off a pretty good Thanksgiving and Christmas meal delivery, which got us good press and interest from the locals.

With the board now set, Duff took charge. Hitting the gavel three times, he said, "I call this meeting to order and call for our first official meeting to be Friday, January 8, in this, our headquarters. Anyone second?" Someone did. "All in favor." Everyone yelled yea. "So be it. I'll put the finishing touches to our by-laws and structure by then. I tentatively set the third Monday of every month as our meeting night for all members and people interested. Do I hear a call for adjournment?" He did, and we did.

"CAMS is born," I said to Shirley on the drive home. "I think we're going to enjoy working with this group. I can also see those wheels turning in your head, Mrs. Herman. Want to talk about it?"

"Rich," she said, "it's twenty-two degrees out and I am freezing. Get me home, start the fireplace, and make us one of your family's famous hot toddies. Then, when I have thawed out, we will talk." She had a good point as a hard freeze was predicted tonight for Camden County.

As planned, neither Shirley nor I took a position on the board. Duff and I agreed it would be best if I stayed just an active member; not having a vote, I would be freer to make suggestions and try to rally support for the group without fear of being called biased or able to bully my way through with my vote. I started contacting businesses, Duff went along most of the time as president and a very good talker, and soon we had over a dozen local companies donating, or at a cut price, lumber, paint, plumbing supplies, etc.

The very first action item by the board was membership eligibility. It was unanimous that anyone wishing to be a member could join, and their annual dues would be what they felt they could afford, which would remain confidential. (Actually, this was my proposal, and I was adamant that Shirley and I would not be members if a person's ability to pay kept them out). We did provide a proposed fee based on a military retiree's rank or a civilian's equivalent pay, but it was for guidance, not as a rule. It seemed to work well.

By the March 15 meeting, we were up to fifty-seven paid members with a dozen more non-members, all active volunteers. There were enough patrons visiting daily that Duff hired one member, April David, as a cook and her daughter, Brandi, who was a sophomore at Camden High, as a part-time waitress. April's husband, Karl, was a senior chief on the Trident USS West Virginia and an active volunteer when in port. CAMS had multiple projects scheduled with more in the planning stages. In one week, I learned how to repair a leaky roof and helped build two ramps for wheelchair-bound members. We also got our first write-up, with pictures, in the local paper. Duff's dream was a reality, and St. Marys, Kingsland, and all of Camden County benefited.

Two days later, I was enjoying my morning coffee when Shirley came into the kitchen beet red. "Rich," she said weakly, taking a seat, "I think it was a good thing you got us registered at base medical. I think my heart is about to explode."

I felt her pulse, which was racing. When I opened her robe, I could see her chest pounding. I had her in the base emergency room twenty minutes later, and she was immediately attended to by a trauma team and rushed into a room. Ten minutes later, a corpsman led me to her room, and I met Dr. Warner for the first time.

"Commander," a tall, thin Navy lieutenant said, introducing himself and shaking my hand. He had long brown hair and I'd guess was in his mid-thirties. "Your wife's blood pressure shot up, but I'm confident we can rule out a heart attack or stroke. I have given her something to bring the pressure down quickly, and we started an IV with nicardipine, which will work over a longer period of time to reduce and stabilize her pressure. I see she is new here as a patient. Does she have a history of high blood pressure?"

"When she had her physical for life insurance several years ago," I said thinking back, "she was told it was slightly elevated but nothing like this. Is she going to be okay?"

"Yes, she is stable for now. I think she may have had an angina episode but have taken some tests to try and find out what caused it. The corpsman will need you to fill out her history, we'll get the test results and go from there. Any questions for now?"

"No, Doctor," I said, "in fact, in all the excitement today I forgot to bring in her health record from Hawaii. I'm known for being organized, but I guess it doesn't help if I forget to provide important documents." Dr. Warner smiled like he understood. "I'll go get the records, and hopefully they'll help." I looked in on Shirley, so she knew I was there, and slightly embarrassed went out to the car.

Three hours later, following a thorough exam and review of her test results, it was determined that it was most likely a panic attack (Shirley had several diagnosed before) that triggered her heart to race out of control. Of a greater concern, her blood tests showed some irregularities with her heart, and a follow-up appointment was highly recommended. Shirley tensed hearing that, and Dr. Warner quickly changed the subject, saying he wanted to observe her a while longer and we could talk later.

Once alone, Shirley and I discussed the situation. I let her vent and lead the way. As always, she talked herself into doing what was right with little advice from me other than taking her hand and saying, "Your health is the number one priority, and don't you dare leave me to face retirement alone." Maybe that was a bit more than a little advice.

When Dr. Warner returned, he agreed to be Shirley's primary care physician. He took her chart, wrote some notes and said, "Done. The first thing we need to do is find out the underlying causes of what happened today and further evaluate your heart and lungs. I'm going to order you a stress test, an EKG, and full blood work-up. The clinic will call you several days before your appointment and tell you what preparations are required. We'll get those results and go from there. Now, I'm sure this is a sore subject—have you given thought about giving up smoking?"

On the way home, I said, "At least he was respectful of your choice, honey. He didn't lecture or belittle you in any way. And, as your doctor now, I'm sure he has an obligation to inform you of the harmful effects smoking could be responsible for."

"Agree," Shirley said. "I really like him, and I can handle people who disagree with my lifestyle but are respectful of my freedom of choice."

While Shirley was in for her blood work, I was able to make my own arrangements for an eye appointment. The base here, and in Jacksonville, had no ophthalmologists attached, so I was told I would be referred to a civilian doctor and that office would contact me for an appointment. I couldn't remember the last time I saw a civilian doctor.

All of Shirley's test results were in, and we met with Dr. Warner to discuss what, if anything, was found. In his office, we found him sitting behind his desk in his uniform without a doctor's jacket. I immediately was intrigued by what I saw, but remained quiet so that he had the floor to talk to her.

"I assume it's okay for your husband to be here?" he started. Shirley said yes. "I also believe you want me to be straightforward, so let me first say that I have a good idea what is going on with you. We know you have had panic attacks in the past, and I can prescribe medicine to help that. Your EKG and blood tests show you are having early signs of heart disease, which I can also help with medication.

"And, being honest, during your stress test, you had a hard time. This is because you are suffering from early stages of COPD. I can also give some relief here, but it is not a cure. Any questions, so far?" Shirley remained stoic and shook her head no.

"I told you what I, as your doctor, can do. Now, what can you do to help yourself? First, and I'm just giving facts, not judging, you need to quit smoking. Not cut down, quit. You can reverse your COPD; that's up to you. Second, take a look at your lifestyle. What is your diet, how much do you drink, and how much do you exercise? All of this matters. I have a folder here with valuable information—but *how* valuable is up to you and how you apply it to your situation. I will help you any way I can and will never abandon you, even if you change nothing."

"Thank you, Doctor," Shirley said. "It's nothing I didn't expect, and now that it has been confirmed, it's actually a load off my mind. I'll take on board all that you said and read your information. I'm pretty set in my ways and not sure what I can or will do. Rich is a great supporter so that is not an issue, and I appreciate your willingness to put up with me."

I could tell we were about done so I spoke up. "Dr. Warner, I notice that you have silver dolphins and a good conduct medal. That means you're ex-enlisted, qualified in submarines, and had at least four years active duty before being commissioned. Very impressive."

"Not many people notice that, Commander," he said. "Yes, I joined the Navy, was an enlisted nuclear-trained electronics technician, qualified in submarines, and got my commission through the Medical Enlisted Commissioning Program. That's why I'm old for a lieutenant."

I smiled. "Having been enlisted ten years before I was commissioned through the Limited Duty Officer (LDO) Program, and a fellow "Mustang,' I sure respect you, sir. Can you be assigned my primary care physician too?"

I received my referral for a civilian ophthalmologist, Dr. Sidney Limmer, and was filling out new patient forms in his office May 14 in North Jacksonville. The same night the referral letter arrived, we had seen an ad on TV for the newest and greatest breakthrough surgery to remove cataracts. The renowned doctor, in the commercial was, a small world, Dr. Limmer.

My name was called, forty-five minutes after my appointment time, and I was shown to a new, modern-looking room with a view of the Jacksonville skyline. I sat in a large leather chair next to many optical machines.

The man from the commercial entered. Dr. Limmer was gray-haired, with a big mustache, and possibly in his early sixties. "I see you're here for a follow-up exam of ongoing glaucoma and a medication refill. Let me take a look." I placed my chin on the plastic holder and followed his directions. A phone rang.

"Yes, dear," I heard him say. "Yes, I know it's black tie. Yes, that's the outfit I have with me. Yes, dear. Yes, dear. Judd is having the limo cleaned and will pick you up at six o'clock and me at six-thirty sharp. Yes, dear, I have the invitation. Bye, dear.

"It's hard to be in demand," he said, sitting back across from me. "Now, let me look again. Okay, sit back. Who diagnosed you with glaucoma? Here it is, 1983 at an Army medical center in Hawaii. Well, I don't think you have glaucoma, Mr. Herman, maybe hypertension but saying glaucoma is a bit of a reach. I can still refill your medication needs; I'm just going to change the eye drops you use to something I think will be more effective."

He smiled and started to write out my prescription. "Too bad, Mr. Herman, you don't have cataracts yet so I can't recommend surgery. My procedure could help and even improve your eyesight."

"He what?" Shirley said that evening, flabbergasted. "Too bad you don't need surgery? What kind of nut is he?"

"A very wealthy one," I said and told her about his phone call. "He gave me enough medication refills for a year at least. Hopefully an ophthalmologist gets ordered into Kings Bay or the Naval hospital in Jacksonville. I'm not comfortable with Mr. Wonderful, the TV eye doctor of the rich and famous." We both laughed. I was serious.

Dusty had been in his townhome almost a year now, and during this time was frequenting the Pub less and less, so we were surprised to see him in his old seat when we entered today. We had given up on asking when a good time was to come down for a tour of his home. He had a fresh haircut and was still looking good.

Actually, we didn't see him at first as our eyes hadn't adjusted, but we heard Lily yell, "Hail, hail, the gang's all here." Beside Dusty was Jack; it was like old times. "If my boss wouldn't fire me, I'd say drinks on the house," Lily proclaimed, laughing, "but you all know her so someone else volunteer." Everyone laughed with her because it was a true statement. Shirley volunteered to buy the next round.

The front door opened, which was rare as most everyone parked out back. In walked two military contractors from Washington, D.C., who always stopped by when in town. The older one, obviously the boss, said, "We saw the new Bigg Redd and knew Rich and Shirley were here so we stopped in early."

We all knew them, and after pleasantries were over, he said, "Hey, Dusty, I heard you moved into a new place down at Pine Lakes. We're here for a week but can take some time off one day to come down and play a round of golf. How about it?"

Two days later, Dusty and I pulled up in his golf cart and, as usual, one of the attendants took the cart to get it ready. We walked into the clubhouse and heard, "There he is. That's Dusty. I told you he was a member here." It was our senior contractor and cohort, standing off to one side like they were being punished. "Tell him, Dusty."

"Mr. Banks," the golf pro said, "these gentlemen were trying to sign in as friends of a member called Dusty. I told them we don't have any members by that name. I'm sorry, Mr. Banks, I didn't know."

"Mr. Banks ... who is Mr. Banks?" I heard one of our guests ask.

"That's okay," Milton, aka Dusty, said. "Some old shipmates call me that name from the old days. I'll vouch for them. Come on, guys, sign in, sorry for the confusion."

I had already left the clubhouse; I was laughing so hard. Trying to be somebody he wasn't had caught up to him, and now, totally embarrassed, Dusty could explain his own way out. I finally composed myself, wiped my eyes, and went to sign in. Everyone was outside waiting for me, and I told them I had to use the restroom before teeing off. Actually, I took a minute to edify one still confused golf pro.

Walking to the first tee, I said, "Shall we draw to see who goes first, maybe go by seniority or do you just want to designate the order, Mr. Banks?" If looks could kill, I was a dead man. I knew I was going to enjoy this round.

I was looking forward to telling Shirley about my morning, but as I turned onto our cul-de-sac I saw her in our driveway, and she wasn't checking the mail. "Rich," she said as soon as I opened the car door, "your dad took a fall last night and is in the hospital. There are no bones broken, and Mom said it was mainly for observation, but he was having trouble breathing and is pretty sore. I told her you'd call as soon as you got home." I was on the phone with Mom right away.

"Okay, Mom," I said, "Dad will be going home tomorrow if he can pass a stress test. Got it." I listened to her once again tell me that smoking had caught up with him and to be thankful that, like her, I had quit. Of course, he still chewed tobacco, which they both seemed to think was okay. "Give me a call when you get him home tomorrow. Thanks, Mom, love you, and tell Dad I love him too.

"That's twice in three months Dad has been admitted after a fall at home followed by breathing issues." I said to Shirley as we walked out to the lanai. "I hate to think about it, but I think there must be something more to this than a simple fall." My answer came sooner than expected.

"He'll be in the hospital another day to make sure he can maintain an oxygen level using an at-home machine or portable bottles," I reported to Shirley after the next phone call. A pulmonologist had been called in and determined Dad's oxygen level was too low to sustain breathing on his own; he would require oxygen 24/7. "At least they know what has been causing his getting faint and falling."

I never did get around to telling my story about my golf morning. Somehow, it just didn't seem important anymore.

CHAPTER 30

January 1, 2000, Little Yellow House

"HAPPY NEW YEAR MORNING," I GREETED SHIRLEY AS she joined me on the lanai. "Apparently, the world has survived the calendar changing to the year 2000."

I poured two fresh cups of coffee from the thermos I brought out and handed my sleepy wife one of them. She slumped into one of the high-backed rattan chairs and still hadn't said a word. We were in bed before ten o'clock last night, and I didn't even hear any of the fireworks or other celebration noise.

"Morning," she finally said, "I slept like a rock. I think our nightcap might have had something to do with it." I smiled and said nothing. "I don't know how we ever survived the partying we used to do on New Year's. Or any of the things we used to do. Kind of nice waking up without a hangover or wondering if we did anything embarrassing." I don't know what flashed through her mind, but she suddenly had a big smile on her face.

"With that smile, can I assume your new year is off to a good start. Care to share?"

"Just think about it," Shirley continued, now wide awake. "Even with all the medical issues our families faced, especially Kim being diagnosed with breast cancer, 1999 was a pretty good year. We've kept busy volunteering and made some good friends along the way. Duff heard from the Vietnam Veterans Memorial group, and St. Marys is on the short list for the Moving Wall to visit. We visited Mom, Dad, the Nelsons, the Irenes, Mar, Jim, and kids—plus my baby, Jeff, and your oldest, Chris, were here and got some good golf in. What did I leave out?"

"When you put it that way, we were active for sure. Like you said, we had some medical worries, especially with my eye scare."

Last November, the clinic had called and said there was now a Navy ophthalmologist stationed here so I had my six-month follow-up exam there. Dr. Neal, a Navy commander, conducted my eye exam and was not impressed. In fact, he was downright mad.

"I cannot believe," he said, "that Dr. Limmer even examined you. He's not a glaucoma specialist, he's a glorified cataract surgeon and probably only did a basic course in glaucoma as a resident thirty years ago. You do have glaucoma, Commander, and I'm getting you back on the right medication immediately. Hopefully, six months on what he gave you hasn't done any real harm—and I don't think it has, and we can recover. He will hear about this." I knew I didn't like that Dr. Limmer, but I never thought I was in danger. I pondered what the physician's oath says: First do no harm.

Lifting my cup of coffee toward her in a gesture of congratulations-we-made-it, I added up some of what we'd been through, including Shirley's heart and lung scare, which was now getting under control, Dad and his lungs, and Mom's recent heart concerns. Our biggest worry had been Kim's battle with cancer: first surgery, then chemotherapy. Hopefully, her last treatment would be next month.

A few months later, we were getting ready for Memorial Day weekend. It was going to be a special one.

"Nice car, son," I said to Chris, giving him a hug as he climbed out of his 2000 Chevy Impala four-door sedan rental car.

"Thanks, nothing but comfort for my parents." Chris always knew how to please. "Dad, Miss Shirley, this is Kent."

We shook hands with his friend, who was stationed with Chris in Pearl Harbor and was partaking in our latest adventure: attending NASCAR's Coca-Cola 600 in Charlotte, North Carolina. "Let me make a head call, you load up, and we'll get going." I knew Chris was excited to hit the road; after all, this was his, and most likely Shirley's trip of a lifetime.

Shirley and I were Rusty Wallace Fan Club members, and last February I gave Chris the club email address. Thinking nothing ventured, nothing gained, Chris emailed Rusty and asked him if he would reenlist him for his next tour in the Navy. Not only did he hear back from the club, two hours later he got an email from the driver himself. Rusty said he would be honored to do the reenlistment ceremony, giving Chris the personal phone number of his public relations director to work out the details.

Shirley had thought Chris was playing a joke on her when he called to ask her if she would like to meet her hero, Rusty Wallace. When he walked in the house this morning, before she would let him go to the bathroom, she said, "Show me the tickets and VIP pass, Chris."

He laughed and handed her the race packet he received from Rusty, and as soon as she saw it was real, she gave him another hug. "Hurry up, let's go!" The deal we worked out with our son was that he would get a rental car—Bigg Redd not being a good car for four adults to travel in—and provide the tickets to the race.

The main reason for the reenlistment being scheduled this weekend was NASCAR had proclaimed the Coca-Cola 600 Fan Appreciation Day. To accommodate the fans, all track activities would be stopped at ten a.m. All the top drivers were holding autograph sessions at their home racing facilities, and that is where we were to meet Rusty.

I'm not sure what we were expecting, but over 30,000 fans converged on Concord, North Carolina, to attend one or more of the thirty open houses. We left the hotel three hours before our scheduled meeting time and still had to park four blocks away. The crowd reminded me of a state fair.

We finally made it to Penske Racing and saw one of the number 2 Miller Lite Fords on display out front. There were easily 500 people in line, many with a Miller Lite in one hand and a model race car or something in the other, hoping to get an autograph.

Not making any friends, we walked down the line toward the

front door. I'm sure people were curious as to why three uniformed sailors and a lady with Rusty gear on, were going to the head of the line. Luckily, as questions started being yelled our way, the front door opened and someone called out, "Christopher Herman here?"

An older man ushered us inside, closed and locked the door, and said, "Welcome, I'm Buck Flair, Rusty's helicopter pilot and retired Army warrant officer." He shook hands with each of us. "I'm not very good at Navy ranks, but are you a colonel, sir?"

"Navy commander," I said, "equivalent to your lieutenant colonel. Please call me Rich. Kent here is a Navy chief petty officer, and Chris is a second class petty officer and star of our party. This young lady in the Rusty Wallace shirt, a huge Rusty fan, is my wife, Shirley."

"Thanks, Commander, and call me Buck. Rusty has asked me to be your escort for today, and I want you to know I am thrilled he asked me. This way—the boss is waiting for you."

We followed him down a hallway and as we neared the end, Shirley let out a little gasp and gripped my arm, tight. I looked where she was pointing. Rusty Wallace, in person, came out of an office and was heading toward us.

"Where is Shirley?" he said. He walked straight to her and didn't offer his hand; he just bent down and hugged her. "Chris told me he was bringing his best friend, father, and beautiful step-mom. He wasn't lying, I see. I like your shirt, Shirley."

He continued to shake our hands, Shirley worked on keeping her jaw up, and it was easy to see why he is so well-liked and popular. Maybe 5,000 fans would soon be waiting outside and he made us feel like the most important people in the world. "Come on, I'll give you a tour of our shop, and then Buck will show us where he thought would be a good spot for the ceremony."

For over forty minutes, we toured Penske racing while Rusty explained all the different workstations and their importance to the team. "I'm one of the people who believe if you are blessed with the talent to drive in NASCAR, you should earn your ride through hard work and an understanding of all facets of the sport," he said. "And racing is a sport. My father taught me, and I'm teaching my kids, don't expect to be given your future, work for it. I'm proud to say I can build a car from the bottom up, and I know this gives me an advantage."

"Rusty?" Buck pointed to his watch. "I don't want to stop either, but we do have a schedule to keep."

"Okay, Buck, lead the way." Rusty followed him but didn't stop talking. "Did Buck tell you he was a helo pilot in Vietnam? Flew over 140 rescue missions and received a Bronze Star and Purple Heart. I trust him with my life." You could sense the admiration between the two.

"Buck flew, and you guys dive. I'd love to go on a submarine some day. What's it like being underwater weeks or months at a time?" Chris took over, giving a great explanation of submarine life. "Wow, you sold me, Chris, maybe I should enlist too and go back to Hawaii with you."

"No, you won't," Shirley blurted out, then looked embarrassed. "Ah, your fans want to watch you race every Sunday, you won't have time." It was too late; we were all laughing already.

The ceremony spot was by one of many trophy cases, and Kent explained to Rusty how to administer the oath. Buck was given our cameras to take pictures, and Chris was sworn in for another four years. Amazingly, Rusty did not stumble on a single word, and the ceremony was not only serious, it was very professionally performed.

Kent, who was taking care of all the administrative duties, showed Chris and Rusty where to sign and had to intervene when, pumped up, Rusty wanted to also sign as "Officer overseeing the swearing in."

"That's why Chris's dad is in uniform, Rusty," Kent said respectfully. "He's the officer witness."

We were told we could bring one item to have Rusty sign, the same as the thousands waiting outside, but we had pushed our luck and brought more. As it turned out, Rusty had already signed authentic cars, hats, and T-shirts as gifts, and he handed them to us. With Shirley's permission, he signed the shirt she was wearing, and I figured it would be tough to get her to take it off.

At the door, Rusty told us, "I have a great appreciation for the military, and honestly, it was my honor to perform your ceremony, Chris. I have your number so don't be surprised if I call for a tour on a submarine the next time I'm in Hawaii." Buck opened the door and led us out, into ninety-degree heat and a crowd that went crazy seeing Rusty with us. I turned and he was holding Shirley's and Chris's hands in the air. "Let's hear it for the military," he shouted over the cheering crowd.

We went back to the motel to safely store all our souvenirs and change out of our uniforms. We only had one room, with two double beds, so Shirley was allowed to go in first and clean up while we waited outside, sipping on much-appreciated ice-cold beers. We thought about trying to get two rooms, but Shirley said she thought she could deal with three sailors in the same room. Chris and Kent couldn't have been more accommodating and excellent roommates.

It was almost dinner time so we headed to the lounge/restaurant to meet up with Kim, John, and Katy. Kim, who couldn't figure out why her mother liked auto racing, now had become a big fan. Tomorrow, we all would attend the NASCAR Busch Grand National Race (junior circuit race teams) and on Sunday the Coca-Cola 600. It was a wonderful evening; Chris and Kim (step-siblings) hadn't seen each other in years, and Shirley couldn't stop beaming as she sat next to her now fourteen-year-old granddaughter, showing off her autographed shirt.

We survived the heat wave, basking in the bright sunshine for five hours Saturday and eight more on Sunday, then a four-hour drive to go three miles in a traffic jam as 183,500 fans left the track and the disappointing eighth-place finish by Rusty.

We were a tired group of four when we arrived back in Kingsland. Later, we saw Kent and Chris off to the airport to catch their flight back to Hawaii. A great experience and a lifelong memory was made. I wondered how long Rusty's biggest fan would wear that shirt?

I received a call from a very excited Michael Duffy on July 5. "Rich, I couldn't wait until you came in. We're approved, the Vietnam

Traveling Memorial Wall has been placed on their schedule to be here from October 25 to the 31st. We have until September 5th to provide them with all our plans to provide a safe location for viewing, adequate guarding, and our schedule of events with names, times, and all sorts of things. We have our work cut out for us; I'm calling an emergency meeting for tonight." He finally took a breath. "Can you come down here today and help me get started?"

"I can help, Duff," I told him, "but, remember, I'm not on the committee. We have good people, who have a lot of contacts and pull in town that I don't have, who already started planning, so let them do their thing. Of course, I'll attend the meeting, and Shirley and I will help where we can. And, Duff, call the mayors of St. Marys and Kingsland, and the base commander first to make sure they are on board and will have representatives on the committee. Without the military, police, fire, and city officials, we'll never pull this off."

"Civilian and Military Society, come to order," Duff said, banging the table with his gavel on August 31 for the special meeting addressing the Vietnam Moving Wall project. "We will be approving our Operation Order to be sent to the Vietnam Veterans Memorial organization tomorrow." Kingsland and St. Marys mayors, the base's commanding officer, presidents of the city councils, and fire and police chiefs were in attendance.

The meeting lasted three hours and ended with Duff, CAMS executive director and president, officially signing our Operation Order, as witnessed by others we thought would show our serious commitment. Both the cities and county official seals were applied.

A week later, we received official approval and a set of parameters that must be met. You'd think we were hosting a visit by the president of the United States. Police, military and motorcycle personnel, in dress uniforms, are required to meet the wall five miles before it exited I-95 for St. Marys and escort the truck carrying the panels making up the wall to its final location where it will be erected. Ten volunteers, properly indoctrinated, must be available to the truck driver who will supervise the wall erection. Two armed military guards must man the wall at all times. The list was exhausting, but CAMS and the civilians and military of Camden County were determined and the work began.

The Moving Wall arrived, with motorcade, and all the officials were there to make sure the right emphasis of its importance was noted. After numerous prayers and a few short remarks, the wall came to life. The weather was beautiful and the forecast was promising. Let the visit begin.

Several thousand people showed up for the opening ceremony. The keynote speaker was not a submariner, which many expected, but an aviator. Rear Admiral Boyce Johns, Vietnam veteran and war hero, had flown over 400 combat missions in support of Navy Riverine Forces and SEAL units in Vietnam, receiving the Silver Star and Distinguished Flying Cross medals among his 98 awards and decorations.

When he mentioned flying over trying to give cover to river boats, a gentleman in the audience, wearing a Vietnam War Veteran officer designated ball cap, stood and yelled, "I was one of those river boat sailors, and I brought you some friends." Six other gentlemen stood up and in unison said, "We were too, sir, and you saved our lives," as they all gave a salute. The audience stood, and the applause and cheers, even outdoors, were deafening.

We all have heard about the Vietnam Memorial Wall in D.C. and this Moving Wall replica, but until you actually touch the wall and view the over 58,000 names of those who lost their lives in Vietnam, you never will feel its full impact. I served during the Vietnam era, and although I never served in-country Vietnam, I spent months training with the Marines who did. That day, I recognized several names of those who gave it all. Shirley joined me when I was done, not a word was said, and we, as I think most of the visitors did, walked away with tears in our eyes.

The visit of the Moving Wall to St. Marys, Georgia, would be one of the greatest events I was ever part of. After its visit concluded, and the wall, with motorcade, was escorted out of town on to its next destination, one thing was certain. As we waved goodbye, I think I can safely say, every one of us was proud to be an American.

CHAPTER 31

January 1, 2004

"YOU'RE UP EARLY," I SAID JOINING SHIRLEY ON THE lanai. "Not often you get up before me. You okay?" As usual, we had stayed home and were in bed before ten o'clock last night, leaving the New Year partying to those young at heart and willing to brave the drunks on the road.

"Physically, I'm fine," she said, waiting for me to finish pouring coffee. "Mentally?" She paused and I just let her have a moment. "It's hard to explain, but I feel like the last few years have been consumed by so many medical issues, and the country still recovering from 9/11, that we haven't been able to plan or enjoy our retirement while we're still young."

I wasn't sure how to respond. Six more of Shirley's siblings had passed away in the last three years; of the eighteen Stephenson children, six were still alive, four in their seventies or eighties. Shirley had cataract surgery on both eyes, one year apart, which actually was a positive; however, her blood pressure was still not under control, and I worried about her shortness of breath getting worse. After 9/11, two of her nephews had joined the Army and were now flying Black Hawk helicopters in the same unit in Iraq, risking their lives daily.

I couldn't just tell her all families have issues, not when my parents had both been hospitalized at least a dozen times each; Mom now had congestive heart failure and Dad's lungs were getting worse. Of course, his falling again and this time breaking his pelvis was a major blow last June. And today, I sat here with a face recovering from a thirty-day skin cancer chemotherapy treatment which basically burned off forty percent of my skin.

"We've had our fair share of setbacks, that's for sure." I decided to agree with her, then change the subject. "On the bright side, we have had some positives—Chris and Adrienne got married; Jeff met Tami, who we adore, and you told him he better not lose her; Kim was cancer-free; Mom turned ninety and is still sharp as a tack; Dad received his twenty-five-year sobriety pin; I officially passed the ten-year no-smoking date.

"On top of that, I bought you Bigg Redd 6, one of the last 2002 Chevy Camaros made before production stopped; the Civilian and Military Society is thriving; the Submarine Museum is doing well; Saddam Hussein has been captured, and I love you." I smiled, and she actually grinned at my ending.

"Your cup is always nearly full," Shirley said, "and you're right. Time to stop feeling sorry for myself." She took a closer look at me, "Do you want me to get a cool cloth? I wish you'd never done this treatment. I'm not sure in the long run it will be worth it. You've been miserable for weeks."

"Water over the dam now," I said, trying not to use hindsight. "Oh, how could we forget another positive; all five Robinsons survived their house fire. That alone is a major blessing. Remember, the insurance investigator and fire marshal are coming tomorrow for our formal statements." Deacon and Fran Robinson and their three sons, who lived on our cul-de-sac, had lost their home to a massive fire in November. Shirley and I were directly involved with reporting, and I was first on scene.

"It was about 2310, or ten after eleven, Thanksgiving night," I said into the microphone that the fire marshal placed on the table to record our statements, "and I was heading to bed when I saw flames coming out of the roof on the attached garage of the Robinsons' house. I yelled to call 911, and I ran to the house to take a look." The fire marshal nodded to me and gave a thumb's-up.

"Coming out the front door were Deacon and the oldest boy, who is mentally challenged. He was in a daze, and when I asked him where the others were, he didn't respond. I got them safely in the grass and went through the front door where I found Fran and the baby coming down the stairs. I made sure they got out to join Deacon and went back in. The fire department was arriving.

"I found Raymond, their six-year-old child, in thick smoke at the top of the stairs and was carrying him back down when a fireman met me, covered us both up, and escorted us out. By this time, the fire department was getting the fire under control, the medics were tending to the Robinsons and the police were doing crowd control." I pushed the mike toward Shirley, who made a short statement about the 911 call and rapid response time.

"That wraps it up," the fire marshal said as she finished. The insurance investigator asked if I thought there was anything suspicious about the family's reactions, and when I said no, he said he had enough to agree with the fire marshal that the fire was started in the clothes dryer, an electrical component shorting out and a complete accident. Case closed.

"That certainly starts the year off," I said as our guests left. "As bad as everything is, and the Robinsons displaced, at least the case is closed, they're all fine, and they were fully covered. I even heard them say it was possible to rebuild. Should be interesting."

A week later, more bad news arrived. "I love you too, Mom," I said, hanging up the phone. Shirley was sitting next to me, knowing this call about Dad wasn't good. I turned to face her.

"He fell again. Tripped over his oxygen tubing and re-injured his pelvis. January 9, thirtieth and final day of my chemo treatment, and suddenly, I don't feel like celebrating." My face looked like a rotten radish, red with black-burned skin, which would hopefully fall off, and I'd be free of skin cancer. That was our hope anyway. A follow-up appointment in three months would determine the actual results.

Dad remained in the hospital over the weekend and on Monday was moved into a rehabilitation facility to get his strength back and ability to walk, even if with a walker. Tuesday night, Marlys called to inform us that he had taken a turn for the worse, his lungs were failing, and he was back in the hospital. Mar had traveled to Minnesota so many times this past year and, definitely feeling guilty, I felt it was my turn to do my fair share of family support.

Against my dermatologist's better judgment, he understood and respected my request, I was medically cleared to travel to the below-zero weather. I assured him I would cover my face with Vaseline when outdoors.

On January 21, Chris, now stationed in Washington D.C., arrived at the Brainerd airport as I did from Georgia. We were greeted with an actual temperature of twenty below zero, wind chill minus forty. Scott drove up from Minneapolis, and we all gathered at the hospital the next day.

I talked to the nurse about the pain Dad was in and asked if there wasn't something his doctor could do. I was told everything possible was being done. Early in the evening, the head nurse took me aside and said he was going to look in on Dad. When he came out, he nodded to me. I knew what he meant and started the farewell conversations.

Each grandson took fifteen minutes alone with their grandfather to say goodbye, and as they joined their grandmother in the family waiting room, I went in for the final time. Mom followed me and would be the last person with Dad when he passed. I never told anyone about my last conversation with the nurse, and no questions were ever raised. It was my father's time and a blessing he was no longer in pain.

Chris went home with Scott, and I stayed with my mother in her assisted living apartment and helped make family and friends notifications, as well as arrangements for Dad's celebration of life. After several busy days and tons of phone calls, we felt we had completed our task and settled for a simple meal of grilled cheese sandwiches, tomato soup, and glasses of milk the night before I departed. It was then my turn to have the talk I always hoped would take place, the timing just had to be right.

"Mom, why don't you rest and we'll have a private talk?" At ninety-one years of age, she was still as sharp as ever, and a little smile appeared on her worn but still beautiful face. I brought us fresh cups of coffee and placed hers on the end table within easy reach.

"That sounds like a line I used the day you returned from your first enlistment," she said, getting relaxed in what once was Dad's chair.

"Yes, I confess, I stole it from you," I said quickly, and she let out a little laugh. "I don't feel bad though, didn't a lot of people use your lines, even Hubert Humphrey at the 1948 Democratic Convention?" Now, she was all-out laughing.

"Seriously, Mom, you told me things you had never shared with anyone else, and I haven't breached that trust. Now, I would like to do the same with you. You said someday I would face a turning point where I had to make a decision and, no matter what I decide, don't look back. Two things: You were right about my coming to that fork in the road and making a difficult decision, and I have never looked back."

"Too bad we don't have something to drink," Mom said out of the blue, catching me off guard. "Don't look surprised, Rich, it was your dad who had the drinking problem, not me, and he never batted an eye when I occasionally had a little social pick-me-up. Marlys usually joined me."

I excused myself and when I returned, I had a bottle of merlot. "You mean like this? I thought you couldn't have alcohol in your residence so kept this in my suitcase for another time."

"The heck with them," Mom said. "Crazy to tell people over seventy-five they can't have a drink if they want. I'm ninety-one, what're they going to do to me. Pour me a glass, would you, a small one. It wouldn't be good if I have a heart attack tonight." She looked forty years younger.

After pouring us our wine and Mom making a toast to Dad, she asked me to continue. I told her what I was really thinking during my first six months back in 1970, how the Vietnam protests closed down schools and my plans for the future, and then finding myself married and no set path into the future. I told her how I had been getting ready to have a serious talk with Mary when I got the call for an interview with the CIA and was offered a job that would provide a wonderful career opportunity. My mother never interrupted me, just smiled, and I knew she understood. I had come to that fork in the road, made my decision, and never looked back.

Our talk lasted almost two hours, and I shared other little tidbits about my life, some personal and some behind-the-scenes background, declassified, of several events I was involved in and unable to discuss, none of which I ever shared with anyone else. Nothing surprised her that I did, only what I sometimes got into, or away with. I'm sure most children have a close bond with one or both their parents, but I don't think many reach the level of love and respect my mother and I had together. *Call me biased; I am. No one can hold a candle to Angie Herman.*

My cab arrived to take me to the airport, it had warmed up to a balmy five degrees below zero, and as we were walking to the outside door, Mom and I hugged and said goodbye. Walking out I heard my mom say, "I have to ask, son, do you ever regret not taking the fork in the road and going with the CIA?"

I smiled, waved, and said, "Who said I didn't?"

Months went by, and September brought a big day for the Herman family. I drove up to the gate at the entrance of the Office of Naval Intelligence (ONI) Command, Washington, D.C., and a Marine in dress uniform rendered a smart salute. I was in my dress white uniform, which still fit well, and returned the salute. My retired ID card was screened, and I was handed a VIP parking permit and directed to my parking destination.

"How does that feel, Commander?" Shirley said. "Been a long time." She was being a little playful, but I knew she was still proud of our military connection.

"Feels normal, actually," I said. "But this is Chris's big day. You and I are just reaping all the benefits of that—and then seeing our granddaughter."

Chris's mom was going to be here, but Scott and Hannah, newlyweds still, were in the process of moving to King of Prussia, Pennsylvania. They had been married August 28 at a small ceremony at his mother's house. We'd have to plan another day to see them.

It had been a busy couple of months for Chris and Adrienne. Alexis Kaiulani Herman was born August 25, and Chris had found out he was chosen for advancement to chief petty officer just weeks before. Every year, September 16 is the worldwide Navy Chief Advancement Day, and today we would witness one of the greatest moments of any enlisted sailor's career: taking off the dungarees and donning khakis for the first time, and discarding the well-known dixie cup hat for the combination cover. Today, the members of this group would become that person they have heard about for years, "Go ask the Chief."

The ceremony was well organized and professionally done, like the dozens I had been to before. We couldn't have been prouder of Chris, and, although his wife was an Air Force tech sergeant, I think she knew how special this particular advancement is to the Navy.

Following the festivities, we went to the kids' home and met our granddaughter, Alexis. Chris' mom and stepdad were here too, and after greeting them, Shirley and I got to meet and spend some time with the other proud grandparents, Leo and Barbara Marks. Two things for sure were evident this day; one, Alexis was a beautiful child born into a wonderful family; and two, there would be no problems between the grandparents.

Driving back to our hotel, I took Shirley's hand. It had been a wonderful day. "As much as things change, there's still many that stay the same," I said. "I hope they never change this tradition of the chiefs' initiation and advancement ceremony. Every time I attend one, I feel so proud of our military heritage and pray we never lose it."

I was getting emotional, turned right at the next light, and followed the signs for the Washington Navy Yard. Shirley knew exactly where we were going. It was time to dangle our feet over the pier and watch a sunset. It had been a long time since we had been here: our private place.

CHAPTER 32

January 1, 2006, Little Yellow House

"A BEAUTIFUL AND WARM MORNING TO START A NEW year," I said, pouring a cup of coffee for my bride. "This might be our last day out here on the lanai for a while, though ... cold front coming in."

"Enjoy it while we can then." Shirley sounded chipper. "Today, I'm good just taking it easy and starting the year making calls to family. What time do you want to call Mom?"

"I think she's having dinner and watching all the football games with the Irenes. Let's call around two this afternoon, and we might be able to talk not only to her but also Gary, Jackie, and their family."

We wanted to see how their daughter, Sonya, was doing, after her kidney transplant about a year ago; fortunately, Wayne, her brother, had been a match. It was a blessing—and a big step to donate one of your organs. I was also remembering how amazing it was that, during testing for a donor match, doctors found an infection in Gary requiring life-saving surgery.

We planned our calls for the day, and first on the list were Jeff and his bride of four months, Tami. It's always interesting when some people become race fans, and these two were no exception. Jeff, like his sister, Kim, had become a die-hard Jeff Gordon fan. His new wife had been a long-time Dale Earnhardt fan, and after his tragic death at the 2001 Daytona 500, like many, she became a Dale Jr. fan. It was only fitting they were married on 8/24 last year—in honor of their driver's car numbers—and we attended their beautiful wedding at the home of a friend of theirs in Orlando on a golf course. Shirley and Jeff had become very close again these last few years, and I loved him and Tami like my own children.

On a chilly day in February, I hung up the phone and looked at Shirley. "That was a strange call from Mom. She said how much she'd like to see Chris and Adrienne after their second baby is born." Adrienne was due in two months.

"At first, it was like any other call and then she seemed to get very serious, and sounded solemn when she asked me to fulfill one more request. When she said goodbye, she said, 'I love you, son.' How often has she ever said that aloud? Almost like a goodbye." Shirley gave me a hug and nothing more was said.

Mom passed away five days later, February 15, 2006, at age ninety-two. Shirley was fighting a bad cold and fatigue so we decided she should stay home. I flew to Minneapolis and joined Chris, Scott, Marlys, and Jim to plan her memorial service. Or, should I say, we followed Mom's directions. Her pastor from the St. Paul Unitarian Church, and friend of many years, Reverend Arthur Armstrong put it best during his sermon.

"We gather here today," he started, "to celebrate the life of Angeline Aldea Herman; mother, grandmother, great-grandmother, sister, aunt and known to most as just Angie. Usually, I meet with the family to gather notes and their thoughts to prepare for my talk, but with Angie that was not the case. You see, she had already choreographed her funeral service from the music we'd hear, passages to be read, right down to the seating assignments, I think." The audience roared with laughter because that was her.

"In fact, almost every word I am about to speak was approved by her. Of course, this is why so many are here today, Angie told us to be." The crowd not only laughed but cheered, all in deep respect for this brilliant, wonderful woman.

After what may have been the most upbeat funeral service any of us had ever attended, the large crowd assembled for a social gathering in the church basement. I took a moment to visit my mother one last time.

"You'd be proud of Reverend Armstrong and your family today, Mom. Chris wore his chief's dress blue uniform, and Scott and I joined him to honor you with our own private Navy farewell salute. Your final wishes were carried out without a flaw and the sadness and crying was replaced by happiness and laughter, just as you hoped. And I haven't forgotten what turned out to be our final talk. I found the box; the letters are intact, and one day I'll fulfill your request and write that book."

"I know you're happy with your doctor," I said in my most understanding voice, "but we don't have a choice. The new rules say when you turn sixty-five, you must start seeing a civilian doctor. My understanding is the military is trying to lessen the burden on the military care system and dependents are being forced into the civilian world for health care."

"They should grandfather it," Shirley said adamantly. "All these years going to the clinic and now they are turning us away like we don't matter. And they're charging us now to boot. What other promises are they going to break?"

Shirley had a good point. Military retirees, like myself, had been promised free health care for ourselves and families (spouses as long as they remain a dependent and children until at least eighteen) after twenty years active-duty service. I retired in 1997 with thirty years service and we had Tricare Medical Insurance coverage. At first, our health care was free but then we started being charged $130 a person or $260 a family annually. I even heard they were thinking of charging for prescription drugs. Technically, Shirley was right about breaking their promise but it was hard to complain when some of our civilian friends were paying over $800 a month for less coverage than we had.

"Good argument, dear, but let our service representative and politicians fight it out. Bottom line is, you turn sixty-five this month and we need to pick a doctor from the list we have on those that accept Tricare Insurance and are accepted as Primary Care Providers by the government. There are only four in our area."

Shirley looked at me and smiled. "Let me see the list." She had vented enough and now would do what she always did, accept the inevitable and move forward. "One of these is a pediatrician so I hardly think she is in consideration. One is family practice medicine but it says in practice over forty years so likely older than me, let's rule him out. That leaves two. I would like an Internist if possible. A Dr. Thomas C. Windsor III is listed here and he is an internist. It also said he recently opened a new practice in St. Marys. Would you call his office and see what you can find out?"

I looked at the paper in my hand with all of Shirley's information I thought they may ask for. Little did I know, as my call was answered, this would be one of the most important phone calls of our lives.

"Hello, Mrs. Herman," the nurse said entering the exam room. "I am Sharon and I'll be asking you a few questions and taking your vitals before you see Dr. Windsor. I did give the doctor the copies of your military medical records that you provided and I'm sorry if this seems redundant but, as a new patient, I want to get a good baseline for the doctor. Is this your husband with you and is it okay if I ask these questions, many personal?"

Shirley laughed and said, "Yes, this is my husband and we've been married over twenty-four years. There isn't much he hasn't seen or heard about me so I don't think you're going to shock him now." She winked at me; I could tell she liked the nurse immediately. "Go ahead, Sharon, ask away."

After the pre-exam, Sharon left and said the doctor would be with us shortly. I said, "So far, so good." Before I could continue, the door opened and in walked a big guy, young, over six-foot and built like a linebacker, short brown hair and a no-nonsense expression.

"Mrs. Herman?" he said offering his hand to her. He turned to me, "and Mr. Herman?" I nodded, stood and we shook hands. He pulled up a chair, extended his legs in front of him, placed Shirley's medical chart on them and crossed his hands behind his neck. "First of all, thank you Mr. Herman for your service and you Mrs. Herman for supporting him during his career. I have the utmost respect for the military and their families. Today, we're going to get you established here and, after this examination, see if you still want me as your doctor."

"That's something I never heard before," Shirley said. "If I want you? For twenty-four years I have been treated by whoever is available. Not that I am complaining because I think for the most part, I have always had good medical care, but every time I have a doctor long enough to feel we know each other, they are being transferred."

"Yes, one of the downfalls of military medicine," Dr. Windsor said with a smile. "Believe me, it is just as frustrating for the doctors. I did a quick review of your past medical records, and I want you to know I appreciate you going through the effort to get them, but truthfully, I'll be doing my own thorough exam and making my own determinations of your health issues, if any. Shall we start?"

Fifteen minutes later, after what seemed to be a thorough exam, he made a few notations on her chart and pulled up his chair facing both of us. By the time he finished, Shirley realized she not only found a doctor she liked and trusted, she had found her match on talking straight. She answered every question, even when the answer was not one you wanted to give (smoking, drinking, exercise) and he pulled no punches on what, if she accepted him as her doctor, their goals would be and how to get there. Not only were they on the same page, they were singing the same song.

"Am I dreaming or did I just tell my life history to a complete stranger?" Shirley asked as we drove home. "I have never felt that comfortable with a doctor before. I hope my intuition is right this time, I really like him. He didn't say he'd try, he said he would get my blood pressure under control and get me seen by a cardiologist to better understand my arrhythmia. He's the first one ever to show concern about my bone density and at least he was straightforward and didn't skate around my heart and lung issues." She finally took a breath and looked my way. "That was one good phone call you made, Commander."

I could tell she was excited and I felt good too, saying, "I liked how he said he is an internist and specializes in certain areas but is no expert in all areas, nobody is. He is going to get you seen by the doctor who solely works in the area of concern. Like, he's already asking for a referral to a cardiologist and a pulmonologist in his physician group to look at you. You know how I respect someone who doesn't think they're the smartest one in the room." Shirley rolled her eyes at another one of my Hermanisms.

A month, and five doctor visits, later Shirley was on a new regimen of medicines and Dr. Windsor said he had a good baseline of her complete medical makeup. Her blood pressure would not be completely under control for about six months but they were on the right track. We were so pleased that, with his permission, I called Tricare and was approved to have Dr. Windsor assigned as my primary care physician (PCP) with an appointment in two months.

"We'll see how your blood work comes back but, other than something there, you seem in good health, Mr. Herman," Dr. Windsor said after my physical. "Any questions?" He sat back and was actually waiting to see if I did.

"Just one," I said, looking over at Shirley. "I've had a lot of physicals in my sixty years and this is the first one I didn't get the finger wave. Not that I am complaining, mind you."

Dr. Windsor smiled, "Fair question. Remember when we first met, I said if I see a reason to be concerned, I'll refer you to an expert? I could test your prostate, but I'm not an expert. If I see something in your blood work, where I am an expert, I'll send you to a urologist who does this for a living." Seeing that I was nodding my head, understanding, he continued, "Now, I have a question for you. Is that you I see driving a 2006 Red Monte Carlo?"

"Yes, sir," Shirley answered quickly. "We had six red Chevy Camaros, but they stopped making them after 2002 so we bought this car, Bigg Redd number 7, kind of our trademark. People see it and will stop to come say hi. If they start making Camaros again, we'll be first in line to buy one."

CHAPTER 33

April 16, 2007

WHETHER A HOLIDAY, BIRTHDAY, OR SPECIAL occasion, Shirley had always been hard to buy a gift for. Although she dressed well, she didn't own any designer clothes or ask to get pampered at the spa or get an expensive haircut. She didn't like large crowds; socializing, to her, had been going to the Pub or CAMS for a drink with friends and calling it a day. Unfortunately, those days ended when the Pub was closed and demolished to make a small strip mall and CAMS was forced to close its doors when Duff got too sick to keep it open, and the board just faded away.

The one thing Shirley did enjoy getting was a nice piece of jewelry, and over the years I managed to give her several lovely necklaces, earrings, and bracelets. I had no problem in Hawaii, and she now owned several specially made Hawaiian gold bracelets. One rule though, each piece had to be practical, not flashy or gaudy—a lesson I learned last year. For Christmas I had bought her a diamond dinner ring, which I thought was beautiful. Shirley took one look at it and refused to put it on saying, "What do you want me to look like?" I took it back and downsized, big time.

I wanted today to be one we would remember. I got together with Bradley, owner of Bradley's Jewelry Store in Kingsland, and we designed a unique bracelet, which Bradley himself made, guaranteed to be one of a kind. I then put my plan into effect. Our good friend from CAMS, April David, who now worked at Beaches, a nice lounge/grill in St. Marys and our newest hangout, helped me organize my evening.

"I always dress nice," Shirley snapped when I said let's dress up tonight. "I'm also always on time, stop telling me you want to leave by six." A minute later she walked out, looking great. "It's almost six, let's go then." I could tell she was frustrated with me.

I had to stall a minute so excused myself to go to the bathroom. I heard the doorbell ring and called out, "I wonder who that could be. Why don't you answer the door?"

I couldn't make out what was being said, but when I came out, Shirley was standing there with roses in her hand, being escorted out to her awaiting limousine by our personal chauffeur for the evening. I joined her in the back seat, we each accepted a glass of champagne, and I kissed her on the cheek, whispering, "This day is for you, Mrs. Herman."

When we arrived at Beaches, our limo door was opened and Karl, April's husband, greeted us and escorted us to a private table decorated with balloons and a banner proclaiming, "Happy 25th Anniversary, Rich and Shirley." April served us our usual drinks, a Miller Lite and a Dewar's and water, and the dozen or so customers there cheered and toasted. To make it a David family trifecta, daughter Brandi served us Maine lobster, and I think all was forgiven from my pushing Shirley earlier.

April knew us well and brought Drambuie and coffee after dinner. The atmosphere couldn't have been better, and I handed Shirley her gift. Not often did my wife get emotional, but looking at what she just opened, tears came to her eyes. The single gold band with three diamonds (not too big, not too small) looked great when I placed it on her wrist.

At home, I chatted a moment with the chauffeur, watched the limousine drive off, and, by the time I got into the house, Shirley was already in bed. I smiled as I saw she still had her bracelet on and recalled what she said on the way home, "You outdid yourself this time, Commander." *No, I don't think I did as, deep down, I just knew this night had to be special, one she would always remember.*

The year flew by, and 2008 was upon us before we knew it. For the past several months, more and more I would ask people to repeat themselves, and last month for Christmas, rather than complain, my wife got me a gift certificate for a hearing exam. I never was a vain person, and when it was discovered just how poor my hearing was, I quickly and eagerly accepted the hearing aids.

"Do you hear that?" I asked. We had just left our local Beltone office, and I was now wearing hearing aids.

"That noise," Shirley said sarcastically, "is the turn signal. You just couldn't hear it before. I think you're going to find a whole new world out there, Commander."

I rode along, amazed at all I had missed over the years, and it was wonderful to hear my wife so clearly. "Maybe 2008 will be a good year after all," I said cheerfully.

We were about halfway home when suddenly I could hear well, but I started seeing what looked like dirty water in my left eye. "I think I have a problem." I pulled over, took a deep breath, thought for a minute, and realized where we were.

I drove the two blocks to the office of Dr. Grimm, our eye doctor. I walked in, apologized to the receptionist for not having an appointment, explained what was happening, and two minutes later Dr. Grimm was in the lobby looking at me. "Mr. Herman, I think you may have a detached retina."

She immediately took me to a room equipped to handle such an emergency, and after further examination, found three tears to the retina. Somebody was watching over me that day, as her emergency surgery not only saved my retina, but my sight in my left eye.

Amazingly, I was able to drive home, my left eye completely covered, and lay back in the recliner with my head still and facing to the right. Dr. Grimm said I should try to remain like this as much as possible for the next twenty-four hours. When it came to our health, especially eyesight, we followed directions well.

Once settled, I looked at Shirley and smiled. "Maybe I'll regroup on my comment about the start of 2008. On the positive side, I can hear now and still have my sight."

"Hey, Mama," Jeff said, entering our room. It was the week before Christmas, and we were in Orlando to visit him and Tami. He picked his mother up, gave her a swing around, and gently set her down. He turned, shook my hand, gave me a hug, and thankfully, left me on the ground. "Hi ya, Rich. It's great seeing you guys."

"Hi, Tami," I said giving her a hug and getting her into the room and conversation. She looked wonderful as usual. About five-ten and fit, she had long, shiny jet-black hair and one of the greatest smiles I'd ever seen. We were right when we told Jeff not to lose this one.

"You're welcome to stay with us," Tami said. She gave her mother-in-law a hug, and I asked everyone to take a seat. Shirley sat next to her youngest on the couch and wasn't about to let go of his hand.

"We appreciate that," I said, "but you'll soon learn that we always like to stay at a local hotel, not make a fuss, and do things on our own clock. Now, let me get you a drink before we go to dinner."

We were staying at the Crowne Plaza Airport, Orlando, and we were upgraded when we checked in to one of their suites. Along with the bedroom, bath, and kitchenette, there was a visiting area large enough to seat six. This worked perfectly for the reason we were here. Shirley had told Jeff she just wanted to spend a couple of days, the week before Christmas, to see them and relax. She was about to tell them why she really wanted to be here. I served everyone the drink of their choice, and after a few minutes of catching up, I nodded to Shirley.

"Jeff, Tami," Shirley said. "I wanted to see you now because last week I learned that I'm showing the early signs of congestive heart disease, and, as if that isn't bad enough, my lung functions are slowly getting worse." You could see the concern in their eyes, but they let her go on.

"There's no immediate cause for great alarm, but I am realistic and don't want you to wake up one day and be surprised. I have a great primary doctor now, Dr. Thomas C. Windsor III, great name, isn't it, and also two cardiologists who will be following me closely.

After the holidays, I'll be going in for another assessment. Until then, I'm enjoying life and taking it a day at a time."

Driving home, two days later, Shirley seemed relieved she had shared her health with the kids. "I told Jeff I'd call Kim when I got home," she said. "With the two of them being close and talking often, I didn't want him to feel he couldn't talk about it with his sister." She lowered her seat back all the way down and stretched out. "Thank you for supporting me and doing this trip. Now, let's go home and enjoy the rest of the year." A few seconds later, she patted my leg. "Mission complete, Commander."

CHAPTER 34

March 9, 2009, Kingsland

"DR. WINDSOR SAID HE'D CONTACT THE EMERGENCY room and tell them we're coming," I said, as calmly as I could while driving as fast as possible toward the Camden Medical Center.

Shirley had been having coffee, now decaffeinated, and doing a jigsaw puzzle when she felt her heart beginning to race. I called our doctor's office, and he said to take her straight to the ER.

"Here we are, honey, and look, they're already outside." As soon as I pulled up, two medical personnel helped my wife out of the car, and a third was taking her blood pressure and giving her oxygen. In less than a minute, she had disappeared into the ER, and I parked the car. As I walked back to the entrance, I thought about what Shirley said on the way, "You can toss all my cigarettes, Rich, I think my smoking days are over."

I received several updates, thanks to Dr. Windsor, and was finally allowed to see Shirley after four hours—only through the window and waving. She was not only going to be admitted, she was headed for the intensive care unit (ICU). It was seven p.m. before I was allowed to actually see her and hold her hand. Dr. Windsor and Dr. Finney, her lead cardiologist, then briefed me on what was going on. Our doctor had the heart specialist take the lead.

"Mr. Herman," Dr. Finney said, "Shirley's heart has entered stage two of congestive failure. For practical purposes, it just can't meet the demand on its own and needs our help. As usually happens, the lungs are then asked to work harder, and, in your wife's case, they too have weakened over the years and also now need our help. Just how much help is what we need to determine, and that is why ICU. Neither Dr. Windsor nor I want her unattended until we figure it out."

Five days later, I was sitting with Shirley, still in her ICU room, when Dr. Windsor stopped in to see her. "I understand you're making a fuss, young lady," he said, almost smiling. "I know you want to go home; hospitals are no place to be, especially on Saturdays. Let me see what I can do." He motioned for me to follow him out.

"Rich," he said, "do you think you can care for her at home? She'll be going home with a lot of meds and on bed rest for a while longer. You'll need to make sure she eats, takes her meds exactly as prescribed, and most likely have to help her every time she gets up. On the positive side, being at home is good medicine itself."

He handed me his business card with his personal number on the back. "This won't be easy; call me if you need to. I have never given a patient this number, I know a Navy commander would never misuse it." He smiled and patted me on the back.

At five p.m. I was still waiting for her discharge paperwork and list of medicines I needed to pick up. Dr. Windsor had been at the nurses' station over an hour working on it. To be safe, I called the Publix pharmacy and found out they were open until seven. I told them where I was and what I was waiting for, and the pharmacist herself got on the phone and said she would wait for me. At six-thirty, Shirley was discharged, and I drove her straight home, got her settled, and arrived at the pharmacy at twenty after seven. I knocked on the door, and Rachel Mertz let me in.

It was almost nine p.m. when I got home with seven new medications. Not only did Ms. Mertz fill the prescriptions, she went over each one and how and when to administer them. She even made a written schedule out for me and gave me her personal phone number if I had any questions. I had just met not only a good pharmacist but a really caring person.

Shirley was doing well at home until Sunday, March 29, as we were getting ready to watch the NASCAR race, I noticed she was not only starting to breathe heavily, she was losing consciousness. I called 911, and within five minutes the paramedics were on scene and providing aid. I followed them to the hospital, and luckily, Dr. Finney was still doing rounds and met me in the ER.

"Mr. Herman, your wife's lungs are maintaining fluid and causing her heart to have to work harder to keep the blood flowing. I think we're beyond helping her here, and I'm having her taken to Shands Hospital in Jacksonville. They have the best facilities for heart and lung patients. Once she is picked up for transport, I'll call Dr. Windsor and fill him in."

Shirley had a private room in the cardiac intensive care unit at Shands and was monitored 24/7 by one nurse who oversaw only two patients. Visiting was restricted to family only, and I was only allowed to see her five minutes each hour between nine a.m. and seven p.m. I spent a lot of time in the family waiting room watching the Food Channel. She now had a team including heart, lung, and kidney specialists looking over her, which sounds great, but no one was talking to me, or worse yet, the patient herself. Frustrated, Shirley signaled her nurse and expressed, as only she could, her desire to see the head doctor on her team.

"Mr. and Mrs. Herman," an older doctor said, entering the room, "I am Dr. Chen, the ICU department head, and I truly apologize if you feel like you're being left out. I honestly thought my team was keeping you informed. We're a teaching hospital, and sometimes my doctors get so carried away with our interns that we neglect the families." We accepted her apology and asked what exactly was going on with Shirley and was there a plan of action.

"We are having a hard time keeping fluid off the lungs with medication, so tomorrow we will conduct a thoracentesis, a fancy name for draining fluid from between her inner chest wall and her lungs. Taking this pressure away should allow the heart to return to doing its job under less stress. I would expect this to work, and you'll be able to go home in a day or two."

I thanked Dr. Chen for her update, and I was impressed when she saw me again, immediately after the procedure, and when she discharged Shirley to go home two days later.

For the next five weeks, Shirley was gradually getting stronger, and we even managed to get out a few times, twice for dinner and several visits to friends. But one morning she woke up not feeling well and began having trouble catching her breath.

Very soon, I took her to the hospital because of her difficulty breathing. Now, I saw Dr. Windsor entering the ER and waved as he entered exam room 3.

"Her lungs have gathered some fluid," Dr. Windsor said. "I'm pretty sure increasing her diuretic dosage will solve the problem near term, but it's time to face reality, Shirley needs to be on oxygen 24/7."

"Have you told her yet?" I asked.

"Actually," he said, "she mentioned it before I did. When I said it was time, she seemed disappointed but then agreed if it would help, do it." I smiled as we had discussed it being a distinct possibility. He continued, "I've already gotten approval from Medicare, and a medical supply company will be here shortly to show you how to use the portable bottles. They will then set up your oxygen generating system at home and show you how to operate it."

Later that day, I was escorting the owner of James Medical Supplies to his car. "Thank you, Mr. James," I said. "I feel confident we can handle it now."

Not only did he set up Shirley's oxygen system in our home and walk us through using it several times, he also had me assemble and put it online myself. A simple system, once you know what you're doing, but it can also be dangerous if not exactly put together. I thought back to submarine drills, and that night, did it in the dark.

Shirley had been on the oxygen about a week when I woke up one morning and realized she wasn't in bed. I thought she might be in the bathroom so called out to say good morning. Getting no answer, I got concerned and ran out to find her, which wasn't hard because I just had to follow her oxygen tube. I was amazed to locate her actually singing in the kitchen.

"Good morning, sleepyhead," she said. "I decided it was time we had a decent breakfast, on me for a change. Pour yourself some coffee." I did just that and sat at the kitchen table. "This is the first day in a long time I actually felt like getting up and doing something. I think this oxygen has finally started working its magic."

"If you remember what Dr. Bannon said," I chimed in. "The day you quit smoking, your lungs would start to heal. After three months, your lungs no longer bring a further risk to your heart, and the lung functions start to heal." When Shirley was diagnosed with COPD and having fluid on her lungs, I called my friend and now director of pulmonology at the Navy Hospital, and he talked to us about how proud he was of Shirley quitting smoking and what she could expect. "You're past the three months now."

Still not a big fan of his, Shirley did manage to say, "Well, I never said he wasn't a great doctor. After all, I still have you, right?" She served me bacon, eggs, and toast to go with my orange juice and coffee.

"I've been thinking. We skipped over our anniversary; you had no birthday, and mine is coming soon. Let's celebrate them all today while I feel good. I'd like to get my hair done, and if I'm up to it, could we go to Darnell's Landing tonight? It's time I get out and get used to people looking at me, this oxygen isn't going away, and I want them to know I am not either. One oxygen bottle should do."

One thing I have learned the past several years, first with my mother and now with my wife, is women always feel better when they have their hair done. Luckily, the last time Shirley had her hair done, it was at a new salon, where the owner and top stylist, Maurice, hit it off with her. He said he was going to do only a few clients himself; Shirley would be one of them. Even last minute, he would see her that day. I picked her up, and her hair looked great. She was excited how Maurice gave it a little different style, and it was wonderful seeing her with a little extra bounce in her step.

Darnell's Landing was one of the few fine dining facilities in Camden County and provided fantastic sunset views on the St. Marys River. Arriving just as the sun was going down, we were seated at a table with an unobstructed view, and the atmosphere couldn't have been better. It was great getting out again and seeing Shirley enjoy herself. She was relaxed, and I could tell her being seen on oxygen was not going to be a negative factor after all.

We had barely left the parking lot when she fell asleep. I helped her switch from the portable to the home oxygen and helped her to bed. It was a terrific day.

———✦——— 🌳 ———✦———

"Green flag," I shouted as the cars went past the start/finish line. "Go, Rusty," we both shouted and toasted with our beers, Shirley's unopened and symbolic. I put her beer back in the refrigerator and was heading back to watch the race when … *BAM!* It was a car crash, right outside our door. The power went out. "Honey, call 911."

Running to the scene, I found our next-door neighbor slouched over her steering wheel and ran to the driver side door. She had backed out of her driveway, crossed into our yard, and hit the main power distribution box for our cul-de-sac. Her window was down and she looked dazed, but otherwise unhurt. I noticed several live wires and told her not to move. Onlookers were gathering, and I yelled to them to stay back.

The police were the first to arrive; I told them about the live wire, and they started putting up a perimeter tape. Next came the fire department's rescue squad, who immediately got the live wires secured and were able to remove my neighbor and give medical assistance. I suddenly realized—*no power*—and ran as fast as I could to check on Shirley.

"I'm okay," she said, pointing to the portable oxygen. As soon as power was lost, her oxygen machine shut off, and she quickly switched over to her backup system. "Mr. James's training paid off," she said with a big smile. "But this is my last bottle, Rich, good for three hours at most." We had used two of her three backup bottles the other day, and I was going in Monday to have them replaced. "I hope power comes back by then."

The Georgia Power Company was on the scene, and I looked for someone who looked in charge. "Excuse me, sir," I said to a likely candidate, "can you tell me how long it'll be before power is restored?"

"Probably not until tonight," the worker said. "This box only affects your five houses here so our priority is to secure this box wiring, shut it down, and then schedule repair. We have several other calls that need us first."

"My wife is on oxygen," I said, "and her portable system may not last three hours. If I'm going to have to relocate her and all her equipment to another area with power, I need to know now so I can make arrangements."

The worker nodded, "Hang on, sir." He got on his radio. "Dispatch, we have a lady here on oxygen, you need to up this site to a priority one and let me fix it now."

Within twenty seconds he received an emergency work order giving his crew authority to repair this system, and if he needed any additional assistance, manpower would be sent. He turned to me and said, "My crew will have this up in less than two hours." He smiled, shook my hand and went to work. "All right, guys, we have a Priority One, let's get this fixed."

Just over an hour later, power was restored. I got the worker's name and ID number and offered the crew water and sodas. I told them if they came back after their shift was over, it would be adult beverages on the house. They all cheered and waved to Shirley, who stretched her tubing out the front door, before they departed to another priority. Georgia Power's response was awesome, and I hope the letter I would write to the company president and the local district manager made its way down to the workers themselves. I firmly believe that giving a little praise can go a long way, and it costs nothing but a few minutes time to maybe change someone's life.

"I think we dodged another bullet today, Commander," Shirley said. "When the power first went out and I was forced to breathe on my own, I managed, but it was difficult and I don't know how long I could do it. I wasn't scared, but I sure was relieved when I got the bottle hooked up."

I didn't answer right away. The thought of "what if" was too real as I thought about how close we came to having a life-threatening situation. This could not happen again, and I knew what to do. "Lesson learned," I finally responded. "I was scared too, and never again. I promise you."

I made one phone call Sunday, and Monday morning, a Lowe's generator, capable of powering not only the oxygen machine but the whole house, was installed. After a ten-minute training session, I was capable of starting and maintaining our new back-up power system. Hoping we never had to use it, we now had the peace of mind that a power loss, even at the hands of a lousy driving neighbor, would not threaten Shirley's life.

We followed every medical instruction, including small exercise routines and breathing exercises, but Shirley was still showing gradual congestive heart failure. The decision was made to insert a pacemaker, and the procedure was scheduled for the end of July at Shand's Hospital. The day before the operation, she called Jeff and her closest brother, Tom. She was upbeat and wanted to let them know we would be visiting as soon as the old ticker got some needed maintenance. Over the years, I think my cup-half-full outlook had grown on her.

Dr. Finney allowed me to stay with Shirley during her pre-op. The surgery was scheduled for seven a.m. When the transport team arrived to take her away, a nurse intervened and said there was a delay. The anesthesiologist assigned had refused to be part of the team, saying she thought the patient wasn't healthy enough to survive the surgery. Dr. Finney told us she was a very cautious doctor and always refused any surgery that had a chance to have complications. A new anesthesiologist was briefed, signed off on the procedure, and Shirley was transported to the operating room, an hour later.

The noon news was coming on when a nurse came in to brief me. "Mr. Herman?" he said. "Dr. Finney wanted me to inform you that the surgery is taking longer than expected, but your wife is doing fine, and he is still trying to get the pacemaker attached. It'll be a while longer but he'll come see you as soon as he is done."

I thanked him, at least now I knew something, and went for a walk and a fresh coffee. It was after the five o'clock news when another nurse came and gave me a similar report. Nine hours, I knew this was not good.

"Rich," Dr. Finney said, entering the waiting room a little after seven, "she is stable and in post-op." He sat down and couldn't hide his exhaustion. "I tried everything possible, and then some, to get the pacemaker attached for perfect operation, but I was only able to get one of the two leads where they needed to be. The surgery is still a success as far as helping Shirley's ability to pump her blood, but without the second lead attached, she could still experience arrhythmia. I'd say the improvement will be around eighty percent."

"Once she has recovered from the surgery," I asked, "will she be able to get her strength back and even off the oxygen?"

"Good questions, and she will get stronger, but she will probably need oxygen the rest of her life." I nodded, and he was about to stand, then sat back. "I know you like your doctors to be open and not pull punches. I have given this thought and think you should know, after observing her organs up close, I don't think Shirley has much more than a year to live."

The hospital made an exception to their rules and allowed me to escort my wife to her room a little after midnight. She was intubated, and I was told would be unconscious for several more hours. I knew the night charge nurse, and she gave me a few minutes alone with my bride. "I don't know if you can hear me, but you're back in your room and doing well after your surgery. I'll be back in the morning, and we'll start making our plans to visit our family and friends. Rest now, I love you."

I thanked the medical staff on duty, took the long walk to Bigg Redd and drove home with just one thing on my mind. *Do I, or do I not, tell Shirley what Dr. Finney said?*

"Yes, Charles, I'll pass along your good wishes." Chevrolet was making the Camaro again, and I had just finished ordering the new 2010 Camaro LT, Bigg Redd 8, from his dealership. Over the years, Mr. Calvin had become our friend and always liked to talk to Shirley and give a little extra bonus on our deals. Jerry, still his top salesman, must have told him I was on the phone because the owner picked up to ask about Shirley.

"Yes, sir, I hope to have her home in a few days. That's why I called Jerry on the phone to get my special order in." I listened a moment. "That will be great—you're guaranteeing Bigg Redd will be ready before she's discharged. Fantastic."

"What can I get you?" I asked Shirley. I brought her home this afternoon, after her six-day stay at Shand's following her pacemaker surgery, and got her settled in her recliner. I had made my decision on my dilemma of telling her about her prognosis and planned on bringing the subject up right away.

"I'd say our new Bigg Redd was enough, Commander. What a beautiful car and a great surprise." I was about to say something when she continued, "It's time we have that conversation I think is important for all couples to have, before it's too late. I know my operation was a hard one and not totally successful. I also know I will be sixty-eight years old in a couple weeks, and my family history shows a longevity of around seventy, so let's be realistic. I am probably looking at one, maybe two more years. You're doing well and hopefully have many years left. I'm ready to deal with that, are you?"

I should not have expected less. "No secrets between us, that's always been our rule. Dr. Finney told me about the same thing after your surgery." I waited for her reaction, and got none. "Yes, I am ready to deal with that. No one says we have to like it, but we're in this together, always have been, always will be." Shirley put her arms out, and I went over and gave her a hug.

"Thanks, Commander. This conversation will stay between you

and me. I need you to be strong with me. Now, let's take a look at what we want to do and how we can do it for the next year. I will do all I can to help keep me healthy and prove them wrong by living a lot longer, but I want quality of life, not just more of it. First, I want to see Maurice to fix my hair.

"Second thing, get an appointment with legal on base. Let's update our wills and get our estate in order. We both have always said that is our responsibility, not our children's. Third, and yes, I am saying this, let's go see Lori and make sure all our banking is in order and take a look at the status of our investments. I don't want you to go homeless and starve to death once you're on your own." She said that in such a matter-of-fact tone, I wondered if she actually believed it.

CHAPTER 35

January 1, 2010, Little Yellow House

"WELCOME TO 2010," I SAID AS SHIRLEY JOINED ME IN the living room. "Too chilly for the lanai this morning; in fact, I think staying inside today will be a good idea." I was concerned that we were doing too much as, although she wouldn't admit it, I could tell she was tiring easier and had also lost some weight.

"That's fine with me," she said. "We've been active enough for a while. Not that I'm complaining, mind you, but a break for a few days will be fine." I had to allow her to judge her own body and set her limitations. To a point.

The past six months, since her heart surgery, we did just what she wanted and made quite a few trips to see family and areas we were always interested in visiting. Checked off our list were a visit to Kim and John's in Florence, Kentucky; several visits to Jeff and Tami in Orlando; a four-day visit to the Stephensons in West Virginia when Shirley's older brother Tom passed away; and Chris and family (Alexis, now five, Aliyah, three) had come to our home for a day. We had also gone to Daytona Beach, including a tour of the raceway; Cocoa Beach, Florida; Hilton Head, South Carolina; and finally, Tybee Island and Savannah in our home state, Georgia.

Every two weeks, Shirley would go in and have her pacemaker checked. We were always amazed how the technician would place a round disc over her heart and it would give a read-out of every skip in her heartbeat, every time the pacemaker was activated and for how long, and even predict her heart functions for the next several months. Other than a few dosage changes to her medicine, Shirley was doing as well as could be expected.

During her March visit with Dr. Windsor, he asked if she was having trouble swallowing. When she told him about her throat constantly being sore, he immediately got her an appointment to see an ENT specialist.

"Mr. and Mrs. Herman? I'm Dr. Stiles. Your doctor asked me to take a look at you. It's nice to see you here, Mr. Herman; for some reason, most spouses don't like to be present for my exams." He took a look in Shirley's mouth and felt around her neck. "I've been at this a long time, and I'm afraid your throat soreness is due to cancer, Mrs. Herman."

"I knew that was a possibility. Have we caught it early?" Shirley asked with a steady voice. "What's the next step?"

"We need to do a biopsy, find out what stage you are in, and go from there. I don't like to speculate this early because I don't want to alarm you any more than necessary, but I don't want to sugarcoat it either and pretend all is going to be okay. I can call Dr. Windsor for you, but he will agree with me that the sooner we start aggressive treatment, the better. I recommend you let me do the biopsy today."

A week later, Dr. Stiles gave us the results of the biopsy: two tumor masses, stage four. As much as we had hoped for stage one, and being able to treat it like my floor of the mouth cancer by just cutting it out, Shirley's had progressed too far and required more extensive treatment. Radiation and chemotherapy would both be required. After a referral, an initial assessment appointment for cancer treatment was set for two weeks later with the Southeast Georgia Health System.

"They just entered the hotel," I called out. We were back in the same Crowne Plaza suite we always booked in Orlando, and through

our view of the lobby I could see Jeff and Tami arriving. I had their drinks ready by the time they knocked on our door.

"Hello, Mama!" Jeff, with his usual gusto, picked up his mother and, noting her oxygen tubing and machine, set her down gently and kissed her on top of her head. "Impressive, Rich, hauling that big machine and getting it set up."

I was already serving everyone's favorite adult beverage, and we settled in the same spots as before. "Thanks," I answered, "the medical supply company just told me to be careful and they were fine with it making the trip." I didn't tell them how difficult it was to fit in Bigg Redd and haul up to the room.

"Shirley," Tami said, "you look good, but we are a little concerned. This is like déjà vu."

"I know, kids," Shirley said. "Sorry to be the bearer of bad news again, but I've been diagnosed with throat cancer and will need to go through a series of radiation and chemotherapy. I wanted to tell you in person so you know I'm doing okay and ready to fight this next battle." Jeff moved closer to her and put his arm around her. "There's nothing any of you can do, but I owe it to you to be up front. You know I have Rich and he is giving me all that I need for support, but I may need you to look after him some too."

We had dinner, reminisced and enjoyed some laughs. Shirley was like her old self and never let on she was in pain or anything was wrong. There were tears when they said goodbye, but I think that was a good thing. I walked the kids to the elevator.

"She's one strong lady," I said as we waited. "Seeing you both and getting your love and support goes a long way in helping her. And she may not ask, but all prayers and thoughts these next few months are welcome." I wiped my eyes before going back into our room. Shirley was already asleep.

I was in the family waiting room at the Southeast Georgia Health System Hospital in Brunswick, while Shirley was having surgery. Last week, we met with her team leader and head oncologist, Dr. Morrell, and Dr. Skipper, lead oncology/radiation specialist. It was determined that eight chemotherapy and thirty-five radiation sessions would be required to fight her cancer—an aggressive schedule. Yesterday, she was fitted with the precision mask she would put on when receiving radiation. Today, she was getting a port inserted in her upper chest that would receive her chemo fluid and, because eventually she would need it, a stomach feeding tube.

"Mr. Herman?" a nurse said. "Your wife is in recovery and should be able to go home in an hour or so. I'll take you to her."

Shirley was lying in a bed, still hooked up to a monitor taking her vitals and an IV still in her arm. She was dozing so I just stood by her side and held her hand. The nurse came back an hour later and said, "Okay, Mrs. Herman, you can get dressed and go."

I was almost speechless, but recovered quickly. "Go home? Is anyone going to tell us about the surgery, what I need to do when I get her home? And I haven't a clue how to use this feeding tube."

"I thought you were trained, Mr. Herman," the nurse said, "I apologize. I'll show you what you need to know before you go. First …" The nurse demonstrated how to use the tube and had me practice several times, to the amusement of Shirley, who laughed every time I poured fluids all over the dummy I was practicing on. I hoped I'd be more proficient at home when actually feeding my wife.

Next, a technician came in and trained me on handling hazardous materials as I would be required to clean her chemo port and her wounds. Luckily, the Navy had trained me well so I had no problem, and was not skittish, doing what had to be done. They loaded us up with waste bins, bags, and everything required to meet safety regulations.

The next morning, April 14, I took Shirley to her first chemotherapy treatment. The staff in this unit was outstanding and explained every step along the way. I was amazed at the storage requirements and rules for handling chemo materials. It would even make a nuclear-trained submariner proud. The amount in the bag was checked, double-checked, and then signed off by a third person before it was hooked up to Shirley. Each of the eight patient stations had a small TV to watch and magazines to read. I remained at her side the entire time, which I found was an exception and not the rule for most patients.

Finished with her chemo, about four hours, we went to her first radiation treatment and found the same degree of expertise and control over the procedure. We were here less than an hour, the treatment itself just twenty minutes long. This was a Wednesday, and, after a seven-hour stay, day one was finished. In the future, Monday would be the day she would receive her weekly chemo, while radiation would be daily, Monday through Friday. Dr. Skipper would meet with us weekly to discuss the treatment's progress.

On May 3, halfway through her chemotherapy and with one-third of the radiation treatments done, we met with both Dr. Morrell and Dr. Skipper. We learned her tumors had decreased almost forty percent, and physically, she was doing as well as could be expected. I was becoming immune to "as well as expected" because no one could ever tell me what was expected. I saw my wife needing a wheelchair to go farther than fifty yards, losing weight, losing hair and getting weaker, with recovery after each session taking longer and longer. Her throat was getting to the point she could only handle soup and soft foods. And she was just halfway.

Shirley deserved something positive, and I placed a call to Maurice to ask a favor. When I explained where she was in her treatment, how weak she was, and the loss of some hair, Maurice didn't hesitate and made a time to see her when his salon would be closed. He met us when we pulled up, took over pushing her wheelchair, and told her he had a special afternoon set aside just for her. I went to do some much-needed grocery shopping.

"Hi, Rich," Rachel said as I passed by the counter in the Publix pharmacy. "By yourself?"

"Hi," I said in return. "Yes, Shirley is getting her hair done. I'm taking advantage and picking up some things. I hate to leave her alone for very long."

Rachel motioned me over to the end of the counter, away from other workers and customers. "Rich, I would never pry, but we go over all of Shirley's medications, and as your pharmacist, I know exactly what she is fighting and how sick she really is. You can't do this by yourself much longer or we'll be taking care of you too. Have you thought about hospice care?"

"We're not giving up yet, girl," I said maybe a little too strongly. "She has two more chemo sessions and two weeks of radiation. God willing, she'll start getting stronger and better."

"Hospice is not giving up," she said calmly, and I felt bad I had snapped at her. "It is just care for a patient to give them a better quality of life and, in time, they may be able to get off it. I'm going to give you some information to look over. Feel free to discuss it with me any time." She gave me her home phone number. "We all want what's best for Shirley, and you too, so don't be too quick to turn it down. Okay?" I took the information, gave her a hug and thanked her. She truly was a good friend.

"Wow, you look great, young lady," I said as Maurice wheeled my smiling wife out to the car. "And I mean that, honey. Maurice, you are a magician." With a big smile, he patted me on the back, helped me get her into the car, and stow the wheelchair.

"It's easy to make beautiful women more beautiful," he said. "And I enjoy my time with Shirley. She has given me lots of tips about taking care of our four-month-old baby boy. My wife will be impressed." I thanked him again as I entered the car. I noticed he had tears in his eyes, maybe thinking …

Shirley rang the bell after her last chemotherapy, and today she did the same as her thirty-fifth and last radiation session was over. The entire staff signed her mask and gave it to her as a going-away gift. Apparently, some patients display their masks, making them into planters or a showpiece. I had a feeling the one in her lap would find a home in her closet.

In the car, she fell asleep immediately; I knew she was having difficulty staying awake more than a couple hours at a time. We would meet with her doctors next week for another assessment on how to proceed with treatment.

"Shirley is in a lot of pain, and it's not only her throat," I said. Dr. Morrell had asked her how she was eating and, as it was too painful for her to talk, I replied for her. "Eating is very difficult, and I have gone from cutting food into small pieces to using a blender and getting one can of Ensure, her nutrition drink, into her through the feeding tube. Will her throat eventually get better now that the treatments are over?"

Shirley tapped me on the arm and made a hand motion. "She wants me to tell you that we did pretty good with the first couple of bottles of Ensure and then—I guess the line wasn't clear enough— one came back at me, and I was covered with a chocolate nutrition drink. It was the first time she had a good laugh in a long time and enjoyed every minute of me cleaning up." Everyone joined in for a moment of humor that released a lot of tension.

"Yes and no about eating," Dr. Skipper finally said. "Her tumors are still going down, which is a good sign. However, we cannot for certain say if we are in remission for several more weeks. As for the pain, I'm going to prescribe a fentanyl transdermal patch. It's applied directly to the body, and the medicine gets absorbed through the skin rather than having to take a pill. You will change it every five days. It's been very effective in many of our cancer patients.

"You have to follow the instructions, but as a submariner, I think you can handle one more thing." He smiled, knowing Shirley liked it when I was picked on. "I'll also get her other medications in liquid form so they're easier to swallow. If it's still too painful, use the feeding tube."

Dr. Morrell said, "We will monitor the progress weekly. Rich, so you don't have to take time coming here, rinse her port out every two days, and keep a close monitor on her incisions. If any sign of infection, come in immediately. We're doing what we can and will continue to do so. Any questions?" He started to get up.

"Yes, I do." I think I surprised him as he sat down quickly. "When Shirley's team was first started, I asked that our primary care doctor be kept informed, and you both said you would. I know you are the cancer and radiation specialists and in charge of her care for that, but I want him informed because, when you are done with your responsibilities, Dr. Windsor will be caring for her and he shouldn't have to ask us her medical condition. I don't really care about egos; I want professional courtesy shown to him."

"What did you say to Morrell and Skipper?" Dr. Windsor asked as soon as I answered the phone. "I just got a thirty-page report on Shirley covering everything diagnosed, prescribed, and recommended for further care of her. I have never gotten a report from those guys before."

"Maybe no one ever asked," I said, "or maybe it's just my dynamic personality. I did challenge their egos though, so be prepared for some backlash."

"Not a problem, my friend," he said. "The next time she's up to it, stop by and let me have a chat. I'm leaving word at the front desk that you have an open-door appointment, which means I'll see you at your convenience. Hope to see you soon."

We showed up the following week, on Shirley's sixty-ninth birthday, and were shown to Dr. Windsor's office, not an examining room. She was wearing one of her attractive new wigs; I had bought several real-hair styles for her to choose from, and if you didn't know it, you'd think it was her natural hair. Dr. Windsor came in, told her how impressed he was that her hair had grown back and wished her a happy birthday; then, let her tell him about how she was doing.

The bond these two had formed was amazing, and I couldn't have gotten her any gift that would have matched this visit. When we left, it was obvious we not only had the best doctor, but a dear friend.

CHAPTER 36

August 4, 2010

I LOOKED AT THE SPEEDOMETER, 135 MPH. I SLOWED Bigg Redd down to take Exit 29 off Interstate 95N and sped up again en route to the hospital in Brunswick. I had just fallen asleep, about ten p.m., when Shirley woke me to say she wasn't feeling well. I had applied a new fentanyl patch earlier in the evening, but neither of us thought that was the problem. I called the emergency number her team had provided and, to be on the safe side, was told to bring her in.

After getting her dressed and a new oxygen bottle hooked up, we left for the ER. I had gone about a mile when Shirley cried out in pain and was struggling hard to catch her breath. Already committed to the drive, I sped up in hopes of a police car seeing me and helping out. Murphy's law, no police in sight, and I pushed Redd. I made the forty-minute drive in just under twenty minutes and was met at the ER entrance. The first person on the scene yelled something out, and people appeared from everywhere to assist. It would be two hours before I knew what was going on.

"Mr. Herman, ah, Rich," Dr. Morrell said, "I happened to be making some late rounds and was able to take care of Shirley as soon as she came in. She is stable and resting now." We found a place to sit.

"Based on her symptoms when she came in, chest pain, hard to breathe, and the slower blood flow in her veins, I did an ultrasound and found a pulmonary embolism, or blood clot, had passed into her lungs. It's treatable, but with her heart condition, I'm calling in our team cardiologist for a second opinion." He looked to see if I was going to ask something, I guess. "You see, I can get past my ego." He actually laughed, which I didn't think he knew how to do, as he walked away.

"Hi, beautiful," I said when I finally got to see her. "Dr. Morrell said the cardiologist concurred with his diagnosis, blood clot, and there has been no adverse affect on your heart. They both said it is rare to have a clot when on blood thinners but not unheard of. That was scary, but you're okay now. What are the odds that your cancer team head would be here at midnight?"

"I'll admit I felt better when I saw his face," she said. "He may not have much of a bedside manner, but it sure is nice having him taking care of me." As she started to doze off, I quietly departed, knowing sleep was a blessing for her right now.

I drove home, at the speed limit, asking myself, *Just how much more can be thrown at you, Shirley?* I was about to learn that you shouldn't ask the question if you don't want to hear the answer.

"They're going to keep me another day," Shirley said softly as I walked into her room, expecting to take her home. Her ability to talk was day to day, and when she did, it was slowly and softly. "I have to have another biopsy done."

Caught off guard, I asked, "Biopsy of what?"

"I have a small lump under my left arm." She showed me. "I noticed it yesterday and mentioned it to the nurse. This morning, Dr. Morrell said, to be on the safe side, he'd like to do a biopsy. The reason I have to spend the night isn't because of the biopsy, he's also scheduling me for a full-body PET scan, and I have to fast twenty-four hours. Like I eat anything now. I wish I'd kept my mouth shut." She handed me a brochure titled "What to know about PET."

She couldn't mask her disappointment this time, and it was hard to see her, for the first time so obvious, starting to feel like with each battle she was losing the war. She had been here two days and was upbeat last night when told she would be released today. I looked at the information she handed me. PET, positron emission tomography. Even the name was depressing.

"They're just being cautious," I said, trying to sound upbeat. "It's better to stay one more night now, rather than having to come back. Besides, it'll give me another day to make the little yellow house look great for your return."

We went home the next afternoon. It would be ten days for the results of her biopsy tissue culture to be known, and a meeting was scheduled to discuss that as well as her PET scan results. The cancer team would then address our future treatment options and proceed with the next tailored recovery plan.

Shirley was down to 100 pounds when I got her home. Never big, she had always, except for a short time after returning from Italy, kept her weight between 115 and 118 pounds. I bought a digital scale and weighed her each morning and night. If I noticed a change of more than eight ounces, I would call her cancer team, and they would adjust her medication accordingly. Always giving it her best effort, she was getting weaker and was only taking small sips of liquids. We tried to get four cans of Ensure into her every day, through the feeding tube, but it took longer for her body to accept the fluid each attempt. Throughout it all, she remained positive and we refused to not try.

We met with the team on August 16. Nancy, a physician's assistant with the team who Shirley liked and befriended, attended and sat next to her on the left side, and I was on the right. Dr. Skipper was present, and Dr. Morrell, as team head, spoke first.

"You like us to be up front and honest so I'll just start with, I have no good news to share. Your biopsy came back positive for cancer in the lymph nodes, which has aggressively spread to your breast and the adjacent nodes." Shirley squeezed my arm.

"What?" I interrupted. "Her mammogram was negative just last month." I wasn't sure if that was relevant or if I was just scared and didn't want to hear more.

"As I said, it is very aggressive," he answered. "The PET scan shows that you still show some cancer in your larynx, and there are many spots on your lungs that are most likely malignant. I know this sounds horrible, but I do have a plan of action to help you. It's been over two months since you finished your chemotherapy and radiation. I recommend we start a new regimen next week and see if we can't slow the spread and reduce the size of your cancer. I think you should continue getting treatments."

Shirley, still composed, whispered, "Is there a chance to beat this or are we fighting a losing battle?"

"My colleague has given you the facts," Dr. Skipper interjected. "I think Nancy and I can take it from here and discuss your options." Dr. Morrell looked at him, nodded in agreement, and left. Then, Dr. Skipper turned to us and took off his glasses. He had tears in his eyes. Clearly, this man, with years and years of experience, still showed compassion for his patients.

"Rich, Shirley," he said, "Dr. Morrell wants you to go through another round of chemo/radiation so he can extend your life maybe a couple of months and his statistics look better. I recommend you say no to any further treatment; your body and mind have suffered enough. Go home and enjoy what life you have left." He wiped his eyes.

"I think you should consider hospice care, starting immediately. I know that sounds like you are giving up. You aren't. You are telling the world that you will go out on your terms, with best care for your quality of life and with dignity."

Dr. Skipper stood, walked over, and knelt next to my wife. He gave her a hug and said, "You're a beautiful woman who I have grown to respect and want only what is best for *you*. Not for this hospital or any cancer study. Nancy is our hospice coordinator and can tell you more about the program and how to transition to it, if you choose to. Whatever you decide, I will support you all the way. Go enjoy your husband and do it your way." Shirley hugged him back and he left.

I asked Nancy to give us a few minutes, and after she left it was just the two of us. "It's decision time," Shirley said softly. "I think we both knew this day wasn't far away, so no big surprise. Still tough to hear though." I felt it took everything in her to remain so composed and utter those few words.

Then, while I was thinking I should say something, she continued. "Have Nancy come back, and let's see about hospice, Rich. You can't do this by yourself any longer." Now, she had tears in her eyes.

Nancy returned, explained the hospice system provided by the Golden Isles company, as well as another hospice provider, and answered every one of our questions. At the end she said, "My job is to coordinate the transition to their care, I have no vote and don't want to sway you to one service or the other. It's your choice. If you don't want hospice care, I can help you get home care to meet your needs." She left again to let us have some time.

"I know you're exhausted," I said. "Let me do the talking, and you can nod or write down your thoughts." Shirley smiled and gave me a thumb's up. "In a nutshell. If we get home care only, nurses will come on a preset schedule based on your needs, but we will still have the same doctors responsible for your care, and they are limited by laws and ethics on just what they can do." Shirley nodded in agreement.

"With hospice care, we'll get the same nurses' care plus a 24/7 on-call service. Our team of doctors turn over your care to the hospice doctors, who decide your treatment based more on quality of life than prolonging life. Without saying it, Nancy inferred that they are not as constrained by strict laws with your medication dosage and, trying to give you comfort, can ethically push the envelope."

Shirley agreed. I made a quick call to Dr. Windsor and asked his advice before I asked Nancy to come back.

"We'd like to have Shirley transition into hospice care with Golden Isles," I said decisively. "We chose their service because our primary care physician, Dr. Windsor, supports them as do several of your staff doctors that are on their board." We signed some paperwork and the wheels were set in motion.

Dr. Skipper came in to give his support for our decision and wished us well. He then asked if he could walk us out and, pushing the wheelchair himself, he told us a little about how, this past year, he had to make a similar decision with his mother. He was thankful that, with hospice care, the few months his mother had left were much more comfortable. As we reached the door, he shook our hands and said, "Rich, I think I heard Shirley is a Dewar's connoisseur, I think you should make her a nice drink to enjoy tonight. Doctor's orders!"

After I got Shirley settled into her recliner, she was able to accept about twelve ounces of Ensure. I went to the kitchen and returned with two drinks. A Dewar's and water for her and a Miller Lite for me. She looked at me, confused, and then I showed her two straws. "Doctor's orders."

I put the straw in her drink, trapping some scotch in the lower part, then placed the straw gently between her lips and let the fluid flow. "Is that a smile I see?"

Her eyes were twinkling. I alternated dipping between my beer and her drink, filling each straw with the small amount and placing it in our mouths. It wasn't fancy but that didn't matter, we were having a date and nobody had to drive.

CHAPTER 37

August 30, Little Yellow House

GAIL, THE WEEKDAY DAYTIME NURSE, ASKED ME TO walk her out. I knew this wasn't for a chat about the weather. Shirley had been home in hospice care almost two weeks now.

The first day, a hospital bed was put in the living room, giving her a look out onto the lanai, the front bay windows, and her kitchen. I put the TV where she wanted it, and the Food Network had been on ever since. Receiving at-home caregiver training, I had to demonstrate I could effectively handle medications, feeding, personal hygiene, and handling of materials considered biohazardous.

The second day, after Gail had departed, a new prescription needed to be filled and, not willing to leave Shirley alone, I was trying to figure out a way to get it without calling the hospice service and asking for help. As I was thinking, the phone rang, and our friend, pharmacist Rachel, came to the rescue once again. She let one of her technicians off long enough to deliver the meds, which had to be signed for, and when I went for my wallet to pay, I was told Rachel had taken care of it. I made a note to write the Publix home office with a letter of commendation.

Each morning, Gail would visit, and the third day I had to call the emergency number for the night nurse, Richard, because I was having trouble getting her feeding tube attached properly after cleaning. He responded in half-an-hour and, after getting the tube operating again, stayed and talked to me for over an hour. After the fiasco with her first medication, hospice was now delivering all medications in person to our door.

One person Shirley liked and trusted the most was Margaret, a nurse's assistant, who came every Monday, Wednesday, and Friday to bathe her and change the bed. Last Friday, once it was cleared with hospice, she stayed while I went to get much needed groceries, and as Shirley said, "He needs a break." She was still worrying about me.

In the driveway today, Gail said, "Mr. Herman, Shirley needs to get more nourishment. I was able to get one can of Ensure into her, but she needs at least four a day." I nodded in agreement, and she continued, "I know it's hard and you're doing a great job, just push her a little more, and hopefully she'll respond. Right now, she is just tired and, frankly, who wouldn't be. She's a real fighter."

"I don't want to put you on the spot, Gail," I said, "but you said you've been doing this a long time. Realistically, how long can she hang on? And please call me Rich."

"Every patient is different, and that is the truth, not a cop-out. I will say, make sure your papers are in order, and if anyone wants to see her alive, they better plan to do it soon."

I went back in and sat on the edge of the bed. I picked up Shirley's purple foam brick with the Minnesota Vikings logo on it and tossed it in the air. With her unable to talk above a whisper, I had started sleeping on a mattress next to the bed and, if she needed me at night, she could throw the brick at me and wake me up. It worked well and she had used it several times.

I looked at her, still of sound mind, so tiny physically yet full of fight, and thought about what Gail had said. "Hey, honey, is there anyone you'd like to have visit?"

She nodded her head yes and whispered, "I don't want just anyone to see me like this. I would like to see the kids and," she hesitated, "Lori. But first, call Killebrew Funeral Home and see if they will send someone to see us. I don't want you to have to worry about me when I'm gone, and, like your mother, I'll do it my way." She actually had a little smile.

"Mrs. Herman," said Audrey Killebrew, co-owner of the funeral home with her husband, "you are the easiest client I have ever had. We will follow your instructions, including cremation, to the letter, and may I say again, I'm sorry we had to meet under these circumstances."

"You never cease to amaze me," I told Shirley when I returned from escorting Mrs. Killebrew to her car. "I'll do what I can—no, I will make sure every detail is followed. I'd make you a Dewar's right now, but I don't want to be accused of elderly abuse." I looked over and she was asleep. I called Lori and Jeff.

"Shirley," Lori said, coming through the door the next afternoon, "I'm honored you wanted to see me." She was bubbly as ever and jumped up to sit on her bed. "What can I do for you, my good friend?" She took the frail left hand into both of hers.

Shirley smiled the best she could and waved for me to go away. I took the cue and closed the sliding glass door behind me as I went out on the lanai. Almost an hour later, Lori opened the door and asked if I'd see her to her car. She kissed the top of her friend's head, and we walked out.

"Thanks, Rich. She just needed to talk to another woman for a minute. I can't tell you how much I admire that lady. God is taking her too soon, but I guess he has a plan." She hugged me, kissed me on the cheek, and drove off. I knew she would never divulge her conversation with Shirley, and I totally honored and respected that.

"Do I look okay?" Shirley said for the umpteenth time. Yesterday, she had Margaret bathe her, make up her bed, and fix her hair. Jeff and Tami were on their way. The doorbell rang and her eyes lit up.

"Hello, Mama," Jeff said as he sat next to her on the bed. "You look amazing ... what did you do, spend all day at the beauty shop?"

"Just for you," Shirley came back with, and her voice was stronger than it had been in weeks. "You don't look too bad yourself."

The kids planned to take us out to dinner but, when they saw that was a non-starter, Tami suggested she and I go get takeout. I knew I loved her for a reason, and we departed, leaving Jeff with his mother alone for a much-needed visit.

"Wow, I get to ride in Bigg Redd," Tami said.

"If you behave, I'll let you drive him home," I replied. She laughed and said she'd stick to driving their truck and motorcycles. While waiting for our to-go order at Applebee's, we sipped on cold Miller Lites.

"We won't be spending the night, Rich," Tami said. "We discussed it and think a good day visit will be all Shirley and Jeff could handle. He is having a hard time accepting his mother is sick, and truthfully, I'm worried how hard he is going to take losing her. I'll get him through it though." She patted my hand. "Now, how are you doing?"

It was a great visit, and Shirley managed to stay awake the whole time. She was fading by the time they were leaving. "I wanted to tell you, Tom came to see me the other day," she said. "He said we needed to talk."

We were all confused by her comment as her brother Tom had passed away last November. We let it go and goodbyes were said. At their car, I told the kids that I knew this was a tough visit and how much I appreciated their coming. Jeff went back in to hug his mother one more time. Before they left for good, Jeff returned two more times to say goodbye. Tami took the keys, and they drove off. I needed a moment before going back in, took a deep breath, and rejoined my wife, who I found sleeping soundly. She had a smile on her face.

———

The next two days, Shirley was too weak to sit for more than a minute, and I had to carry her everywhere now. It was just after midnight on Thursday, September 16, when I woke up to the purple foam brick hitting my head— and a strange noise that turned out to be her hands hitting the bed. I tried calming her but finally had to call the emergency night number.

Gail responded, arriving in twenty minutes. She thought Shirley was having a reaction to one or more of her medications and called the doctor. He agreed and told her what to do. He also said, he was calling Golden Isles to transport her to their facility. He decided his patient was too much responsibility for the husband and was no longer going to get home care.

"Gail," I pleaded. An ambulance had arrived with orders to pick up a patient for transport. "Don't let them take her. My wife, who has given much more than she's received in her life, wants to pass peacefully at home. I owe her that and I can handle it. Isn't hospice all about quality of life? She's resting now, let it go, please."

Gail looked at me and turned to the EMT. "She'll be staying here for the night, guys. I'll take responsibility for the decision and sign your release form. It's all on me." She signed a form, and they left. "I'll stay with you until morning, Rich. Get some sleep; tomorrow you may be giving that speech to the hospice board."

I actually slept several hours and when I woke, Gail was on the phone. "Yes, Doctor, I agree." She motioned for me to join her. "I will let Mr. Herman know. Yes, sir, and thank you." She hung the phone up, smiled and said, "Shirley can stay home a little longer. She is stable now and moving her could do more harm than good. I used your quality-of-life line, and it worked, as it should. This is what hospice is all about."

I sat next to Shirley on the bed, kissed her forehead, and took her hand. "Hear that, beautiful, you're still going to have to put up with me after all." She squeezed my hand and gave a little nod. I walked Gail out to her car.

"Rich," she said as soon as we were outside. "What happened was Shirley rejecting her medicine. It is part of the process, and her body is shutting down. All you can do now is be with her and carry out any of her last wishes. It's impossible to predict, and I'll have my phone at all times, but I think she may not make it through the weekend."

There it was. No more conjecture, no more wishful thinking or last-minute miracle drug would suddenly appear. It was reality. I thanked Gail and joined my wife. However long she had left, I would let her know how much she was loved.

For most of the day, Shirley slept, and I talked to her about everything we had done over the years. When she was awake, I would get an occasional eye blink or weak squeeze of the hand, but for the most part I just rambled on. I dozed on and off, my head resting on her mattress and holding her hand, and was awakened by the phone ringing at six a.m.

"Hi, Rich," Lori said. "I just got back from running and thought I'd call to see how our girl is doing." I gave her a quick recap. "I'm on my way."

Ten minutes later, "Hello," Lori called loudly as she walked through the door. She jumped up on the bed and took both of Shirley's hands into hers. "Hey, I didn't come over to watch you sleep. Say hello at least." I think she and I both saw Shirley's eyes blink, and Lori said she felt a little squeeze. "That's my girl, you rest now while I talk to your husband." She hopped down and sat across from me in the other recliner.

"Thank you for coming," I said. "I can tell she knows you're here, and that's great."

"Don't get soft now, Rich. Let me ask you something. Have you told Shirley that she prepared you well, that you're going to be okay, and you understand she has to go? She needs to hear that. And her comment last week makes sense. She said her brother Tom had come to talk to her? He probably came to guide her. It's called faith, Rich. Who's to say that she didn't see him? Certainly not me, and it's actually nice to hear. Comforting knowing someone is watching over her."

I sat back and just listened. What she was saying made sense. Lori stayed another hour, we talked, and I showed her photo albums covering my career. It was probably kind of corny but, just what I needed. When she left, I thanked her for being such a good friend. Little did I know when she departed, the impact she would have on my life in the near future.

I took Lori's advice. I lay down next to Shirley, put my arm under her shoulders, and cradled her the best I could.

"Hey, beautiful, I need to let you know something. You have been not only the greatest wife I could ever have asked for; you are my best friend. There is a new definition to be added to infinity: my love for you. You've given us a wonderful life, and you have prepared me well for this moment. I know you are tired and it's time to leave me. For now. Go when you're ready, and I'll be seeing you again. Tom, if you are here, guard over your sister and show her the way. I love you, beautiful wife."

Shirley Ann Stephenson Herman, sixty-nine, passed away in my arms, peacefully, at seven-fifty p.m., September 18, 2010.

Following her guidance, a small celebration of life was held a week later at the Killebrew Funeral Home. Shirley had talked to Reverend Tobias, and he officiated the ceremony. She had also talked to her favorite nephew, John Hicks, who made the trip from Arizona to say the eulogy for his beloved aunt. Attendees were asked to wear Hawaiian attire or something casual.

Chris flew in from Hawaii and Scott from Minnesota, joining me on the front row with Jeff, Tami, Kim, and John. Marlys flew in from Michigan and sat by my side. John, who had fresh leis flown in from Hawaii, placed them around the necks of the family. I was overwhelmed by the support as I viewed the crowd: Lori, Dusty, April and Karl, Mr. Henry, Deacon and Fran, pharmacist Rachel Mertz, active and retired military who knew and respected Shirley, and many others.

The Reverend had written a song for the occasion and sang it *a cappella*. I don't think there was a dry eye when he finished. Before his beautiful eulogy and tribute to his aunt, John read several telegrams, including two from admirals I served with. The love and respect shown my wife was absolutely wonderful and, I knew, heartfelt. It was a very appropriate ceremony and one that Shirley would have been proud of; simple, serious, yet with a lot of humor, and most importantly, short.

Shirley wanted no fuss but she did ask for a simple farewell get-together after the ceremony, to help me get through the day. Adam, a retired Marine and owner of the Beaches, authorized April to open the lounge and hold a private party to honor our loss. Marlys and the kids made a collage of our pictures, which was a great representation of our lives. On a table there was a pack of cigarettes, a glass of Dewar's, a Rusty Wallace shirt, and a 1,000-piece jigsaw puzzle. These items were mainstays and part of her life, just as much as was her legacy of kindness, compassion, faith, and generosity.

"We propose a toast," Jeff said as he and Kim stood. April had made Dewar's and water drinks, and Brandi served them to everyone who asked. Once everyone had a beverage, Jeff continued, "To the world's greatest mama." Everyone cheered and joined in. I noticed one person who had taken a drink but didn't touch it. I knew why.

"Mr. Henry," I said as I arrived at his table, "you didn't want to toast Shirley." Sitting with him were the Reverend and Crystal, who toasted with sodas. I was impressed and honored that they came into the lounge to join in. "I'm sure Reverend Tobias will not look poorly on you if you do." I had a big smile, and Mr. Henry was totally embarrassed.

"Go ahead," said Crystal. "Rev, look the other way so he can honor Miss Shirley." He did, and Mr. Henry drank his scotch straight down. He handed me the glass with a big smile, like he got away with something.

I thanked everyone, told them to enjoy themselves, and Marlys and I went home. To accommodate those who came from out of town, I had rented a block of rooms at the LaQuinta Suites, only six blocks away. Shirley was adamant that no one should have to pay to show their respect. It turned out well as the kids and John Hicks were able to spend a few days together with comfortable lodging, a lounge and pool on site. Over the next few days, they left on their own schedule with Scott being the last to leave. Marlys and I took him to the airport and when we got back to the house, it was just the two of us.

"Sis," I said, "you don't have to stay. I know you've got family to get home to, and I have to be on my own sooner or later."

"Jim and the boys are fine," she shot back. "I'm staying to help you until I think it's time to go. Now, tell me how you are really doing." I broke down, wept, and held my sister. She was right, as always; I needed her to stay.

The next several days we talked a lot, and Marlys helped me gather all of Shirley's clothes and other personal items, donating them to Goodwill. "You don't need to look at them every day," she said. "You have her picture and keep what you want, but we're getting rid of some things while I'm here. If we don't, you'll never get around to it or be able to move on." We drove to the hospital in Brunswick and donated Shirley's wigs for Dr. Skipper and Nancy to give to patients who needed and couldn't afford them.

On the fourth day, after we had our daily coffee and bagels, I said, "Dress comfortable. We're going for a ride." Three hours later, we entered the Daytona Speedway Experience. We saw all the race cars on display, including Rusty Wallace's car, Midnight, that won thirteen races, watched the "Experience Movie," where we found ourselves leaning into the curves and high banks, rode the trolley around the two-and-a-half-mile track, and splurged getting photos in the Daytona 500 winner's circle.

I think I gave my sister a memory of a lifetime. I knew it would be for me. We made it home around eight p.m., exhausted. It was a wonderful day and broke me out of feeling sorry for myself, for now anyway.

"Mar," I said, "I can't begin to tell you what your staying has done for me. Once again, you've come to my rescue. Do you ever think I'll be able to pay you back?"

"I hope you never have to, but if you do, I know you'll be there for me." She took a sip of her drink. "After we see Lori at the credit union tomorrow and bring the gold into Bradley's, I think we've accomplished what we needed to do. Will you be okay if I make plans to go home the next day?" I nodded and we clinked glasses.

—————✦—————🌳—————✦—————

"Finally, I get to meet your twin, although five years older than you," Lori said, smiling. Marlys and I were meeting her to take care of any paperwork that needed changes regarding the Herman banking accounts.

"Rich, I took the liberty to just print out everything that needs to be done. There's not that much, but it's important, especially for taxes, to get it done and recorded." It took less than ten minutes, and while I signed paperwork, the two girls talked. I had asked Marlys to be with me so she had a general idea of where to go and who to see if anything happened to me.

As we left the credit union, Marlys said, "What an impressive lady. I wish Jim and I had a banker we were close to like that. I also know from the funeral that she's a good friend and will take good care of my baby brother."

Next stop was Bradley's Jewelry. A supporter of the Christian Appalachian Project for many years, Shirley wanted all her gold jewelry, that was not designated to go to someone, to be melted down and sold—with the money being a one-time donation to help the mountain children. Bradley had discussed this with her before, so when I arrived, he was well versed on her request. I had Marlys with me for a specific reason.

"Let me take a look," Bradley said. He had designed most of what Shirley had, except some Hawaiian pieces, and knew what he was looking for. "Is this the piece you wanted me to check and clean?" I nodded yes, and he took one of the necklaces, with a diamond pendant attached, and went to the back of his store.

When he returned, he said to Marlys, "Let's see how it looks on you to make sure I got it right." He came around front and placed it around her neck.

"Perfect," I said. "In fact, it looks so good, just leave it." Marlys suddenly caught on to what I said and gasped. "For all you've done, Sis, Shirley wanted you to have this." Before she could respond, I asked Bradley, "Can you just let me know how much that comes to, after your fee of course, and provide the check and paperwork for me?"

"Can I make a suggestion, Rich?" He held up a bracelet. "We designed this for your twenty-fifth wedding anniversary, and Shirley told me it was her favorite. I think she would have liked you to hang on to it. I can take it, remove the three diamonds, melt down the band, and design you a ring. I think it'd be a great remembrance." I remained silent. "There will still be a good donation left for her charity." I told him to do it.

After taking Marlys to the airport the next day, I entered my empty house. I got a beer and placed the cars in their starting positions for tomorrow's race in Dover, Delaware. I brought Shirley's picture, put it on the table, and placed her signed Rusty Wallace T-shirt on her recliner. I wasn't hungry. I wasn't anything, but lost. This would be my first night alone in this house.

I took another beer out to the lanai. I was trying to figure out how I could move on; the emptiness and loneliness was beating me down. Finally, I sat up straight and, talking to no one, said, "Stop it, Rich. Life goes on, and yours will too. Figure it out!"

MOVING ON

October 2010 – January 2014

"I saw a car parking next to Bigg Redd ... A tall blonde got out and headed my way. 'I hope you're Kathy,' I said, trying not to be too forward."

CHAPTER 38

October 12, 2010, Little Yellow House

IT HAD BEEN WEEKS SINCE SHIRLEY PASSED, AND I knew I wasn't doing well, but I really didn't care. It was easier to drink a few beers than to cook or go out and eat. My only outing had been to Bradley's to get the check, for more than I expected, to send to Shirley's charity. I also received the ring Bradley designed and made from the bracelet. It was a man's gold ring with three diamonds, the largest in the middle and two smaller ones on each side. It was absolutely beautiful, a one-of-a-kind, and a gift from Bradley in remembrance of his friend. It was amazing how much she impacted people's lives.

That same afternoon, I would receive another unexpected gift. "Commander," the voice on the other end of the phone said when I answered, "it's Denise Diamond."

My hand started to shake. My administrative assistant from my last duty station. "Denise, it's great to hear your voice. How are you doing."

"I think the question is, how are you doing, sir? Admiral Staten called me and said Shirley had passed away. I'm so sorry."

"Thank you, and would you please call me Rich?"

"Yes, sir," she said. "Again, how are you doing?"

"I'm not going to say as well as expected because I've learned to hate that phrase." Denise was so easy to talk to. "Actually, I'm probably not doing that well but taking a day at a time. Ugh, I hate that phrase too."

She laughed a little. "Good to see you still have your humor, sir.

I'm working in human resources now at Fort Snelling, in St. Paul. A question, sir. Do you have anyone helping you with the grief process?"

"No, I didn't know there was such a person." I didn't.

"Yes, sir, and I am one. I would be more than happy to be yours until you find somebody local. You have to have someone, Commander. Don't go through this alone. Let me give you my private number here at work, and if you'd like to talk, call me at five-thirty a.m. my time. I'll come in early each day so we can chat. Would you do that for me?"

I wrote down the number and said I would call her one way or the other. I felt like I was no longer alone. I took a much-needed shower, shaved, and ate a little food. I then tried to call Admiral Staten, my last boss, who spoke at my retirement.

The day after Shirley died, I had called a local friend, Karl David, still in the Navy. I asked him to use his contacts to locate and call the admiral and say, "Lady dolphin-wearer Shirley Herman has passed." He did, and the admiral called me several hours later and followed with a telegram read at her funeral. Obviously, he knew Denise would want to help her old boss and friend. No wonder he made admiral.

I talked to my new guidance counselor every workday morning for the next two weeks, and she gave me the shoulder I so badly needed to cry on and the positive outlook I refused to accept. We had always worked well together, and she probably knew me better than anyone, other than Shirley.

At her encouragement, I finally went out one evening for dinner. It felt strange to sit alone and try to enjoy a meal, but I made it through, and Denise said that was a major step. I had gotten a new cell phone and met Brandi at Beaches for a lesson on how to use it. It was a breakthrough getting me out of the house, and I got some quality time with April and Karl.

I made an appointment at base legal to update my will and other legal documents. The lawyer I had was great but I wanted a second opinion so I met with Lori and asked her to look them over. "Everything looks good, Commander," she said. "I know this wasn't easy, and I'm proud of you. You look pretty good too." Her smile was contagious.

"Thanks," I replied. I told her about Denise, who she was, and how she was helping me.

When I finished, she got up and closed her office door. "Rich, Denise probably has kept you from doing something stupid and she is right. You need to find someone local to be your grief counselor. I'd like to be that person if you'd let me."

I looked at her and shook my head. "You have to be kidding me. I never knew that."

"We don't advertise," she said. "A grief counselor is only effective if they are trusted by the person grieving, who is also willing to be helped. I would love to meet Denise; she is obviously very good and a dear friend."

"And she looks like Julia Roberts," I said, chuckling. "A little joke Shirley and I had. Yes, she's wonderful. Lori, yes, I'd love to have you on board."

She gave me her personal number, and we set up a time to talk when she was off work. I went home on a high note and called Denise the next morning. "That's great, Commander, I'm happy for you. Still, take my cell phone number and stay in touch." I thanked her, told her how much her caring and guidance had helped; I would keep her number on speed dial.

I found in Lori exactly what I did in Denise, and then some. She was a great listener and picked up helping me understand the process I was going through. Where she was probably a little better for me was that she had no problem slapping me down. I was no longer in denial and angry about losing Shirley, but I wasn't helping myself move on. I got very good at excuses and finding ways around doing what was required. Three weeks after we talked the first time, Lori made her value obvious when she visited me at home.

"Welcome to Casa Herman," I said, holding the front door open for her. She smiled and not only came in; she started going from room to room on an inspection tour. I trusted her and took a seat in the kitchen.

She joined me in the kitchen. "It's been over two months since Shirley passed. It's time to take the shrine down. Her picture on the mantle is fine, you don't want to block her out, but all these other items, they need to go." She pointed at all the other pictures, Rusty's jersey still on her recliner and items reminding me of her.

"Maybe other family members would like some things, good, send them, but you have to find a balance to have memories of your wife, but accept she's gone. Every time you see all her things, it will keep you depressed. Break the need to hold on to what is no longer there, and you can come out of your depression."

I wasn't angry with her, but she seemed a little cold about my not wanting to let it go.

"Oh, get that look off your face. Stop feeling sorry for yourself, you're going to be just fine. Stick with me, I won't let anyone or anything hurt you. You have to trust me, Rich."

She went to the mantle and pointed to the sealed box. "Shirley's ashes?" she asked softly. I nodded yes, not looking forward to what she would say to that. "You told me she gave you two options to spread her ashes. Have you given any thought to carrying out her wishes? What are you waiting for?"

She wasn't being mean; I knew it was part of the process. I had no answer, I hadn't given it any thought.

"Rich," Dr. Windsor said, "good to see you." I was here for my annual physical. "Shirley has been gone three months. How are you doing?" I remained silent. "Are you sleeping and eating?" I just sat. "Getting out to golf or exercising?"

When I still didn't say anything, he put his clipboard and pen down and rolled his chair toward me, stopping with his face within a foot of mine. "Commander, talk to me. I can only help you if you let me."

"I'm starting to sleep and eat a little better, this past month anyway," I said. I told him about my grief counselors and where I was in the grieving process. He listened and didn't interrupt. "A couple of weeks ago, Lori inspected my house and gave me a good talking-to. Told me my grace period was over and to start getting my act together. She even told me to get off my butt and spread the ashes so I can move on."

"Three months and you still have the ashes?" Dr. Windsor said in disbelief. "I'm with her, what is stopping you? What did Shirley want?"

"She asked I either spread her ashes in her family's grave site in the West Virginia Mountains or take her to Hawaii and spread them into the Pacific at a favorite place we used to visit on the North Shore. If I chose Hawaii, she wants me to fly first class because she never had a chance to and wants to go out in style."

I'd never heard him laugh out loud, until now. "That's Shirley. I vote for Hawaii, let me check my calendar, and maybe I'll take the wife and go with you." I joined him laughing. "Seriously, I agree with your grief counselor. Unless for some reason you can't, plan your trip and carry out Shirley's wishes. Doctor's orders."

"Aloha, Dad," Chris said as I deplaned at the Honolulu airport. "I kept looking at the weather reports and didn't think you were going to be able to land. In fact, you're the last flight they allowed in. The airport is shut down until tomorrow. They predict major flooding and possibly the worst storm in forty years."

"I was lucky for sure." I hugged my son. "We were the last plane allowed to fly out of Atlanta before the snowstorm hit. The air was so turbulent when we got airborne, they closed all food and drink service, and we stayed buckled in."

To make it worse, the storm front on the East Coast stretched all the way to the Mississippi River; then we hit another front on the West Coast. When the crew was about to open service, the pilot had announced it would be too rough the rest of the way.

I held up Shirley's ashes. "The first time we fly first-class, and I didn't get a single free drink or anything to eat the last twelve hours."

I could stay with Chris at his place in Aiea, but, as customary for me, I chose to stay at the Hale Koa Hotel on Waikiki Beach and got an ocean view room. I placed the ashes on a table near the window. We planned to head to the North Shore on Saturday, weather permitting. Our goal was to hold our private farewell to my wife and his stepmother, who he had grown to love so much.

The predictions were right, and Hawaii, especially the Island of Oahu where we were, had record storms and flooding. Saturday morning it was still raining on and off, but the storm itself had moved on. Chris came for breakfast with his friend Mari, a local girl who offered her support and a traditional Hawaiian farewell for Shirley. Debris had blocked the main road, but he thought we could make it by another route. I came here on a mission, and nothing was going to stop me now.

In my almost twelve years living here, I had never traveled the roads we were on. It rained the entire trip, and several times we almost turned around. Once, it took the three of us to remove a fallen tree on a muddy back road. I don't know if we were that determined or the submarine can-do attitude just took over, but the three of us managed to get through the thick brush and made it to what Shirley and I called our private place. "Stop!" I said.

It was cloudy and drizzling as I took Shirley's ashes out of the case and cut through the seal on top. Mari walked out into the ocean with me, and Chris was close behind. We waded out about forty feet when all of a sudden, the rain stopped, the clouds opened, and the sun shone through, only to where we were standing. It was magical, and Mari smiled and nodded like this was the sign she was looking for.

Looking up, I saw a perfect wave coming and told Chris to snap the picture when I signaled. Mari opened a plastic bag and took out a handful of freshly picked plumeria flowers. As the wave crested, I spread Shirley's ashes and Mari threw the flowers. I signaled and Chris, unbelievably, captured the moment perfectly as the wave accepted the ashes and flowers, took them to shore and then back out to sea. It was January 15, 2011, and this was my final goodbye.

As we watched Shirley heading out to her final resting place, I said, "Farewell and following seas."

CHAPTER 39

April 2011

THREE MONTHS AFTER RETURNING FROM HAWAII, I was just going through the motions one day at a time. I was going out and being more active, but the grief still followed me.

Home watching TV, on April 12, my phone rang. "Rich," I heard that familiar Boston accent say. "I'm so sorry to hear about Shirley."

"Thank you, Rose," I said, "How did you find out?"

"I was attending a senior executives seminar today on human resources and military responsibilities, and the lecturer was Denise Diamond. Boy, has she come up in the world, and her presentation was fantastic. Sharp lady. Anyway, we remembered each other from Hawaii, and she told me about Shirley."

"I apologize, I should have called you. You might say I haven't been myself, but that's just an excuse for my being disrespectful. You deserve better than that."

"Not at all, Rich, and I'd like to make you an offer. Why don't you come spend some time with me? I've got this huge house I talk to myself in, and you'd be able to rest, think, and do whatever you want—without being in, frankly, an environment full of memories of Shirley."

I arrived in San Diego ten days later and was met by my friend of over thirty years. When I saw her pull up to the curb, it was like a ton of pressure was going away; for the first time since losing Shirley, just as Denise and Lori had told me, I felt it was okay to be here. After lunch at the Marina on San Diego Bay, we drove up the mountain in El Cajon, where Rose lived. She had divorced years before, and her four daughters were grown and had lives of their own.

After I settled into a spacious guest suite, she gave me the grand tour of her property that I first visited more than twenty years ago. Her home on top of this mountain had a 360-degree view of the cities below, all the way to the Pacific Ocean. Breathtaking and priceless.

"I had forgotten how beautiful it is up here, Rose. You've outdone yourself on the landscaping." The perfectly trimmed flowers, shrubs, and trees made her yard a showpiece. "You may never get rid of me." We laughed, and she took me by the arm.

"Come, let's get a drink and sit out on the lanai. Tell me everything … that you feel you can talk about, anyway."

Rose and I talked for a while before going in for dinner. Taking our after-dinner coffee to the den, we talked until almost midnight, when Rose decided she needed to get some sleep if we were to get up at six in the morning. That's when she told me tomorrow was her birthday, and we were going on a short trip, with three of her children, to celebrate. I think we were about the same age but, being a gentleman, didn't ask.

The next morning, we drove with two of her daughters and a son-in-law to Palm Springs, California, where we would stay with her oldest daughter and husband. There, we experienced a wonderful birthday dinner at the Hilton Palms Resort.

I learned Rose likes to gamble and is very good at it. I limited myself to losing $100, to be sociable, and was broke playing the slots and blackjack an hour later. I followed the birthday girl around, carrying her drink and acting like a bodyguard, watching her leave the casino over $700 richer. It turned out, five of us played, and I was the only loser, which everyone made sure I heard over and over. We had a great time.

The next day we went to the Colony Club for Easter Sunday brunch and then relaxed around the pool at the house before heading home. Rose and I were back on top of the mountain, exhausted, around one a.m. She needed to be up in four hours to make it to work at her normal time, and Rose Emon was never late.

I was very comfortable here, with no pressure or demands, and I was looking forward to the project I was about to begin. I slept like a rock, or is it a baby?

I was up at eight a.m. and, once I figured out how to operate the Keurig, I made a cup of coffee and enjoyed it on one of the lanais. Feeling refreshed and relaxed, I went in and set up a work space in Rose's office. I unpacked the cardboard shoebox I brought along, dumped out all the letters my mother kept from my first enlistment, and went to work. My initial reaction was, as my grandma used to say, "*Uffda!*"

While Rose worked each day, I, at my own pace, started putting together my letters and organizing them into a manageable database. It was slow going, but I was in no rush and took many breaks to enjoy where I was. I even started, after receiving explicit instructions, to water the flowers and all the other flora, which took two hours a day. I actually enjoyed it.

One evening, Rose hosted a seafood buffet dinner for forty military and civilian personnel from the U.S., Britain and Australia navies, who were involved with the latest upgrades to our submarines' communications. She had asked me beforehand if the affair would bring back memories too soon, but I told her I would look forward to it. The event was a huge success. Rose thought of a great idea, and she and I played hostess and host together, meeting everyone at the front door as they arrived. As I knew most of the attendees, from my active-duty days as the Submarine Force Communicator, it was like a class reunion to me. I was in my element, and Rose knew it.

"Quite the evening, Rich," she said, kicking her shoes off and flopping on the couch. "You seemed to be enjoying yourself." I grinned; she knew me well. "You are highly respected by this crowd, Commander. Want to give second thought to taking me up on my offer? The job is still yours."

I got us a nightcap and we changed the subject, watching the caterers finish cleaning up. As she headed up to bed, I said, "You're a tough recruiter, young lady, sleep well." I heard her laugh all the way to her room.

Rose and I got along well, never once getting on each other's nerves. My letters and book planning kept me busy during the days; in the evening, I would greet her with a beverage, and we would take time to sit and talk, vent sometimes, about the day. She never pushed me to discuss anything about Shirley, yet she listened intently and offered advice when I did.

After ten days, I had organized my letters, made a computer file of each one with the date written, and gave it a title and a short recap of its contents. Rose showed me how to download them onto a flash drive. I told her I was ready to go home and get on with my life. She smiled, said she agreed, and all seemed well with the world.

Four days later, I was packing to leave when Rose called. "Would you do me a favor, Rich? I have a colleague, a good friend, who I'm meeting for dinner and then taking her to the airport. Would you go with me? I hate that area and don't want to be alone." How could I possibly say no?

Rose picked me up, said her friend would meet us, and we drove across San Diego to Fleming's Steakhouse. We were met at the door by a man in a tuxedo, and that should have been my first clue. "Your table is ready, Ms. Emon," he said, escorting us to a large booth. "Enjoy your meal, and if there is anything I can do, please let me know."

Rose guided me onto the bench on the left side of the table, almost pushing. I slid over, and there was a woman already sitting there. Next to her sat a man who looked familiar, and next to him another man, who also looked familiar. Rose slid in the right side. As my eyes got accustomed to the dark, I looked again at the person sitting next to me.

"Doris? Doris Fields?" I said, surprised. Doris, Rose's top software analyst in 1989, had installed a software patch in the submarine communications program in Hawaii, saving millions of dollars, and more importantly, keeping communications available to our strategic submarines. However, installing the patch got her fired for not having approval from her superiors. I had called her boss and basically threatened his career if he didn't change his mind; she had been rehired and eventually promoted to Rose's position.

I then recognized Barry Stills and Damien Spanos, two of the best officers who ever worked with me. In fact, they gave credo to my Hermanism—*if you want to be successful, put good people around you.* Retired now, they were civilian contractors, often working with Rose on submarine projects.

"You got me, Rose; I never saw this coming." Everyone here knew Shirley well, and all were sincere when they offered their condolences. I managed to tap Rose with my foot, and she smiled and blew me a kiss. It would be another wonderful evening, as well as a reminder how much I enjoyed my naval career.

"Rose," I said before getting out of her car at the airport the next day, "I will never be able to repay you for the last two weeks. You're a great lady and a wonderful friend." I reached over, we hugged, and both had tears in our eyes. As she was about to pull away, through the open window, I said, "Tempting, Rose, but it's still a no to your job offer." She smiled, and drove off.

I returned from San Diego fresh and invigorated. My first task was to give the little yellow house a thorough cleaning, and that was one thing I was good at. It was the second day when I was dusting Shirley's nightstand that I opened the top drawer to clean it out.

On top, I found a letter in protective plastic. I recognized the beautiful handwriting and saw the note at the top: "Please read this when I'm gone – you will feel better and closer to me. Shirley." I sat on the bed and read the letter, at least a dozen times. I knew what I had to do.

The Stephenson family had always been nice to me, and I enjoyed my visits to the West Virginia mountains. To the core, they were die-hard patriotic Americans, honest, hard-working, and would give you the shirt off their backs. A handshake meant something here, and they liked their small towns and local stores. Don't tell them Walmart, or Wally's World as they called it, was progress. Most of the men worked in the coal mines, as did their ancestors. Ninety percent of the family, men and women, smoked, while only a few had ever tasted alcohol. The only cuss words they ever spoke came when quoting the Bible.

Other than nephew John, none of the family members from where she was loved and raised were able to make it to Shirley's celebration of life. Travel for funerals isn't allotted for in the family budget. I felt it was necessary to go to the family reunion this year; they deserved to hear this letter.

Over a hundred Stephensons attended the annual Father's Day reunion, and I think every one of them made sure they told me, personally, what Shirley meant to them and how much she was missed. One great-niece told me about the time when she didn't have a dress or any shoes to go to her senior prom, until she received a package from Hawaii. It was a dress, underthings (her words), make-up kit, and shoes for the prom, with a note: "Enjoy yourself. Love, Aunt Shirley." I never knew she had done that, but was not surprised.

She had also ordered and had engraved headstones placed on every grave in the family graveyard. You had to walk or ride a horse the final block to it; the roads couldn't handle a car. My wife never talked about or took credit for her generosity and compassion for others.

When it was time for family announcements, her nephew John stood on a picnic table and led this very religious family in prayer, dedicating it to Aunt Shirley. I stood with oldest brother Bob, wearing a T-shirt with the American flag, his retired Air Force hat in his hands. John asked me to say a few words.

I stood on the picnic table and said, "I have brought a letter I found and, although it was left for me, I want to share it with all those who loved her." I pulled out the letter, still in its protective plastic. All eyes, from the youngest to the oldest, were on me and you could hear a pin drop. Composing myself, I read:

"When I come to the end of the road and the sun has set on me, I want no rites in a gloom filled room, why cry for a soul set free.

Miss me a little, but not for long, and now with your head bowed low, remember the love once shared, miss me, but let me go.

For this is a journey we all must take and each must go alone, it's all a part of the master plan, a step on the road home.

When you are lonely and sick at heart, go to the friends we know, bury your sorrows in doing good deeds, miss me, but let me go.

As the day ended and I said goodbye, I wasn't sad, I was content. I had done the right thing and shared my wife, their sister, cousin, or aunt, with them one last time. I could feel the love they had for me, and that cannot be put into words. I was about to start my drive home when I stopped the car.

I made a call on Bigg Redd's On-Star and changed my destination. There was someone I needed to see in Michigan. As I drove off, I took one last look at this beautiful place. *Fret not, my family here, West Virginia will always be on my mind.*

I figured I could make it to Marlys' house in under two days.

I arrived back home just after the Fourth of July weekend. Last January, when I was in Hawaii, Chris had told me it was time to join the rest of the world and, probably thinking I would never get there, ordered me a computer system. It arrived months ago, but I had yet to open it. It was time.

While on active duty, I worked with and, as the senior submarine communications officer, was responsible for some of the world's latest technology. I could talk the talk but not walk the walk when it came to the newest technology. Since retirement, I had gone without not only a computer but also a cell phone and even a wristwatch. I opened my new Dell laptop, and my world changed.

Like everything else I've ever taken on, I put good people around me (Hermanism). I called Karl David and his daughter Brandi, asking for help. Karl, still on active duty and technically savvy as an electronics technician, hooked up my hardware. Brandi, now attending Georgia Southern University and a computer whiz, installed my software.

After getting my email account set up and an hour of initial instruction, I knew enough to be dangerous. She gave me her personal number and I hired Brandi, paying a retainer up front, to be my social media consultant.

I arrived early and took a seat in the lobby. Lori had called yesterday, asking me to come see her at work around noon. She even gave me homework, which was not uncommon this past year while helping me through the grieving process. I was to write down my accomplishments since we started and assess, honestly, my progress. I quickly realized this was another one of her lessons to bring me to reality.

"Sorry for the wait, Rich," Lori said as she waved for me to come to her office. "With Thanksgiving tomorrow, we have a long weekend, and a lot of people want to get in their banking." I sat across from her. "How did you do with your assignment? I cleared my calendar, so we have no time limit." She smiled as I handed her my notes.

"It's fine you got held up," I started. "It gave me a little extra time to gather my thoughts."

For the next hour we had one of the best talks ever. When I thought we were about done, she said, "I think you have gotten through the grieving process. You were always a positive person and saw your cup half full. You may not realize it, but I see that again. You are ready to move on.

"First, a question I have after our months of talking. Who do you consider friends, who you can turn to, trust, and would go to their side when called, no questions asked?"

I wasn't expecting this and gave it thought before saying, "You, of course. Rose Emon, Denise Diamond…"

"Stop," Lori said and leaned forward. "Do you see a pattern

here?" I didn't. "They're all women. Rich, you relate to and trust women more than men. I'm not a psychologist, but I'd think your Uncle Sherm would agree you got this from your mother. Nothing wrong with that; if you think about it, it was the exact opposite for Shirley. She turned toward men." She was right, we had even talked about it once.

"You're not a very good loner, Commander, you need female companionship. It doesn't have to be sexual, just the association. In her last words to you, the letter you found, Shirley said miss her a little but not for long. It's been over a year; we need to find you a date."

"Whoa, young lady," I said. She was looking at me as if asking, *Well?* "When I think of moving on, it's with my life solo and with family and friends. You and I have talked about expanding our helping the homeless, people who just need time to get through a tough patch. That in itself will keep me busy. Another thing, I'm sixty-five years old, and I was never a great catch in the first place, let alone now."

"Don't sell yourself short," Lori fired back. "Just give it some thought, and if you do meet someone you'd like to take to dinner or whatever, do it—you're ready. I'll even take a look at some of the ladies at church." Apparently, I had quite the look on my face. She burst out laughing. "Seriously, I'm proud of you. Have you made any plans for the holidays?"

"As a matter of fact, I have. I'll keep you posted. How about you?" Lori had never talked much about her private life, and I had never met her husband, Joe. I did know he was retired Navy, now in law enforcement, and they had two daughters. She was also an avid long-distance runner, had won numerous races around the country, and even competed in the Boston Marathon. I suddenly realized— Denise Diamond was too. Interesting coincidence.

"Joe and I will be going to Michigan to see our oldest daughter and grandkids for Christmas," Lori said, "and then we'll spend New Year's quietly here, visiting our other daughter and Joe's mom. Thanks for asking." As I was leaving, she gave me a hug saying, "Enjoy the holidays, Rich, and give what I said some thought. No rush to do anything, but keep your options open."

Unlike last year, I actually shopped for cards with meaning and got them sent to arrive in time for Christmas. I even put up a little tree on my coffee table. Wanting to keep in touch, and because I genuinely missed them, I made arrangements and visited Jeff and Tami December 22 and 23, staying in the same suite we always had at the Crowne Plaza. I never wanted to lose contact with my stepchildren, and this was a good start to make sure we didn't.

I spent New Year's Eve much like those of the last twenty years, quietly and safely, but this year alone. There was one other difference too. I made it to midnight, welcoming in the new year with a Dewar's and water, and a simple wish: *I hope 2012 is a good year, and as I look for a new path, may I always remember Shirley is looking down, smiling on me. May I always make her proud.*

CHAPTER 40

January 14, 2012

IT WAS HALFTIME IN THE NFL PLAYOFF GAME, AND the commercial playing was for the online dating service, eHarmony. Usually, I would ignore it, but today, maybe thinking about Lori's advice on dating, I jotted down the 800 number. *I think my nephew Steve met his wife, Mary, online, and they're a great couple.* Deciding it cost nothing to listen, I dialed the number.

"Your name and all personal information remain confidential," the recording said. "All emails go through ..." It went on with other information. I signed up for a thirty-day trial period.

I found my new project more interesting than the football game and answered the minimum number of questions required to be screened and accepted into the system. When I logged in, I was amazed at how many women's profiles found their way to my personal queue. In my questionnaire, I set my own parameters on ages, interests, education, likes/dislikes, etc., so only the profiles meeting these were there for me to look at. I got a beer and started reviewing the more than 100 already in the queue.

I had looked at twenty or so profiles and found one that I wrote down as a possibility. She was sixty-two, a widow, mother of two grown children, a retired bookkeeper, and looking for a companion, not necessarily a husband. She lived in Brunswick, Georgia. I continued on and heard a ping. There was an email from eHarmony.

Someone had replied to my site and wanted to contact me. Under the rules, eHarmony already filtered the request, found it legitimate, and passed it on, asking me to review it and let them know what I would like to do. The email said a fifty-three-year-old female, divorced with three sons, living in Fernandina Beach, Florida, wanted to chat. I thought she was pretty young—but, then again, she already knew my age. I sent my reply, and three minutes later we were hooked up in a chat room.

I started: *Hi, my name is Rich, and like my site said, I am retired from the Navy, a widower, two grown sons, and live alone in Kingsland.*

She answered back immediately: *Hi, Kathy here. You answered my request so my profile hasn't scared you off. I liked what I read on yours and want to know a little more about you.*

We texted questions and answers several more times and, as recommended by eHarmony, ended our session after fifteen minutes, agreeing we should chat again soon. I enjoyed it and called Lori. As my grief counselor, she said an online dating service had never crossed her mind, but she was happy for me to have someone to chat with. As my friend, she warned me not to believe everything you read online.

I was beginning to watch the next playoff game, the Giants winning the first game in overtime, when I heard my computer ping. Opening it, I saw another eHarmony request asking if I would like to continue my chat with Kathy. Two minutes later, she was in my chat room.

Hi, Rich, I was sitting here thinking, why do we have to wait to chat again? We're not teenagers. In fact, I know it is against the rules but if I give you my phone number would you like to call and we can talk in person.

I dialed her number. "Nice to meet you in person, sort of," Kathy said, answering the phone.

"Same here." I liked the sound of her voice. "So you are a rule-breaker, are you?" I was sure she knew I wasn't being serious.

"Not always, but the way I see it, your life is as long as a ruler and we're both past the halfway point. Why work on a timetable?"

"You did say on your profile that you were honest and straightforward," I came back with. "Anything else you think I should know up front?"

We talked another twenty minutes and it was relaxing, informative, and definitely intriguing. I decided why not. "My turn to break the rules. The dating guidelines say we aren't to meet again in person for two weeks. Tomorrow is Sunday ... how would you like to have lunch? You choose the place you would be comfortable."

"Deal," she said immediately. "Do you know where Chili's is in Yulee?"

"I will tomorrow." I didn't even know where Yulee was.

Thank goodness I had a TomTom GPS. It turned out Chili's in Yulee, although in Florida, was only eighteen miles away, and I arrived fifteen minutes early. Five minutes to noon, I walked to the entrance and started looking for a gray Toyota Scion. I had never heard of this car, but she said it looked like a toaster on wheels. I saw a car parking next to Bigg Redd. What were the odds? A tall blonde got out and headed my way.

"I hope you're Kathy," I said, trying not to be too forward.

"Car is a dead giveaway, isn't it?" she said with a big smile.

I opened the door, and we found a booth for two, away from other customers. Her shoulder-length hair was well styled, and walking in, I realized we were about the same height. We picked up our menus, immediately taking up where we left off last night. She was a very attractive, professional, and obviously very bright woman.

We ordered lunch, and I, at least, was enjoying our first date. But I'm also realistic and knew she was out of my league. As we finished our meal, already fifteen minutes over the recommended hour set by eHarmony for a first date, I knew what I had to do.

"Kathy, I've really enjoyed meeting you, and I can tell you are a wonderful person, but I'll be honest with you. We maybe could have a few fun dates, but I'm looking for companionship, and it wouldn't be long before you would want to move on. I am sixty-five, you know."

"Yep," she said. "I knew that, and if it mattered, I wouldn't be sitting here. I already raised four adolescents—husband included there—and have no desire to raise another one. I want a good, well-rounded man who is confident in his own skin, that I can rely on and be comfortable with. Let's ask each other this question. Why did you reply to my first email?"

Good question, and I started. "I liked your responses, nothing sounded phony, and I wanted to meet the person who sent it." Her turn.

"I saw one thing on your profile that made me overlook everything else. You answered the question about who has had the biggest impact on your life the past year, saying, 'my two grievance counselors without a doubt.' That answer is honest, compassionate, and from someone who has a lot to offer. I've enjoyed this too, let's give it a try."

I didn't hesitate. "Want to break another rule?" She flashed a big smile, nodding yes. "It's only one-thirty, you said you liked the St. Marys waterfront in Georgia, and haven't seen it in years ... want to go on a tour?"

As we walked to our cars, I asked who should drive. She pointed to her Scion and asked, "Where are you parked?" We headed out in Bigg Redd.

We walked the beautifully restored waterfront; I pointed out the St. Marys Submarine Museum, its history, and my involvement, and we decided it would be great to tour one day. It was four o'clock when, heading back to Chili's, Kathy said, "Because of your glaucoma, you don't drive at night. You better show me where you live." Confused, I looked at her.

"Let me clarify—in case we decide to go on a night date and I have to drive." I laughed, we definitely broke another rule, and I gave her a tour of my home. "You were right, you are a good housekeeper. Do you hire out?"

When I dropped her off at her car, we decided to try a second date the following weekend and I'd give her a call. Before getting into her car, she lightheartedly said, "I know where you live, why don't you follow me home and I'll repay the favor." She lived in a gated community not far from Chili's and just west of the Shave Bridge that led to Amelia Island.

I got the tour and met her best friend and roommate, Maggie, a twelve-year-old Boston Terrier. Maggie and I bonded immediately, and another check (as I would find out later) was made on her list of requirements. As I was leaving, I saw a shooting range target on the door to her garage.

"Oh, that," she said. "Before our date, I cleaned my 38-special and went to the firing range to brush up on my shooting." There were a lot of holes in the target. "By the way, all three of my sons, my brother, and my father are marksmen. I have them all on speed dial." She smiled but then broke down laughing. I took note to remember that.

The next night, Kathy broke another rule. She called me. "I know it's only been a day, but why wait until the weekend for a second date? Why don't I come to your place for dinner tomorrow night? My treat. Do you like Popeye's chicken?"

I couldn't help picturing her smiling on the other end. "I think that's a great idea, but I will cook for you. Do you like seafood?"

The next afternoon I called David, my nephew, who was now the executive chef at Michigan's Tahquamenon Falls Lodge, located at America's second largest waterfall after Niagara Falls. I told him what I had gotten myself into and after laughing at my predicament—I hadn't the faintest idea how to cook a fancy shrimp dinner—he gave me a list of what I needed to buy and the exact cooking instructions he used for gourmet shrimp entrees.

"Wow," Kathy said, "that was fantastic. I never would have guessed you could cook like that." We had just finished dining on delicious shrimp, with garlic bread, a Greek salad, and glasses of chardonnay.

I never liked being phony so told her about David, his being a chef, and his background. As had been the case with everything these last four days, she didn't let me down.

"That's even better," she said. "Most guys wouldn't have 'fessed up to that or would've just taken me to a restaurant. You actually went through all that effort just to please me. You get another box checked off." Obviously, I didn't know what she meant and gave her a blank look.

"Okay, I have a list of traits and requirements that are important to me. So far, you're checking all the boxes. I have a friend, who will remain anonymous, who has connections and ran a background check on you. It was impressive." She seemed quite satisfied with herself, and I couldn't think of a good comeback. "Let me pick our next date. Pick me up Saturday morning at seven, and dress casual and warm." We shared our first hug at the door, and I watched her drive away.

"Welcome aboard Amelia Island Cruises," the boat captain and guide said.

Kathy and I took seats on the starboard side of the catamaran boat, and for the next three hours were entertained listening to the history and many stories of Amelia Island's earliest settlers and historical events while observing dolphins, seabirds, marsh life, and wild horses on nearby Cumberland Island. Kathy had been on this tour several times, learned something new every time, and thought it was the best way to educate me about where she was born and raised. I absolutely loved it, and we agreed, if the time ever came, we would put this on our things-to-do list with visitors. We docked just before noon, and my next surprise began.

Brett's on the Waterfront was a restaurant at the Fernandina Beach marina on the Amelia River. We had a table outside with a view of the river and all its activity. Although my date would say it was just a coincidence, a couple stopped by to say hello.

"Rich," Kathy said, "this is my older," stressing *older*, "sister Judy and her husband, Rod." *Coincidence, the lady who ran a background check on me?*

"Would you please join us," I said, standing and shaking their hands. I could tell no one expected that, and I enjoyed catching them off guard.

"Oh, no," Judy said. (I later would learn she was actually eight years older, and Rod was my age or a little older.) "We were just passing by, and when I saw Kathy, I wanted to say hi." *Sure.* They said we'd have to get together soon and departed.

"They seem nice," I said. "Who else are we going to run into?"

"Busted," my date said, unable to keep a straight face. "No one else. Actually, for the record, Fernandina is like a fishbowl when it comes to running into someone you know."

We spent a lot of time together over the next few weeks. She seemed to enjoy hearing about all the places I had lived, and I was impressed to learn she had home-schooled her boys. We never held back on answering each other's questions and, not agreeing on everything, we found we were compatible, comfortable, and most importantly, happy with our relationship going to another level. I had never, in my wildest dreams, thought I could find or even wanted closeness with another woman; it felt good, and I accepted it, not feeling guilty.

My immediate and extended family was spread out across the U.S. (Hawaii, Michigan, Minnesota, Virginia, West Virginia) while Kathy's was within fifty miles of Yulee. She got to know mine through my talking about them, although I was able to introduce her to Lori, April and Karl David at Beaches Lounge, and neighbors Reverend Tobias, Crystal, and Mr. Henry. One thing stood out with every encounter, everyone immediately liked and accepted her. Lori was a little protective, which we both found understandable and a sign of great caring, but I knew she would be supportive in time.

Meeting Kathy's family was a whole different story. Shortly after meeting Judy and Rod, we did get together for dinner, and I met her fifteen-month-older brother, Danny. There was no doubt who was the baby of the family, and she was deeply loved. I really enjoyed how her family all talked at the same time, yet they seemed to hear every word. And they all had a great sense of humor. The oldest sister, Diane, lived in Yulee with husband Tom, but I hadn't met them yet.

Her brothers Ronnie and David had passed away when they were still young.

Kathy's three sons all lived in the area. Her oldest, Matt, worked in Camden County as a fireman—as did her middle son, Justin, who lived in St. John's County, just south of Jacksonville, Florida. The youngest son, Jon, was a senior at the University of North Florida majoring in mechanical engineering. Matt and wife Lacy had three children, Gabriella (eleven), Dawson (eight), and Macy (six). Justin and wife Tori were expecting their first child any day. Jon and his fiancée, Hannah, were getting married on Kathy's birthday, March 17.

Her parents, retired, still lived in the house where she was born and raised in Yulee. Her father, called Bo by his friends, served in the Navy during World War II as an aircraft mechanic; after his honorable discharge, he worked in the same field for civil service at Naval Air Station Jacksonville. He was so good at his job that he was in high demand and often flew to other locations to fix aircraft. Since retirement, he and his dogs had fished every day.

"Dad, I want you to meet Rich, he's retired Navy," Kathy said, introducing me. I shook the hand, strong and with a firm grip, of this older veteran and told him it was an honor to meet him. It was. He had white hair, and even sitting I knew he was at least six feet tall, with a strong build. He didn't say a word, but he did look me in the eye and nodded.

Her mother, Elizabeth, was just the opposite. She had a big smile and a twinkle in her eye. I immediately liked her. "Nice to meet you," she said. "Do you live around here?" I answered, and we made small talk for a couple of minutes. Then she put her hand out and said, "I have a bad finger, it always hurts. I also have a titanium knee." She showed me both.

"Okay, Mom." Kathy rolled her eyes. "That's way too much information for a first meeting." She changed the subject. "Dad, Rich's father was in the CCCs."

"Really," he said, definitely liking what he heard. "The Civilian Conservation Corps helped save this country back in the thirties.

Gave young men a purpose, a job to support their families, and taught them a trade. What did your dad do?" He was sitting straight now, fully engaged and smiling.

"He built bridges in northern Minnesota," I said. "And he said the same thing about how it helped our country. He also served in the National Guard and was drafted, but didn't see combat because the war ended. He said the CCCs helped all the men grow up and instilled patriotism."

"Got that right," he agreed. "Young people today should have to serve in the military to learn how good they have it and why this country is great. What did you do in the Navy?" He asked Kathy to get us each a fresh cup of coffee. *I think I found a new friend.*

Kathy and I had been dating, almost daily, for five weeks. Visiting the St. Marys waterfront by myself, I walked from one end to the other and back again, taking a seat in the pavilion overlooking the St. Marys River. Although I couldn't dangle my feet in the water, which was ten feet below, I was able to experience the feeling I always got when in such a place; peace, contentment and freedom to think.

I held a serious conversation with myself and at the end, looked up and asked someone for her blessing. Later that evening, I asked Kathy to join me on the couch, and I shared my thoughts from the day. There was no hesitation when she let me know her feelings were the same.

CHAPTER 41

March 3, 2012, Downtown Kingsland

KATHY AND I WERE MARRIED, EXACTLY SEVEN WEEKS from our first online contact. It was a small ceremony attended by Judy and Rod, Danny, and our witnesses, April and Karl David, and officiated by a justice of the peace. Short, simple, but elegant in its own way, we exchanged our vows and devoted our lives to each other. We hosted a wedding lunch at Brett's on the Waterfront and decided we would celebrate all special days here.

We didn't inform the rest of our families of our marriage and delayed our honeymoon so that Kathy could be here for Jon and Hannah's wedding and all the festivities leading up to the big day. She thought, and I agreed, that announcing our being married would be a distraction from the couple's big day, and holding off was the right and only decision.

Kathy attended the wedding, and I joined the reception following the ceremony, sitting at the family table. Here I met Matt, his family, and Justin and Tori with newborn Payton—it was her first outing and her introduction to most of the family. She was, understandably, a bigger hit.

After the toasts and roasts, especially by Matt who had the crowd in stitches telling stories about his little brother, the party began. And in the style only my new wife could get away with, she introduced me to her sons, daughters-in-law, and grandchildren, as her new husband.

Matt was the first to shake my hand, congratulating us and hugging his mother, followed by a stunned Justin, and finally making his way to our table, Jon. I think Jon said it the best when he and Hannah were about to depart a couple of hours later. Taking me aside, the youngest son, at about six-three and 220 pounds, said, "Just don't hurt my mother."

"I found a picture of my dad in the CCC," I said, "so hopefully it'll be a good place to start a conversation with your dad while you visit your mom." We were headed down Highway 17 to Yulee; Elizabeth wanted her daughter to check her finger.

I looked over at Kathy in the passenger seat, and she seemed to be in a trance, looking straight ahead. "Honey, you, okay?"

Suddenly, she started shaking and threw up. I had seen this look thousands of times with my brother; she seemed to be going into a coma. She started to fall forward, and I reached to pull her up, got the seat belt adjusted higher on her chest to keep her head up and her face out of the vomit. I decided the emergency room at Southeast Georgia Medical Center was my best option, did an illegal U-turn, burning the tires, and drove the half-block back to I-95N toward Brunswick.

I managed to dial 911 and as I entered the highway, I explained my situation to the dispatcher and requested to be met at the ER entrance. Kathy was breathing, but it was shallow and slow. She was unresponsive to my voice. Bigg Redd passed 100 mph several times, and I came to a screeching halt at the ER where an emergency crew met us. The last I heard as they rushed her through the doors was, "BP sixty over forty and falling. We're losing her…"

I called her eldest son, Matt. He was on duty at the Camden County Fire Station not far away and said he would be there as soon as possible. Next, I called Justin, who also was on duty, and I got the same response. I was sitting in the ER waiting room when, five minutes later, I saw a Fire Rescue Squad pull up at the ER entrance, followed by a fire engine. Within seconds, Matt and Justin arrived, nodded to me and headed straight into the room where their mother was being treated. I sat and could only wait. I thought, *Married less than a month and what did Jon say? Just don't hurt my mom.*

"Mr. Herman?" a woman in scrubs asked. When I nodded, she continued, "I'm Dr. Frye, and I believe your wife had an adverse reaction to a medication she took, going into anaphylactic shock. She has responded to an epinephrine treatment and is stabilizing. She was able to say she took an allergy medication earlier. We'll have to identify exactly what it was so that we can get it into her health record."

When I entered the room, Kathy was sitting up with Matt and Justin on each side of the bed. She smiled at me; they didn't. "You look a lot better than when you arrived," I said. "Wow, scared me to death, honey."

"We've got to get back on shift, Mom," Matt said. He and Justin both hugged and kissed their mother. They turned around in the doorway and Matt said, "That was an impressive response to Mom's condition, Rich. Getting here so fast probably saved her life—we can't thank you enough for that." I hoped they passed that on to Jon. Once they left, I finally got to hug my wife.

Kathy ended her lease on her townhome and was fully moved into the little yellow house, with Maggie, by the end of March. Our first visitor was Marlys, and after scolding me for not holding off on the wedding until she got here, she and her new sister-in-law were chatting like old friends.

Over the spring and summer we enjoyed visits to the Florida Keys and Savannah, Georgia. Other visits were to Mackinaw Island, Michigan, traveling over the world-famous Mackinaw Bridge connecting the lower and upper parts of the state, and a relaxing week with Mar and Jim at their beautiful home on Lake Michigan.

We topped off the summer with—we called it our official honeymoon—a trip to Hawaii. Chris, still on active duty and stationed here, met us at the airport, and Kathy was greeted Hawaiian style, a lei around her neck and one special flower for her hair, behind the left ear—meaning unavailable. We stayed at the Hale Koa Hotel on Waikiki Beach, and for the next ten days I showed her around, going places most tourists never see.

The trooper and adventurer she is, my bride tried every Hawaiian food and talked to the locals, who loved being respected, about their heritage and culture. We also attended two authentic luaus, and I snuck in a little shopping, presenting her with a handmade gold Hawaiian bracelet as a remembrance of our visit here. To say it was hard to leave was an understatement, but we knew we would be back when Chris retired, a trip we were already looking forward to.

CHAPTER 42

October 2012, Little Yellow House

FOR THE PAST YEAR, KATHY HAD BEEN IN CHARGE OF her parents' medications. She would ensure they didn't run out and each week took plastic containers, divided by weekday and morning/ afternoon slots, and put the pills they should take inside. She and Judy also tracked their medical appointments and, between the two of them, provided transportation and directly talked with doctors about their current health and required care.

When we first met, Kathy's dad was ambulatory, but Elizabeth used either a walker at home, or wheelchair when out, to get around. I can only imagine how hard it is to give up one's independence, and their kids had already convinced them they could no longer drive; now they informed them that being alone at night was no longer an option. I was amazed, and very proud of them, as they each agreed to take every third night to stay at the house and care for them. No one complained, they all deeply loved their parents and did what had to be done.

One evening in early October, we brought up the subject of all the travel we made back and forth to Florida. If not to her parents, it was to visit one of the kids or grandkids. One thing led to another, and we asked ourselves, "Why are we still living in Georgia?"

It made logical sense to find a home in Florida and move closer to Kathy's close-knit family. We looked at what seemed a hundred homes when I finally said, "Let's write down what we really want and think about building our very own retirement home." The following weekend, we visited a new community between Yulee and

Fernandina Beach, in the early stages of development, and toured the Amelia Concourse model home.

Kathy, looking around the master bedroom, saw me standing in the kitchen. "Everything okay?" she said.

"This is it, gorgeous, this is the house we've been talking about."

The floor plan met what we envisioned as the perfect house with the master bedroom and bath on one side, guest rooms and full bath on the other, and living spaces in between. The contract allowed us to choose what colors for both the exterior and interior, also the roofing, flooring, ceiling design, all bathroom hardware and kitchen appliances; basically, we controlled every aspect of our home.

"I know we said we were going to downsize and this house will be twice as big as the little yellow house, but if we can get a piece of property on the lake, I say let's make an offer. Today, right now."

Our home was being built and all was going well when Kathy's father's health took a turn for the worse and, unable to fight any longer, he passed away peacefully, December 12, 2012. The family patriarch, William Richard Beazley, ninety-one, World War II Navy Veteran, preceded in death by sons Ronnie and David, was laid to rest with military honors in Bosque Bello Cemetery, Fernandina Beach. His wife of sixty-six years, Elizabeth, children Diane, Judy, Danny, and Kathy, other family members, and many friends looked on. A reception followed, and the stories told—of a man known to some as Dad, Rich to his wife, Bo to friends, and PaPa to his ten grandchildren and nine great-grandchildren—would ensure his memories would forever live on.

With full respect for this man and veteran, I whispered, "You stood your last watch, let someone else take the helm. Fair winds and following seas, may you forever rest in peace."

I knew Kathy was a woman of many talents, but she really showed off her abilities as she single-handedly designed and decorated our new home. Meanwhile, at our Kingsland home, she rewired and repaired all the electrical problems, painted where needed, and with the help of brother Danny, fixed plumbing issues. We quickly sold the little yellow house.

On April 19, 2013, we moved into our new home: 2,500 square feet, four-bedroom, two-bath, living room, dining room, entry/parlor room, kitchen and kitchenette, family room with two-car garage. And yes, it was located on a lake.

With our newest family member, Roxy, a three-month-old Boston terrier to keep thirteen-year-old Maggie company and active, this capped our first action-packed year and started a fresh new life, the Hermans in Nassau County.

Our first holiday season in the new house, Jon and Hannah with seven-month-old Sawyer, now living in Wisconsin, stayed with us for the holidays. On Christmas Eve morning, Kathy and I were in Walmart buying groceries to deliver to the homeless in Kingsland, as I had done for two years. Justin called and said he, Tori, and twenty-two-month-old Payton would be dropping by to visit, in two hours.

We hastily finished our shopping, delivered our goods, and headed home. We made a quick stop at Publix, bought what we needed, and pulled into our garage, with a half-hour to prepare.

While making sandwich trays and other buffet type foods, Kathy got a great idea. She called Matt, Judy, Danny, and the sister I had not yet met, Diane, inviting everyone to stop by. I was getting into a festive mood, this was bringing back fond childhood memories of my family's annual Christmas Day brunch, and I created a bar to open when the first guests arrived.

It is amazing what a little ingenuity can do. With the help of Jon and Hannah, by the time our seventeen guests arrived, we looked like this day had been planned forever. I made mimosas and eggnog, with or without brandy, to serve with plenty of non-alcoholic beverages too. The family couldn't believe how Mimi (Kathy's family name as grandma) put on such a great spread. The grandchildren opened gifts from their cousins, and we all relaxed and felt blessed we were able to be together.

As everyone departed, Kathy and I gave each other a high-five. A simple, unexpected phone call turned into a family event, and it was decided: Christmas Eve mornings would be at Mimi's and PopPop's (the name baby Sawyer was being taught to call me and one I would learn to love). I hoped the brunch buffet would be a tradition carried on through generations to come.

CHAPTER 43

December 31, 2013, Fernandina Beach

AS 2013 AND THE HOLIDAY SEASON CAME TO AN END, I found myself sitting alone on a lounge chair in the back yard, enjoying the view, and waiting for nightfall. Here, as I had throughout my adult life, I would find a spot, a private place, to call my own.

During my initial enlistment in the Navy, on the fantail of the USS Cambria, watching sunsets glisten in our wake as we sailed the mighty seas, I found my first such place. On the USS L Y Spear and USS Richard L. Page, once again the fantail was where I would be. On shore duty in Italy, Sardinia, and Hawaii I would find the same setting, sometimes even dangling my feet in the waters around me, many times from the end of a pier. The St. Marys waterfront on the Georgia coast was another place that met my needs, and now, looking over our lake, I had my latest and possibly last, private place.

I thought about how I was drafted while in college and chose to join the Navy. On active duty, I grew in body and mind, experiencing the different people and cultures of the world, including the good and some bad. I met, fought, and prevailed over prejudice and saw first-hand the perils of war.

Honorably discharged, I returned to school, married, started a family, and faced the reality of the times. I still saw my cup as half full and hoped I always would. Thirty-three months later, I reenlisted in the Navy to provide for my family and make it a career.

My first tour in the Navy, I was young and made some mistakes, several reaching the level of international incidents, but I was always honest, owned up to my errors, and with a good work ethic became a valuable asset. It had been at a court-martial hearing (where the charges were vacated) that the board's senior member gave me the moniker, "Work Hard, Play Hard." An old adage, and whenever you see that on a Navy Amphibious Force recruiting poster you can thank me.

I had reentered the Navy with the goal of becoming commissioned an officer, and exceeded expectations. I persevered through being a non-qualified submariner with a submarine officer designation. At every new duty station, I had to prove myself, going against the current, and I did. At my retirement, Rear Admiral Steven Staten III said I was the guru, the oracle, the Jedi master of submarine communications.

Along the way, and through retirement, a family was raised, countless friends made, and I am content with my life's accomplishments. Losing Shirley, at the time, was something I never thought I could recover from.

I met the right woman at the right time. Kathy Beazley, my angel in waiting, came into my life, and as they say, the rest is history.

I smiled as I thought about how we got here. The naysayers who had their doubts we'd last. How could a couple, meeting online, breaking all the rules of protocol, dating just five weeks before marrying, possibly have a future together?

Even Kathy had almost second-guessed herself on our first date when, on the way to St. Marys, Georgia, she realized she was with someone she only knew by his first name, going to another state, and no one knew what she was doing or where she was. She prayed I wasn't a rapist or worse yet, a serial killer. When she told me this, I couldn't help but think—I would probably come out on the short end of the stick if I ever stepped out of line.

Kathy and I, maybe older and wiser, knew exactly what we were doing, and to use her analogy of the ruler as a timetable, we were both well past halfway. Little did the outsiders know what we knew; we found love, respect, honesty, trust, acceptance, and a friend in each other. It didn't take long for us to draw the obvious conclusion.

I looked up and saw my bride of almost two years coming to join me.

"I realized it was almost sunset and thought I'd find you out here," she said, getting comfortable on the lounge chair next to me. "We've been married long enough for me to know when you are looking to do some reflection."

I smiled. "Yes, some things don't change, and thankfully, this is one of those times I look forward to. How about you? Anything on your mind?"

"Always, especially as the holidays end. This time of year, I get mixed emotions. I enjoy the festivities, the kids and grandkids visiting, yet I get down and moody when I think who is gone. My dad, brothers, your folks and friends that have moved or passed on. It's hard to explain."

"Some things don't need an explanation. One of the things I was thinking about was how many people are probably amazed we are doing so well." I told her what I thought was the reason, and she smiled and readily agreed.

"I'm very happy, gorgeous, and I thank you for coming into my life," I said. "Accepting what I was going through at the time, understanding the loss I felt, and knowing just what I needed. No doubt in my mind, the next dictionaries printed will have your picture by the definition of compassion."

"It works both ways," Kathy said. "I think it was fate, that day in January. I have not regretted a second of our decision and look forward to next year and the years after. As many as God has planned for us."

"Kathy, I feel the same way. Speaking of the future, my boys are doing well. Chris plans to retire next year, and still wants us to be there. I look for him to stay in Hawaii." I knew he thought Adrienne and the girls might eventually settle in Valdosta, Georgia, only about 150 miles from here, so they would be a lot closer. I smiled, thinking of Alexis and Aliyah, my two lively granddaughters.

"And I think Scott has a future as a fitness instructor or personal trainer. It's just a matter of time before he finds his niche and true happiness. I also want to keep contact with my extended family, Jeff and Kim. They've been part of my family since 1981, and I never want to lose touch. Any predictions for your boys?"

"Always." As she grinned, I could see the wheels turning. "Matt and Justin will always be first responders at heart. Interesting how both their wives are hair stylists. I wouldn't be surprised if all four of them started their own businesses someday. Matt and Lacy probably have their family set, but Justin and Tori want a brother or sister for Payton, and I hope Jon and Hannah will want another child. One thing for sure, they all have bright futures ahead.

"And our grandkids," she continued, "all growing up so fast. Gabriella is so curious and adventurous. I look for her to go into the medical field when the time comes. Dawson is growing just like his daddy, taller and thin. Believe it or not, Matt was built just like that; now he's six feet plus and a big man. Macy is a fireball—I told Lacy she's going to be the family tomboy, carefree and one to keep an eye on." She sat back, and the sun was getting lower behind us, casting long shadows on the water.

"I'll never understand," she said, "but do respect, how you can go so long without seeing your boys, granddaughters, and the rest of your family. I'm selfish, though, I like my family close to home. That ten years in Brazil was trying on me, and hopefully, never again." I could sense the pain and regret she had felt being away from the rest of her family those years abroad during her first marriage.

Then Kathy began to smile. "I definitely think you should write that book. After all, didn't your mom ask you to?" I just shook my head, not knowing what to say.

It was about time to see the last shadows on the water as the sun set. I stood and with Kathy's hand in mine, I opened the back gate and we walked to the water's edge. I gently squeezed her hand. "I want to end this year with the woman I love and to share the rest of my life with you, respectful of all we've had and will have. Thank God, we found one another. I love you, Kathy B. Herman."

My hand was squeezed back, "And I you, Richard William Herman, my Commander. I'm happy to be here with you, sharing our own private place."

EPILOGUE

December 24, 2023, Fernandina Beach, Florida

"DO YOU KNOW WHY I ASKED YOU HERE?" I SAID TO Alexis and Dawson. It was the eleventh annual family Christmas Eve morning celebration for Mimi and me, this year with twenty-five members here. Like last year—except this time I had called the meeting—we three took a break from the gathering and were sitting in my office again.

"We hope we know why," D replied, a bit anxious and looking at his cousin.

What a difference a year makes. Now a sophomore at Florida State College Jacksonville, he was still growing. Alexis, a sophomore at Valdosta State University, was as cute as ever and now showing even more stature and maturity.

"I have completed the manuscript for book three," I announced.

They both smiled, leaned over to hug, gave high fives, and this time Alexis spoke. "That's wonderful, Papa. I'm proud of you." She came to give me my own hug. "What can you tell us about it, and when will it be available to buy?"

"Buy?" I laughed. "This book will fill in the blanks and connect the dots of my life before my first enlistment, between my enlistments, and after my military career. I hope to launch later next year, and the story covers my life from birth to New Year's Day 2014." I saw their curious looks.

"Before you ask why I stopped at 2014, I'll tell you. When I wrote the first book, the reason was to leave a tangible work my descendants could physically hold to read about their family history.

I did that. Then, I succumbed to the pressure and wrote book two to answer questions book one didn't address and to continue the story of my naval career. I did that." Wide eyes were still on me.

"As you two know, I had no intention of book three, but I did tinker with a couple of possibilities. That speech you gave me last year, which I guess I now thank you for, convinced me to go forward with it. I wrote part of it and stalled.

"Then, Gary, my cousin Jackie's husband and my good friend of sixty-two years, passed away this fall, and I spoke at his celebration of life service. I met with their children and grandchildren that evening and, through their asking more about the family and showing encouragement, I came home energized and wrote every day. I hope what I've written will provide more answers, maybe even some closure in some places, and it'll live on a long time."

My grandchildren gave me big grins and thumb's-up, making me feel honored by their approval.

"I have no intent or inclination to add a book four to this," I told them firmly. "My hope is that one of you, my descendants, will pick up the torch and continue the series. If someone does, they'll have a good place to start. Yes, New Year's Day 2014.

"Mimi and I have been married now almost twelve years, we have ten grandchildren, one will be a nurse soon, and you two are in college ... I could go on and on. There's already another ten years of family history that's been lived and will provide a good foundation to work from—with plenty more ahead."

Alexis and D seemed to take what I said on board, and even if they didn't discuss it soon, hopefully it will be in a conversation in the future. They congratulated me again on finishing the book and then left to be with the others. I took a moment to compose myself before joining in for the rest of our celebration.

Each year on this date, we are reminded and humbled by how much we have been truly blessed. Kathy and I choose to embrace and enjoy the future with whatever it should bring, knowing what matters most in our lives: Nothing is more important than *family*.

I looked around my office and smiled. Five years ago, this room had been a spare bedroom. One day, Kathy surprised me as she had converted it into my space, with a newly assembled wood desk, computer, printer, and all the accessories to go along with a book for beginning authors—and a note: "When you are ready, you will know."

Closing the door and walking out now, I looked up. *I hope you're proud, Mom; your request has led to a trilogy. All because you asked.*

ACKNOWLEDGMENTS

To be perfectly safe and avoid offending someone by missing a name, an author could refrain from writing a page acknowledging anyone. However, using that as a safety net might lead the reader into thinking the writer has gotten so full of themselves that they need not share the credit for the incredible amount of work by others that goes into making a manuscript into a book. I fall into the category that this page, if I gave credit to everyone where credit is due, would be the longest chapter in my book.

Those who know me will attest that I take no personal credit for the success of my books, as they would not even exist if not for the supporting cast I had along the way. It took my second gold medal before I accepted the title author in place of writer.

I do take credit for one thing: I follow my own Hermanism, and I know how to put good people around me. If you are one of the cast of hundreds, throughout my life, who fall into this category, I am grateful. To you all:

THANK YOU!

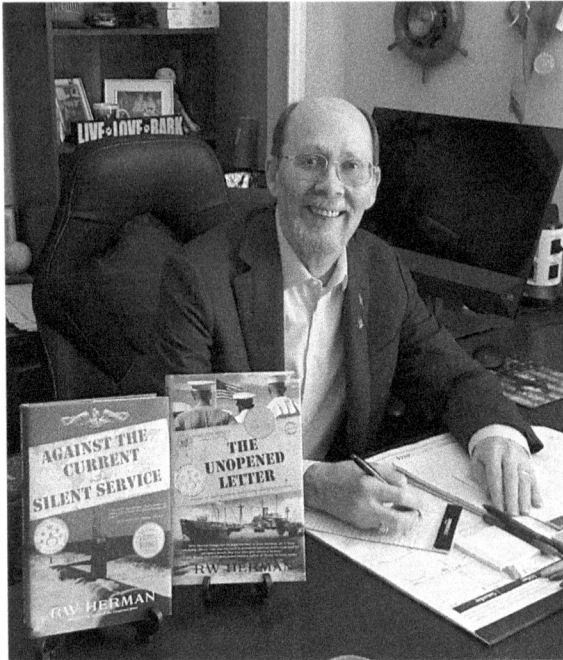

Commander Richard W. Herman, winner of the 2021 and 2023 Florida Authors and Publishers Association President's Awards GOLD Medals, was born in Minneapolis, Minnesota. While attending the University of Minnesota in 1965, he received his draft notice and chose to enlist in the U.S. Navy. He served 10 years as an enlisted sailor and then received his commission through the Limited Duty Officer Program, retiring in 1997 at the rank of commander. He is entitled to wear the Legion of Merit, the Meritorious Service Medal with two stars, the Navy Commendation Medal with one star and the Navy and Marine Corps Achievement Medal with two stars. During his career spanning over 30 years, he was a communication specialist and at retirement was the senior submarine communications officer in the Navy. Commander Herman now resides in Fernandina Beach, Florida, with his wife Kathy and their Olde English Bulldog, Sissy and two Boston Terriers, Roxy and Stella.

.

Milton Keynes UK
Ingram Content Group UK Ltd.
UKHW042113111124
451073UK00015B/356/J

9 798990 439894